1957

THE MAKING OF THE ENGLISH LANDSCAPE

THE MAKING OF THE ENGLISH LANDSCAPE

EDITED BY W. G. HOSKINS

1. THE MAKING OF THE ENGLISH LANDSCAPE   W. G. HOSKINS
2. CORNWALL   W. G. V. BALCHIN
3. LANCASHIRE   ROY MILLWARD
4. GLOUCESTERSHIRE   H. P. R. FINBERG

IN PREPARATION

5. LEICESTERSHIRE AND RUTLAND   W. G. HOSKINS

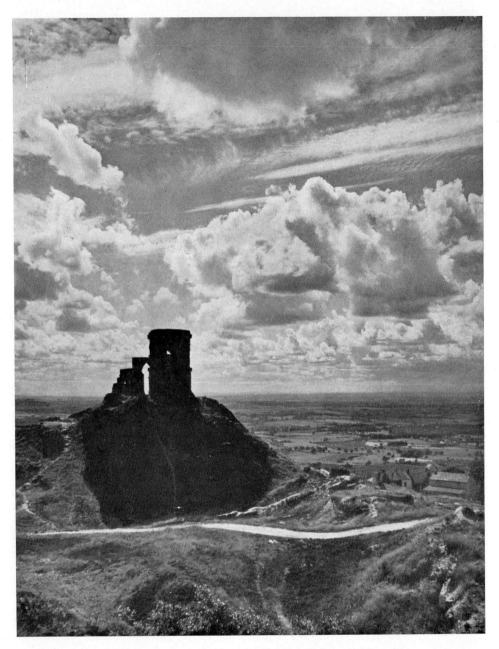

Mow Cop and the Cheshire Plain. This ridge of millstone grit on the boundary of Cheshire and Staffordshire rises to nearly 1,100 feet above sea-level and is still largely a natural landscape. The so-called castle in the foreground is a sham ruin of eighteenth-century date. Northward stretches the immense cultivated plain of Cheshire, the finished product of many centuries of colonization.

THE MAKING OF
THE ENGLISH LANDSCAPE

BY

W. G. HOSKINS

*Reader in Economic History in the
University of Oxford*

LONDON
HODDER AND STOUGHTON LTD.
1957

TO

MY WIFE

First Published - *August* 1955
Third Impression - 1957

Printed in Great Britain for Hodder and Stoughton, Ltd.
by Billing and Sons Ltd., Guildford and London

Contents

Chapter		Page
	INTRODUCTION	13
I.	THE LANDSCAPE BEFORE THE ENGLISH SETTLEMENT	17
	The Pre-Roman Landscape	19
	Western Farmsteads and Fields	23
	Roman Britain	29
II.	THE ENGLISH SETTLEMENT	38
	Villages and their Fields	38
	Hamlets	46
	The Shape of Villages	48
	Some Anglo-Saxon Estate Boundaries	55
	The Scandinavian Settlement	57
III.	THE COLONIZATION OF MEDIEVAL ENGLAND	61
	The Landscape in 1086	61
	The Clearing of the Woodlands	69
	Marsh, Fen, and Moor	76
	Buildings in the Landscape	84
IV.	THE BLACK DEATH AND AFTER	92
	The Abandonment of Villages	92
	New Colonization	97
	New Buildings	99
V.	TUDOR TO GEORGIAN ENGLAND	108
	The Landscape in 1500	108
	The Enclosure of the Midland Fields	114
	The Flowering of Rural England	119
	Country Houses and Parks	126
VI.	PARLIAMENTARY ENCLOSURE AND THE LANDSCAPE	138
	The Extent of the Enclosure	138
	The Date of Parliamentary Enclosure	142
	The New Landscape	143
	The Fields	145
	Hedgerows and Trees	150
	Roads	154
	Farmhouses	157

Chapter   *Page*

VII. THE INDUSTRIAL REVOLUTION AND THE LANDSCAPE   162

    The Early Industrial Landscape   162
    Water-Power and the Early Mills   165
    Steam-Power and Slums   171

VIII. ROADS, CANALS, AND RAILWAYS   180

    Roads   180
    Canals   191
    Railways   197

IX. THE LANDSCAPE OF TOWNS   210

    The Planned Town   211
    The Open-Field Town   216
    The Market Town   224

X. THE LANDSCAPE TODAY   231

INDEX   236

ACKNOWLEDGMENTS

THE author wishes to thank Dr. J. D. Chambers of the University of Nottingham for permitting the use of the map in Fig. 17; Dr. C. S. Orwin for permission to use Fig. 3; Mr. C. W. Phillips, Archæology Officer of the Ordnance Survey, for valuable help with Fig. 2; and Mr. B. Twelvetrees for the loan of the plan in Fig. 16.

The publishers wish to thank the following for permission to use their photographs: Aerofilms Ltd. for plates 1, 6, 8, 9, 10, 21, 27, 38, 44, 54, 55 and 75; Air Ministry for plates 18 and 46; Ashmolean Museum for plates 4, 7 and 59; Air Survey Co. Ltd. for plate 76; F. L. Attenborough for plates 11, 16, 20, 23, 26, 28, 29, 31, 33, 34, 41, 45, 49, 51, 52, 57 and 62; W. G. V. Balchin for plate 3; G. Douglas Bolton for the frontispiece and plate 47; British Railways for plates 58, 67, 68, 69, 72, 73, 74; British Travel and Holidays Association for plates 12, 17, 19, 22, 32, 36, 37, 48, 56, 61, 79 and 80; Central Office of Information for plates 50 and 60; Country Life for plate 35; O. G. S. Crawford for plate 5; Arnold Fellows for plates 13, 14 and 15; K. P. Gingell for plate 82; W. G. Hoskins for plates 24 and 77; London Museum for plate 2; E. T. Long for plate 30; Eric de Maré for plates 63, 64, 65, 66; Roy Millward for plate 53; *The Times* for plate 39; City Engineer and Surveyor, Nottingham for plate 78; the University of Cambridge for plate 25; and Major H. Wake and the Council of the Northamptonshire Record Society for plate 40.

Plates 42 and 43 are taken from John Kip's *Britannia Illustrated* (1709-16); plates 70 and 71 from *Drawings of the London and Birmingham Railway* (1839); and plate 81 from *Views in Devon and Cornwall* (1829-31).

The publishers wish to thank also Messrs. Macmillan for permission to reproduce Figs. 12 and 14 from Gonner's *Common Land and Inclosure*.

List of Plates

Mow Cop and the Cheshire Plain   *Frontispiece*

Plate		*Page*
1.	Dartmoor: the central waste	18
2.	The natural landscape of London	20
3.	Chysauster village, Cornwall	21
4.	Celtic Fields on Fyfield Down, Wiltshire	23
5.	Megalithic field boundary at Castellack, Cornwall	26
6.	Celtic hamlet and fields near Cape Cornwall	27
7.	A Roman road from the air	30
8.	Haxey and its open fields, Lincolnshire	39
9.	A street-village: Combe Martin, Devon	40
10.	Open field fossilized under ridge and furrow, Warwickshire	43
11.	A Saxon farmstead: Westcott Barton, Devon	47
12.	A green-village: Finchingfield, Essex	50
13.	A sunken lane in Devon	56
14.	Saxon boundary bank (Devon): upper half	58
15.	Saxon boundary bank: lower half	58
16.	Launceston castle and town, Cornwall	68
17.	The isolated church: Fingest, Buckinghamshire	71
18.	Fields cleared from medieval woodland at Whitestone, Devon	72
19.	The reclaimed Somerset marshland at Godney	79
20.	Cholwich Town: an early thirteenth-century farm, Devon	83
21.	Medieval frontier and fields at Wasdale Head, Cumberland	84
22.	Rievaulx Abbey (Yorkshire): the choir	86
23.	Ketton church, Rutland	87
24.	Ruins of Calceby church, Lincolnshire	95
25.	A deserted village: Lower Ditchford, Gloucestershire	96
26.	A medieval fishing village: Polperro, Cornwall	98
27.	An Elizabethan fishing village: Clovelly, Devon	99
28.	Fotheringhay church, Northamptonshire	100

Plate   *Page*

29. A characteristic Cornish church: Michaelstow   102
30. Trecarrel chapel near Launceston, Cornwall   103
31. A medieval bridge at Wadebridge, Cornwall   105
32. Bolton Castle, Yorkshire   106
33. A fifteenth-century sheep pasture at Ingarsby, Leicestershire   115
34. Colly Weston village, Northamptonshire   120
35. The Elizabethan manor house at Warmington, Warwickshire   123
36. Elizabethan street at Henley-in-Arden, Warwickshire   124
37. The Old Grammar School at Market Harborough, Leicestershire   125
38. Compton Wynyates, Warwickshire   127
39. Burghley House and park, near Stamford, Northamptonshire   128
40. Courteenhall House and park, Northamptonshire   130
41. Burley-on-the-Hill, Rutland   131
42. Wimpole, Cambridgeshire (after Kip)   133
43. Easington, Gloucestershire (after Kip)   134
44. Blenheim Palace and the park, Oxfordshire   136
45. The field-pattern of parliamentary enclosure, Leicestershire   144
46. Parliamentary enclosure and ridge and furrow, Leicestershire   146
47. Farmstead on the enclosed waste, Yorkshire   148
48. Stone walls of parliamentary enclosure, Derbyshire   151
49. Hawthorns and grass verges, Rutland   155
50. Weaver's cottage at Lumb, Yorkshire   164
51. Etruria Hall near Burslem, Staffordshire   168
52. Strutt's mill at Belper, Derbyshire   169
53. Chemical waste at St. Helens, Lancashire   171
54. Potteries landscape: an air view of Burslem, Staffordshire   174
55. Nineteenth-century housing pattern at Preston, Lancashire   175
56. China-clay landscape near St. Austell, Cornwall   177
57. Tin-mining landscape near St. Cleer, Cornwall   178
58. Stockport Viaduct (1848), Cheshire   179
59. Ridgeway on the Berkshire Downs   181
60. The Fosse Way near Northleach, Gloucestershire   184
61. Packhorse road and bridge at Wasdale, Cumberland   188

Plate   *Page*

62. A prehistoric trackway: Sewstern Lane, Lincolnshire   189

63. Canal cutting near Market Drayton, Shropshire   192

64. A street scene at Stourport, Worcestershire   194

65. A canal bridge by Telford, near Tyrley, Staffordshire   195

66. Canal junction at Great Haywood, Staffordshire   196

67. A Horse Railway (after Tait)   198

68. Making of the Edge Hill tunnel (1830), Lancashire   199

69. Box Tunnel (1846), Wiltshire   200

70. Excavations for the railway cutting at Park Village (Camden Town)
       1836   202

71. Wolverton Embankment under construction (1837) Buckinghamshire 204

72. Chippenham railway viaduct, Wiltshire   205

73. Great Western Railway under construction near Bath   206

74. Crewe Station in 1848, Cheshire   207

75. A planned town: Middlesbrough, Yorkshire   213

76. Scarborough castle and town, Yorkshire   215

77. Stamford from the meadows, Lincolnshire   217

78. A Nottingham court   219

79. Main street at Marlborough, Wiltshire   225

80. Boston church and market place, Lincolnshire   228

81. A Dockyard Town: Devonport, Devon   229

82. The completed landscape   232

Maps and Plans

Figure   Page

1.   Celtic fields in Zennor parish, Cornwall   25
2.   Romano-British settlement in north Oxfordshire   32
3.   The West Field at Laxton (Nottinghamshire) in 1635   41
4.   Plan of Ashmore village, Dorset   44
5.   Plan of Thorverton village, Devon   51
6.   Plan of Middle Barton village in 1795, Oxfordshire   52
7.   Early Colonization in the Lincolnshire Marshland   64
8.   Saxon Villages and Medieval Dispersion in Hertfordshire   74
9.   Medieval Field Pattern on the edge of Dartmoor, Devon   82
10.   Plan of Medieval Salisbury   89
11.   The Deserted Villages of Leicestershire   94
12.   Land without Common Field at the end of the Sixteenth Century   112
13.   The Distribution of Parks in north Oxfordshire   132
14.   The Extent of Parliamentary Enclosure   140
15.   The Pattern of Parliamentary Enclosure in north Hertfordshire   158
16.   Plan of a typical court in Nottingham, 1845   220
17.   Housing development in Nottingham after enclosure   222

Introduction

DESPITE the multitude of books about English landscape and scenery, and the flood of topographical books in general, there is not one book which deals with the historical evolution of the landscape as we know it. At the most we may be told that the English landscape is the man-made creation of the seventeenth and eighteenth centuries, which is not even a quarter-truth, for it applies only to country houses and their parks, and to the parliamentary enclosures that gave us a good deal of our modern pattern of fields, hedges and by-roads. It ignores the fact that more than a half of England never underwent this kind of enclosure, but evolved in an entirely different way, and that in some regions the landscape had been virtually completed by the eve of the Black Death.

No book exists to describe the manner in which the various landscapes of this country came to assume the shape and appearance they now have, why the hedgebanks and lanes of Devon should be so totally different from those of the Midlands, why there are so many ruined churches in Norfolk or so many lost villages in Lincolnshire, or what history lies behind the winding ditches of the Somerset marshlands, the remote granite farmsteads of Cornwall, and the lonely pastures of upland Northamptonshire.

There are, indeed, some good books on the geology that lies behind the English landscape, and these represent perhaps the best kind of writing on the subject we have yet had, for they are concerned with facts and are not given to the sentimental and formless slush which afflicts so many books concerned only with superficial appearances. But the geologist, good though he may be, is concerned with only one aspect of the subject; and beyond a certain point he is obliged to leave the historian to continue and complete it. He explains to us the bones of the landscape, the fundamental structure that gives form and colour to the scene and produces a certain kind of topography and natural vegetation. But the flesh that covers the bones, and the details of the features, are the concern of the historian, whose task it is to show how man has clothed the geological skeleton during the comparatively recent past—mostly within the last fifteen centuries, though in some regions much longer than this.

I am concerned in this book, then, with the ways in which men have cleared the natural woodlands; reclaimed marshland, fen, and moor; created fields out of a wilderness; made lanes, roads, and footpaths; laid out towns, built villages, hamlets, farmhouses and cottages; created country houses and their parks; dug mines, and made canals and railways; in short, with everything that has altered the natural landscape. One cannot understand the English landscape and enjoy it to the full, apprehend all its wonderful variety from region to region (often within the space of a few miles), without going back to the history that lies behind it.

13

A commonplace ditch may be the thousand-year-old boundary of a royal manor; a certain hedgebank may be even more ancient, the boundary of a Celtic estate; a certain deep and winding lane may be the work of twelfth-century peasants, some of whose names may be made known to us if we search diligently enough. To discover these things we have to go to the documents that are the historian's raw material, and find out what happened to produce these results and when, and precisely how they came about. But it is not only the documents that are the historian's guide. One cannot write books on this subject by reading someone else's books, or even by studying records in a muniment room. The English landscape itself, to those who know how to read it aright, is the richest historical record we possess. There are discoveries to be made in it for which no written documents exist, or have ever existed. To write its history requires a combination of documentary research and of fieldwork, of laborious scrambling on foot wherever the trail may lead. The result is a new kind of history which it is hoped will appeal to all those who like to travel intelligently, to get away from the guide-book show-pieces now and then, and to unearth the reason behind what they are looking at.

What I have done is to take the landscape of England as it appears today, and to explain as far as I am able how it came to assume its present form, how the details came to be inserted, and when. At all points I have tried to relate my explanation to the things that can be seen today by any curious and intelligent traveller going around his native land. There is no part of England, however unpromising it may appear at first sight, that is not full of questions for those who have a sense of the past.

I have also chosen to consider the subject chronologically as far as possible, to show how the pattern developed as a whole, even if in patches, rather than by subjects such as Field Patterns, Hedges, Lanes, and so forth, which was an alternative method. It is important to show the logic behind the changing face of the English landscape, and only a chronological treatment can bring this out. Those who are interested in particular aspects of the scenewill find their purpose served by the subject-index to the book.

A few words of warning may be necessary on what will not be found in this book. It touches upon a wide variety of subjects—such as the industrial revolution, the building of country houses, the growth of towns, the construction of the railways—but it does not attempt to give a connected history of these things. Plenty of other books exist for that purpose. I have touched upon their history here only in so far as it has affected the visible landscape, and the reader will find no more than that.

In a book of this modest length, too, covering so large and intricate a subject, much that one would have liked to say in order to bring out the beauty of the detail in the English landscape has necessarily been omitted. It is proposed therefore to follow this general introduction to the history of the English landscape by a series of books on counties of special interest. In these will be found the detailed treatment that the true explorer of England pines for all the time. The first counties to be published will be Lancashire and Cornwall, to be followed by Gloucestershire, Leicestershire, and Somerset, and thereafter by such counties as seem by their peculiar landscape history to call for individual examination. Since this book on The Making of the English Landscape is a pioneer study, in which one has had to feel one's way all the time, one cannot hope to have elucidated everything to the general satisfaction, or not to have made mistakes here and there; but I hope the individual books on the counties will help to fill in the gaps and take us nearer to the exact truth of the way in which things happened.

W. G. Hoskins.

Steeple Barton,
Oxfordshire.

The Landscape before the English Settlement

WORDSWORTH, in his *Guide through the District of the Lakes*—one of the best guide-books ever written, for poets make the best topographers—opens his description of the scenery of the Lakes with a View of the Country as formed by Nature. He then passes, in his second section, to the Aspect of the Country, as affected by its Inhabitants, and this he begins by asking the reader to envisage what the landscape, finished by the great impersonal forces of Nature and awaiting its first human inhabitants, looked like in its primæval freshness. "He will form to himself an image of the tides visiting and revisiting the friths, the main sea dashing against the bolder shore, the rivers pursuing their course to be lost in the mighty mass of waters. He may see or hear in fancy the winds sweeping over the lakes, or piping with a loud voice among the mountain peaks; and, lastly, may think of the primæval woods shedding and renewing their leaves with no human eye to notice, or human heart to regret or welcome the change."

How often one has tried to form these images in various parts of England, seated beside a wide, flooding estuary as the light thickens on a winter evening, dissolving all the irrelevant human details of the scene, leaving nothing but the shining water, the sky, and the darkening hills, and the immemorial sound of curlews whistling over the mud and fading river-beaches. This, we feel, is exactly as the first men saw it when they reached the shingled margin of the river a hundred generations ago. Nothing has changed. We are seeing the natural world through the eyes of men who died three or four thousand years ago, and for a moment or two we succeed in entering into the minds of the dead. Or, on some desolate English moorland it is even easier to feel this identity with the dead of the Bronze Age who lie nearby under a piled-up cairn or under the heathery blanket of a burial-mound. It is easy, too, to feel this kinship while watching the summer morning waves falling with a meditative indifference on a beach still untrodden by the human race. There are many such timeless scenes and there is an acute and melancholy pleasure in this mental game; but it is not always as easy as this. On unpeopled moorland, beside remote estuaries at dawn, or at sea approaching an historic coast, little or nothing is alien to the natural scene. We see it precisely as the first men saw it. The imagination is liberated over the scene.

But there are not many places where one can feel with such complete assurance that this is exactly as the first inhabitants saw it in "the freshness of the early world." Not much of England, even in its more withdrawn, inhuman places, has escaped being altered by man in some subtle way or other, however untouched we may fancy it is at first sight. Sherwood Forest and Wicken Fen are not quite what they seem. The historian, trying to enter into the minds of the first men to break into a virgin landscape, trying to envisage precisely what they saw and no more, is aware of some of the difficulties of his task, if not of all. One needs to be a botanist, a physical geographer, and a naturalist, as well as an historian, to be able to feel certain that one has all the facts right before allowing the imagination to play over the small details of a scene. For unless the facts are right

PLATE 1

The central waste of Dartmoor. This view gives a good idea of the natural landscape of moorland country as medieval pioneers saw it. They were able to colonize the shallow valleys
on the southern half of the moor. Old enclosures may be detected at the left-hand side of
this view, but they appear to represent the furthest limit of reclamation from the waste.

there is no pleasure in this imaginative game, if we clothe the landscape with the wrong kind of trees, or allow in it plants and birds that are really only the product of some recent changes, or if we fail to observe that the river has changed its course well within historic times. We may have to make all sorts of allowances—subtracting here and adding there—before the natural landscape, still untouched by man, is recovered in all its purity and freshness. And if we succeed in recovering this buried landscape, and wish to communicate to others the pleasure it gives us, how difficult it is to do so without intruding the unpalatable jargon of the geologist or the economic historian or some other learned trade.

For what a many-sided pleasure there is in looking at a wide view anywhere in England, not simply as a sun-drenched whole, fading into unknown blue distances, like the view of the West Midland plain from the top of the Malvern Hills, or at a pleasant rural miniature like the crumpled Woburn ridge in homely Bedford-shire, but in recognizing every one of its details name by name, in knowing how and when each came to be there, why it is just that colour, shape, or size, and not otherwise, and in seeing how the various patterns and parts fit together to make the whole scene. One may liken the English landscape, especially in a wide view, to a symphony, which it is possible to enjoy as an architectural mass of sound, beautiful or impressive as the case may be, without being able to analyse it in detail or to see the logical development of its structure. The enjoyment may be real, but it is limited in scope and in the last resort vaguely diffused in emotion. But if instead of hearing merely a symphonic mass of sound, we are able to isolate the themes as they enter, to see how one by one they are intricately woven together and by what magic new harmonies are produced, perceive the manifold subtle variations on a single theme, however disguised it may be, then the total effect is immeasurably enhanced. So it is with landscapes of the historic depth and physical variety that England shows almost everywhere. Only when we know all the themes and harmonies can we begin to appreciate its full beauty, or to discover in it new subtleties every time we visit it. Nor is it only a programme of symphonies that the English landscape provides. One can become satiated with magnificent views over a dozen counties. There is as much pleasure to be had in the chamber music of Bedfordshire or Rutland; perhaps, one might say, a more sophisticated pleasure in discovering the essence of these simpler and smaller landscapes. This book is, then, an attempt to study the development of the English landscape much as though it were a piece of music, or a series of compositions of varying magnitude, in order that we may understand the logic that lies behind the beautiful whole.

The Pre-Roman Landscape

The English landscape as we know it today is almost entirely the product of the last fifteen hundred years, beginning with the earliest Anglo-Saxon villages in the middle decades of the fifth century. The direct prehistoric contribution to the landscape is small. It is more impressive in some parts of England than others, fascinating when studied in detail—as in the remarkable Iron Age villages of western Cornwall or the hill-forts of Wessex—but, considered as an influence on the whole landscape, of little importance. There are, indeed, some counties where it cannot be ignored, but in a general survey of the country as a whole we need not linger over it.

Even in neolithic times (2500-1900 B.C.), to go no further back, the maximum population of Britain was probably only about twenty thousand—about the size of a large country town, such as Bridgwater in Somerset today. Corn-growing was still subsidiary to pasture-farming, life was more or less nomadic, and so it remained until the Late Bronze Age (1000-500 B.C.). The oldest recognizable corn "fields," small irregular plots of ground associated with hut-circles on the western side of Dartmoor, date possibly from the Early Bronze Age (1900-1400 B.C.). There are others on the western slopes of Rough Tor on Bodmin Moor in Cornwall; and similar sites with small, curvilinear plots have been found on the Yorkshire moors, where they are attributed to the Middle Bronze Age (1400-1000 B.C.). These prehistoric fields are, however, only recognizable to the archæ-

PLATE 2

The natural landscape of the site of London (after a drawing by Forestier in the London Museum).

ologist, and then only at certain times of the year, and they can hardly be said to be a feature of the landscape wherever they are. They are interesting only as the earliest known corn-plots in this country, just as the hut-circles of Dartmoor (mainly concentrated in the southern and south-western valleys) are interesting, for our purpose, as the remains of the earliest recognizable dwelling-houses, dating as they do from the Early Bronze Age to the Early Iron Age.

With the Late Bronze Age, and especially the Early Iron Age (from 500 B.C. onwards) the further development of agriculture led to the appearance of settled villages, a revolution in human life comparable in magnitude with the effects of the industrial revolution of the nineteenth century. There had been "villages" of a kind on Bronze Age Dartmoor—as, for example, on Standon Down above Tavy Cleave—but villages as the centre of settled agricultural communities may be said to date from the centuries immediately preceding the Roman Conquest. One of these villages, or more strictly a hamlet of at least eight houses, has been completely excavated at Chysauster in the far west of Cornwall, three miles due north of Penzance. Chysauster is most exciting, even to those whose interest in prehistory is a flickering holiday affair, for here we have a village, still substantially intact, of houses built of granite dry-walling still standing to a height of

PLATE 3

Chysauster (Cornwall): the remains of an Iron Age village in the Penwith peninsula showing the granite rubble masonry of the house walls. It was a hamlet (of eight houses) of a type found all over West Cornwall at the present day, and was occupied until well into Roman times.

several feet. The houses were built in the form of rooms opening on to a central unroofed courtyard, four houses on each side of a cobbled street. The inhabitants of Chysauster cultivated the garden-plots and small arable fields that surround the houses, and also dug and smelted tin. The village seems to have been occupied from about the second century B.C. into Roman times, and was then abandoned. At some later date—but precisely when it is impossible to say—a new site was occupied on lower ground about half a mile south, probably by the medieval colonist and his household who created the present farm of Chysauster. Three miles to the north-west across the moors, near the St. Ives-Land's End road, is the excavated village of Porthmeor, with granite-built houses of the same type, occupied mainly between the second and fourth centuries A.D. Other Iron Age village-sites are known in England, but none is so revealing and impressive to the layman as these two sites in western Cornwall.

The people of the Early Iron Age lived mostly in single farmsteads or in small hamlets, of which Chysauster and Porthmeor are examples. The single farmsteads are revealed in the first instance by air-photography, which detects their presence by markings in the modern crops, but nothing is visible on the surface of the ground and they cannot be said to be significant for our study of the landscape. There is, however, one other relevant aspect of these Celtic farmsteads and that is the distinct possibility that a number of existing farmsteads and hamlets in south-western England (and possibly elsewhere, but of that I cannot speak) represent original Celtic farms which have been continuously occupied ever since their beginning in pre-Roman or Romano-British times. The farmstead itself in such places has been rebuilt over and over again during this long period of time, and is usually of no interest whatever to the archæologist, but as the descendant of a Celtic farmstead on the same site it is a fascinating place to the historian.

The other visible evidences in the landscape of these early farms are the lynchets or cultivation terraces that abound on the chalk downlands of south-eastern England, though they are found sporadically elsewhere also. These Celtic fields represent an immense advance on the tiny, irregular corn-plots of the Bronze Age farmers, for they are more or less rectangular blocks—often approximating to a square—varying in size from half to one and a half acres. They are seldom more than 400 feet long (usually much less), and seldom less than 100 feet in breadth (often more). It is this great breadth which distinguishes them clearly from the arable strips of the "open field" system that followed them in time. Such fields can be most readily seen from the air, as at Fyfield Down near Marlborough in Wiltshire (Plate 4), or on Windover Hill near Eastbourne in Sussex, but they are often easily seen on the ground also. On the Wiltshire and Sussex downs many square miles are covered by these fields. Immediately to the north of Brighton, an area of no less than $11\frac{1}{2}$ square miles is still covered with the lynchets of the Celtic field-system.

These ancient fields survive so clearly today because they were laid out in the smooth turf of the chalk country on a relatively dry soil, and because they were abandoned at some early date when cultivation and settlement moved down into the heavier and more rewarding soils of the valleys. In other parts of England they would be more difficult to find, especially where later cultivation has altered the field-boundaries, but one can detect possible clues on the large-scale maps, in conjunction with other evidence. The present-day field-pattern around the remote Dartmoor farm of Babeny, for example, is highly suggestive of Celtic farming in small square plots. Immediately below these plots flows the Walla Brook, hurrying on its way down to join the East Dart. Now Walla Brook was originally Wēala Brōc, "stream of the Welsh or Britons," a name given by the first Saxon settlers on the moorland fringes to a stream beside whose banks, far up into the Moor, scattered groups of Celtic farmers still survived. It is possible that at Babeny we have traces of one of their farms in the lay-out of the fields. Celtic farmers did not live merely upon the chalk downlands. It is only that the traces of their presence upon the landscape are more visible in that type of country.

PLATE 4

Celtic fields on the chalk uplands: Fyfield Down, near Marlborough, Wiltshire.

We may well seek for signs of their presence in the more difficult terrain of the West and the North, and in the lowlands of southern and eastern England.

Western Farmsteads and Fields

The subject of Celtic farmsteads is difficult to speak about, especially the visible evidences in the landscape. It seems likely that we shall find our surest signs in Cornwall, and above all in the far west of that county, for here the Celtic kingdom of Dumnonia subsisted until the early tenth century. Here a number of

active farms continued in being and come down to us more or less intact so far
as their fields and hedges are concerned. The farmsteads themselves have been
rebuilt over and over again, but the network of small, irregular fields bounded by
miles of granite-boulder walls was almost impossible to change once the pattern
was laid down. The six-inch maps of western Cornwall abound in this pattern,
for example in the parish of Zennor between St. Ives and Land's End. Bosigran
farm shows perhaps the most remarkable of these patterns (Fig. 1). For the dating
of these fields it is probably significant that both east and west of the farmstead
Iron Age houses of the Chysauster type have been found.[1] At Porthmeor, not
far away, the Iron Age village was occupied mainly between the second and
fourth centuries A.D., as we have seen; and at Treen, a little further to the
north-east, another Iron Age village is known to exist (Field 831, O.S. 25-inch
map).

Not all Celtic field-patterns are of the Bosigran type. At Castallack, in the parish
of Paul, the six-inch map reveals a continuous hedge enclosing a large squarish
area roughly one-third of a mile long and nearly as broad. This was later cut up
into about fifteen fields with no particular distinguishing characteristics, so that
the original enclosure has been completely lost sight of except to the observant
map-reader. The large original enclosure was an early cattle-field, covering
about sixty acres. Since a fogou, or sub-terranean retreat, of Iron Age date is
known to have existed immediately north of Castallack farm, and 350 yards
north-west lay a fortified masonry enclosure called the Roundago—probably a
small Iron Age fort—we are probably safe in assuming that the enclosed cattle-
field was of the same period.

At what date was this large enclosure sub-divided into a number of little fields
averaging three or four acres each? I think it likely that this was done in the
thirteenth century when Castallack was re-occupied. It is probable that the farm
was abandoned at an early date, as we know Chysauster and Porthmeor to have
been. The massive original walls of the enclosure remained (Plate 5), though the
interior must have been completely submerged in bracken and furze. We first
hear of Castallack again in a record of 1284, which suggests that it had been
re-occupied not long before, and it seems fairly certain that the small enclosures
within the larger one date from this time. Here, then, we have field-boundaries of
two widely different dates for the historian of the landscape to study.

Nowhere can we *prove* continuity of occupation from Celtic times to the present
day, for no records exist to enable us to do this. It is indeed likely that a great
number, perhaps most, of the farmsteads of Iron Age date have been abandoned
at some date and re-occupied in medieval times under the pressure of a rising
population. This may be true of such Dartmoor farms as Babeny, already referred
to, where the field-pattern and the stream-name both suggest the existence of
Celtic farmers. On the other hand, some farms may have enjoyed an unbroken

[1]Hencken, *Archæology of Cornwall and Scilly*, 311.

occupation. The fact that Walla Brook—"the stream of the Welsh or Britons"—cannot have been so named until the late seventh century at the earliest (when the Saxons reached Devon) is evidence for the continuance of Celtic farming along that stream (as at Babeny) at that comparatively late date, though as a name Babeny does not appear in the records until 1260. I see no reason to reject

FIG. 1.—CELTIC FIELDS IN ZENNOR PARISH, CORNWALL

The Penwith peninsula of west Cornwall is almost entirely of this character: hamlets of the Treen and Bosigran type, and thousands of tiny fields of very irregular shape. These fields are enclosed by rubble walling of unhewn granite blocks gathered from the surface of the land (see Plate 5) and therefore almost irremovable. The fields are of the same date as the numerous "British Villages" which are dotted all over the peninsula. Only two of these have been excavated, Chysauster (Plate 3) and Porthmeor. The latter (not marked on the above map) was discovered in 1933 near the Methodist chapel. Excavation showed that it was occupied from the middle of the first century A.D. until the fifth or sixth century, when it was abandoned. The present Lower Porthmeor and Higher Porthmeor represent a re-settlement, probably of medieval date. The Iron Age fields retained their identity, however, because of the massiveness of their boundary-walls, and were re-occupied. They form a very distinctive pattern, even more tangled and irregular than the medieval field-pattern (see Fig. 9). Indeed, it is possible that the more open, but still irregular, field-pattern to the north of Porthmeor and west of Treen, is the result of medieval clearance, so that we have fields of two distinct periods on the above map.

Reproduced by permission from the 6-inch map of the Ordnance Survey.

the possibility here of continuity of occupation since Celtic times, given a known survival as late as 700 or thereabouts.

Just off the northern foothills of Dartmoor, in the parish of Cheriton Bishop, is a farm called Treable for which some fascinating early evidence is forthcoming. Treable is one of the comparatively few Celtic place-names surviving in Devon: it means "the *trev* or homestead of Ebell," a personal name corresponding to the Gaulish Epillus. Now although Treable is not recorded as a name until 1242, it can be identified quite conclusively with an estate called "Hyple's old land"

PLATE 5

A megalithic granite wall in Cornwall: the north side of Castellack round. A field boundary probably of Iron Age date.

granted by king Edward to his faithful vassal Aelfsige in the year 976. Hyple is a corruption of Ebell, and the reference to "Hyple's old land" suggests that this Celtic landowner (whose name also appears at Ipplepen in south Devon) was in possession not long before, certainly within the tenth century.[1] Here, at any rate, a Celtic estate—in this instance covering an area of six thousand acres—survived almost to within a hundred years of the Norman Conquest, and there is no reason

[1]Finberg, *Early Charters of Devon and Cornwall*, 27 seq., upon which these remarks on Treable are mostly based.

to doubt the continuity of occupation of some part of it at least. A coin of the reign of Hadrian (early second century) has indeed been found in a hedge on Treable farm, but to assume continuity back to that period is hazardous.

The field-pattern of Treable today shows nothing indicative of great age. The Tithe Map of 1842—the oldest we have for this purpose—is disappointing. But there is one aspect of the estate-boundary, as given in the charter of 976, which is

PLATE 6

Celtic hamlet and fields near Cape Cornwall in the far west of the Penwith peninsula. All the buildings and the field boundaries are constructed of surface granite (moorstone).

worth dwelling upon for the light it throws upon a minor feature of the English landscape. At one point on its eastern boundary, the charter takes us "along the way to the old ditch." Walking along this boundary, with the help of the 2½-inch Ordnance map, one finds oneself dropping down a steep hillside along a cart-track which is shut in on either side by an earthen bank several feet high, *i.e.*, a hollow way. This hollow way—"the old ditch"—was already "old" in the tenth century. It can hardly be doubted that it represents the ancient boundary between the estate of Hyple and his ancestors to the west, and that of another (unknown) Celtic landowner to the east. The two hedgebanks, still enclosing the fields of today, are thus of great age—certainly pre-Saxon.

The "hollow way" was made by each landowner digging out a ditch and throwing up the earth into a continuous bank on his own side. So we get a double ditch which forms in fact a track several feet wide and sunk several feet below the level of the fields on either side, thus:—

A's estate   B's estate

Boundary between A and B

A's estate   B's estate

Earthen bank   Earthen bank

Boundary now a double ditch or hollow way

That this is often the origin of the "hollow way" running between two high banks is clinched by the expression in a charter of *c.* 1174 setting out the boundaries between the abbot of Tavistock's estate at Abbotsham in north Devon and that of a neighbouring squire—Richard Coffin—at Alwington and Cockington. Here the bounds begin "from the two-fold ditch" (*twifealda dich*). A Somerset charter of 963, relating to a Saxon estate called Manworthy in Milverton, refers to "the hollow ditch" at one point, evidently the same construction as a two-fold ditch.

The Treable and Abbotsham charters explain the significance and origin of a puzzling feature which all those who walk across country (and do not rush in utter blindness through it in a car) must have come across at one time or another: that is the track, sometimes only a few feet wide, sometimes much broader, which begins suddenly on one side of a field-gate, runs between hedgebanks for several hundred yards, occasionally more, and then stops as suddenly as it began, debouching into a field and losing all identity forthwith. If we regard such lanes as trackways, they are impossible to explain, for they begin and end nowhere, so to speak. They are in fact ancient boundaries between two estates, sometimes medieval, sometimes Saxon or even Celtic, formed by the digging of a double ditch. It should be observed that this does not explain all "hollow ways," some of which are true traffic-routes, but it explains those that appear to go nowhere in particular and to peter out without reason.

There is much more to be learnt about the visible signs of Celtic estates, farms, fields, and hedges, in the English countryside. I have set out above a few of the considerations that have come my way, but patient and minute topographical research—of the sort that is wrongly despised by most historians—will undoubtedly reveal to us in time much more of this distant period still embedded in the landscape around us, if only we have eyes to see, the records to follow up the visual evidence, and the imagination to read the records aright.

Roman Britain

With the spread of settled villages it is possible that the total population of Britain may have risen to something like a quarter of a million before the arrival of the Belgae early in the first century B.C. The spread of the Belgae over the whole of south-eastern England and well into the Midlands, and their cultivation of the loams with the heavy wheeled plough, opened up new kinds of land hitherto considered too intractable for the light prehistoric plough, and there can be no doubt that it resulted in a further substantial increase of population. Knowing what we do of the population of Roman Britain (not much, it is true, but incomparably more than we know of the earlier periods) we cannot put the maximum population of Britain on the eve of the Roman Conquest at more than 400,000— about the size of modern Bristol. When we bear in mind figures of this magnitude, and remember that for the greater part of the prehistoric period in Britain the population was less than fifty to a hundred thousand, we can readily appreciate that even the first two thousand years of agriculture from neolithic times onwards has left little mark upon the landscape, other than a few more or less impressive isolated features. The continuous story can still hardly be said to have begun.

Nor was the Roman contribution to the landscape, or what can be seen of it today, much more substantial. It shows itself mainly in the surviving roads, in the sites of villas, and in a few canals or dykes in eastern England, all of which remained important in their various ways well beyond the Roman period.

The network of the major Roman roads in England is fairly well known, though many gaps even in the known roads remain to be filled in. Besides the major roads, a large system of secondary roads gradually came into existence to serve local needs, and much more remains to be discovered about these. Mr. I. D. Margary's *Roman Ways in the Weald* (1948) brought to light a whole network of these lesser roads in Kent and Sussex, mostly unsuspected until he wrote. East Anglia probably had an equally complex system of local roads to judge by the unrelated fragments on the present map. Most of this still awaits working out. Even so, more than five thousand miles of roads are shown on the Ordnance Survey map of *Roman Britain* (1931 edition).

The Roman road-system, both the main post-roads and the local roads, was important in the history of the English landscape. Not only do many of these roads survive to this day (or more strictly, the line of the road) as trunk roads carrying a thunderous lorry-traffic over long distances (for example, Watling Street, now the Holyhead Road) or as useful secondary roads between villages in many parts of southern England, or in a more intimate fashion as bridle-paths and footpaths for solitary man and beast, but they opened up in their time whole tracts of the countryside on a scale hitherto unknown. Even the lesser local roads pushed through the forested clay lands in all directions, and crossed the high moorlands. This does not necessarily mean that these forests and moors were opened up for clearance and settlement, except perhaps in unimportant little patches. The roads cut through the woods in going from one place to another, but the bulk of settlement was still confined to the lighter and more open soils and was associated with the pre-Roman trackways rather than the Roman roads. The

PLATE 7

A Roman road from the air: the road from Mildenhall (Cunetio) in Wiltshire to Winchester (Venta Belgarum). Near Tangley (Hampshire), looking south-eastwards.

Weald, for instance, remained mostly unsettled and wild, except for clearings where iron-mining was carried on, and the dense forests on the heavy Midland clays show very few sites of villas or native Romano-British villages. The real importance of these roads comes out in the Anglo-Saxon period, for they were, together with the larger rivers, the ready-made routes by which the English colonists penetrated more swiftly and safely into new country than if they had had to hack their way in yard by yard from the edges. There had been, of course, and there still existed, a considerable system of prehistoric trackways, along which settlers and colonists of new land had moved since Bronze Age times, and of which the Anglo-Saxon colonists also made extensive use wherever they found them; but these early trackways kept mostly to the higher and more open ground, on the lighter soils, whereas the Roman roads thrust through the heavier and more fertile soils that offered greater possibilities to the Old English farmers.

The Romano-British villas, of which well over five hundred are known (and many others still await discovery), represent a substantial clearance and taming of the natural landscape. Some of them, like the villa at Ditchley in Oxfordshire, were the centres of estates of a thousand acres or more. The villa was an isolated farmhouse, standing in its own large, open fields, quite unlike the small enclosed fields that surrounded the native villages. Sometimes it was large enough and elaborate enough to be regarded as a country-house, with a correspondingly large estate around it. In some instances excavation has shown that a pre-Roman farmstead stood on the same site (as at Otford in Kent or at Newport in the Isle of Wight), and that the villa represents the rebuilding of an older and more primitive farmstead as some native farmers acquired wealth and a taste for Roman ways of living. Such extensive rebuildings by farmers rising in the social scale occur at later periods in English history, notably in the sixteenth and seventeenth centuries.

Most villas appear, however, to stand on new sites, though they were still built upon the ligher soils—chalk, oolite, and gravel—favoured by men before them. "They tend," says R. G. Collingwood, "to select a rather special type of site: a valley-slope facing south or east, not too high up, with shelter from the wind, exposure to the sun, and water close at hand." Though occupying in the main the lighter and more easily cleared soils, villas were also established in forest-clearings, virgin sites on the heavier soils which the new wheeled plough was able to cope with. One finds such villas in the Cambridgeshire woods, on the edge of the forest in southern Berkshire, and in Wychwood forest in Oxfordshire. The attack on the forests and woods which covered the greater part of England under natural conditions, and above all on the extensive clay lands, was making headway throughout Roman times, though still only slowly and sporadically.

Besides the villas, there was a totally different type of settlement—the native villages, with their small, rectangular fields. These villages, of which a considerable number have been recognized, were simply groups of one-roomed huts: "sometimes pit-dwellings sunk into the ground, sometimes stone-built structures standing wholly above it; they are never neatly aligned on streets or laid out on a regular plan, but clustered shapelessly, generally within some kind of ditch or fence; and although the people who lived in them used Roman pottery and coins to a certain extent, their daily life was affected by Roman ways very little, and in some cases, especially in the highland zone, not at all."[1]

Most of these settlements were so small that they should be called "hamlet" rather than "village." Only eight houses have been recognized at Chysauster in Cornwall, and the Romano-British village on Thundersbarrow Hill near Shore-

[1] Collingwood and Myres, *Roman Britain and the English Settlements*, 209.

Villa .... ▲
Uncertain Villa ... △
Minor Settlement ⊙
Pottery Kiln ...... +K
Miscellaneous finds
(pottery, coins, etc.) .. ●
Roman Road ———
Probable .. ----
Roman Road

Based by permission upon the Ordnance Map of Roman Britain (draft revision)

FIG. 2.—ROMANO-BRITISH SETTLEMENT IN PART OF OXFORDSHIRE

In this comparatively small district (only twelve miles by ten), which is mostly upon the
oolitic limestone there are no fewer than nine villas (and one uncertain villa site),
one minor settlement (Wilcote), a pottery kiln, and a great number of sites where pottery
and/or coins have been found. Some of these sites may well prove to be native villages.
The concentration of sites is particularly notable between the Glyme and the Evenlode.
Just off the map to the west is the important industrial settlement (iron-working) of
Asthall; to the east (off the map) is the Romano-British temple of Wood Eaton.

ham, in Sussex, seems to have consisted of nine wattle huts scattered over an acre of ground or more. Nothing resembling a large nucleated village has been found in Roman Britain: this was to be the most distinctive contribution of the Anglo-Saxons to the landscape.

The distribution of villas and of native villages in Roman Britain is generally distinct. Certain regions, like Salisbury Plain, Cranborne Chase, and the Sussex Downs between the Adur and the Ouse, were apparently occupied exclusively by villages. Such villas as occur in these districts are found on the outskirts. The villas with their large open fields and the villages with their enclosed fields, seem to represent two different economic systems, existing contemporaneously. Whether they are everywhere geographically distinct remains to be seen. In the fairly closely settled region of north Oxfordshire depicted in Fig. 2 they appear to be intermingled.

In some parts of England the landscape was fairly thickly settled and cut up into fields by means of broad low banks. Of the sixty-five square miles of chalk downland between the Adur and the Ouse in Sussex, nearly fifteen square miles show signs of having been divided into fields of the Celtic type; and on this area no fewer than thirty-two occupation sites have been recognized. It now seems probable that this concentrated area of native farming supplied London with its surplus products. Already the Great Wen was going far afield for its food. In recent years areas of close agricultural settlement have been recognized elsewhere in England: in the Fenland, in the Evesham district of Worcestershire, in the lower Trent valley, and on the Yorkshire Wolds near Malton.

The close settlement of the Fens of southern Lincolnshire and of Cambridge-shire in Romano-British times was made possible by an extensive system of dykes or drainage channels and causeways, constructed by the Roman engineers. Aerial photography has revealed many sites of native villages and their associated fields, especially in the silt areas (as distinct from the peat) and on certain 'islands' rising above the general level. The Car Dyke is the best known of these artificial waterways, and has now been shown to be Roman work. It was probably made to provide water transport between the Cam and the Ouse, but Sir Cyril Fox considers that it was also a drainage channel. In Cambridgeshire it forms a wet ditch, five miles in length, best seen near Waterbeach, on the east side of the Waterbeach-Landbeach road and about four miles NNE. of Cambridge. Through the Old West Water the Cambridgeshire section of the Car Dyke is linked with the ditch of the same name and similar character on the western side of the Fens, running from the Nene near Peterborough northwards to the Witham near Lincoln, a total length of fifty-six miles with an original width of about fifty feet.

Long stretches of this ditch may be seen in Lincolnshire, especially just north of Peterborough; again near Bourne, where it runs parallel with the Bourne-Market Deeping road for some distance on its eastern side; and for long stretches north of Bourne. Another good stretch is to be seen from Billinghay north-westwards towards Timberland, about eight miles north-east of Sleaford. Although Roman in origin, the ditch takes its name from a Scandinavian named *Kari* or *Karr*, probably a considerable landowner in the period between the Scandinavian and the Norman Conquests, part of the ditch being in all probability a boundary of his estate. It first occurs by name as *Karesdic* in a twelfth-century charter.

Another Roman canal, the so-called Foss Dyke, was probably also used for both drainage and transport. It connected the Witham near Lincoln with the tidal Trent at Torksey—a cut of eleven miles across a narrow neck of countryside—so giving direct inland communication by water between Cambridge and York. This canal was still of considerable importance in early medieval England, for by its aid the Witham tapped the agricultural and mineral wealth of the north Midlands, and it contributed to the prosperity of Torksey, Lincoln, and Boston as ports between the twelfth and fourteenth centuries.

Down in Dorset, a contour canal brought water from the river Frome below Maiden Newton to the Roman town of Dorchester, meandering through the country on the south side of the river. But this was an isolated feature of the landscape, of only local importance, whereas the ditches of the Fenland were important agents in the transformation of great tracts of land from natural marsh to fairly thickly scattered farms.

There was one other important Roman contribution to the landscape, and that was the town. A few towns had indeed already been founded in south-eastern Britain by the civilized Belgae, who preceded the Romans by about a century. Most important of the Belgic towns was Camulodunum (Colchester), the capital of Britain at the time of the Roman invasion. Other important Belgic towns were Verulamium (St. Albans), Calleva (Silchester), and perhaps Venta Belgarum (Winchester), and there may have been others.[1] But the Romans founded many new towns during the second half of the first century and the early part of the second century, mostly on virgin sites, as at Exeter (Isca Dumnoniorum) which was founded about A.D. 50. By the second century, or the early third, most of these towns were walled around. But the towns were only small oases in a vast extent of countryside: the thirty-three civil towns together added up to only about four square miles of urban settlement. The twelve tribal capitals averaged about a hundred acres each in size, the ten smallest towns about thirty acres each. Roman London covered about 330 acres, but Roman Bath only 23, and Irchester only 20.

We have to record the appearance of towns as a new feature in the English landscape, but they were small, generally far apart, and quite foreign to the mode of life of most of the population of Britain. Possibly some 200,000 people lived in them altogether. As for the total population of the country at this period, it has been put at half a million by Collingwood, and at one and a half million by Wheeler.

[1] I give the modern names in brackets, though the sites of the Belgic town and the modern town (or village) are not quite identical.

Grahame Clark compromises at 600,000 to 700,000. We do not know more exactly than this.

It might seem from the foregoing pages that in the five hundred years that elapsed between the coming of the Belgae and the departure of the Romans the natural landscape had been very considerably altered, tamed, and brought into use as farming land. Wide tracts of marshland had been drained and settled, the forests invaded by roads and by villa-estates in many places, the open downs and some of the valleys dotted with hamlets and isolated farms, nearly a hundred towns (most of them small) planted here and there all over the country, and especially south of the Trent. Over five hundred villas are known: more are discovered every year: the total may well reach a thousand in time. About seven hundred native villages are shown on the map of Roman Britain, and many more await discovery. The map of south-western England, for example, is almost a total blank: only one town (Exeter), three or four villas, perhaps half a dozen villages or permanent settlements: only this meagre sprinkling in an area of more than four thousand square miles. Moreover, this was the important Celtic kingdom of Dumnonia, which was resisting the Saxon invasions (however ineffectively) in a number of pitched battles as late as the closing years of the seventh century. It is clear that there must have been a considerable population in this part of England all through the Roman period of which hardly any record has yet reached the map, and this may be equally true of the northern kingdom of the Brigantes, where the map is almost as barren of evidence of settled life. When these parts of England have been more exhaustively explored by archæologists, we may well have nearer fifteen hundred native hamlets in place of the seven hundred or so now known. Some twenty generations had been colonizing the landscape since the arrival of the Belgae, and must have made a considerable impression upon it before the Anglo-Saxons appeared upon the scene. One would have expected the back of the task to have been broken after all this activity, whereas in fact the Anglo-Saxons moved into a country that was generally still a wilderness, with almost everything yet to be done. In certain favoured regions like the Cotswolds and north Oxfordshire they may have entered a fairly civilized landscape; but in general they had to start (literally) from scratch.

There are two reasons why this should have been so. In the first place we must not overestimate the total impression made by the Romano-British generations upon the landscape. Their clearances, fields, and settlements were locally import-ant, but considered as a whole they made little impression upon the natural scene. There may have been, allowing for discoveries yet to be made, a hundred towns and some 2,500 rural settlements—villas, hamlets, and single farms. It is nearly impossible to say what this rural settlement meant in terms of land cleared and under crops and grass. If we may judge by the Sussex downland already referred to, where 9,000 acres of land show signs of farming in Romano-British times and thirty-two settlements (large and small) have been recognized, we have a very rough average of three hundred acres per settlement. And if we apply this figure (which is almost certainly too high as an average for the country as a whole) to native hamlets and villas alike, we have a grand total of 750,000 acres already rescued from the waste and used as arable or grassland. In 1914 the total acreage under crops and grass in England and Wales (excluding mountain pastures and heaths) was rather more than twenty-seven million acres. In Roman Britain, then, only two or three acres in every hundred capable of bearing crops and grass had been conquered from the natural waste. Such a figure can only be the roughest of estimates, but even if we doubled it—and this would certainly be too high—the Romano-British contribution to the making of the landscape remains unimpressive when considered as a whole.

Moreover, much of this cleared and tamed landscape had reverted, or was reverting, to its natural state when the Anglo-Saxons were taking over. In the Fenland, the artificial drainage system of the Romans had collapsed by the fifth century and the rich farmlands were turned once more into a morass. Either there had been a general sinkage of land-levels, or the elaborate drainage system had been wrecked in the first devastating attacks of the Anglo-Saxons, or by their subsequent ignorance. Whatever the cause, the Fenland went out of cultivation for many centuries, and the first Old English settlers moved through the new wastes to higher ground farther inland. On the Wiltshire downs, large tracts of arable land were being converted to sheep-walks by the latter part of the third century and the upland villages were being depopulated. Possibly, however, the displaced population was being settled elsewhere, perhaps in the Fenland. We do not know. On the Sussex downs the native villages show signs of having been abandoned by about A.D. 400.

All over the country, villas and their estates were decaying well before the Saxon invasions. A few villas were violently destroyed, but most simply decayed two or three generations before the first Anglo-Saxon colonists arrived on the scene. The buildings were tumbled and weed-grown, the fields gone back to heath and scrub. We have all seen in recent years what ten years' decay and neglect can do in a bomb-damaged town. Most villa estates must have been a tangled wilderness after fifty to a hundred years of unpeopled silence, though some survived into a later generation and their land may have been taken over by the Old English without much difficulty, as we shall see in the next chapter. Much farmland went out of use in south-western England when the Dumnonii migrated in large numbers across the channel to Brittany, probably during the first half of the sixth century. It was rescued again from the waste only after many centuries, when the medieval peasant of the twelfth or thirteenth century came upon it again and called it the "old land," for he recognized that someone had been there before him and had once tilled or grazed it. Such is the significance of farm-names like Yelland, Yellaton, Yellowland and Yellowmead, all in Devon.

Much, then, of the work of taming and shaping the landscape by the hungry generations from the Belgae onwards had been lost in weeds, scrub, and ruins by the time the Anglo-Saxon colonists arrived. The work had to begin all over again. Not quite all over again, as we shall see, but the great majority of the English settlers faced a virgin country of damp oak-ash forest, or beech-forest on and near the chalk; and what was not thickly forested was likely to be cold, high mist-wrapped moorland, or water-logged wet heath, drowned marshes and estuary saltings, or sterile, thin-soiled dry heath. Studies of separate counties will correct this picture in detail, and show more clearly what survived from the wreckage of Romano-British rural life; but in the main this is what the picture looked like to those land-hungry invaders as they penetrated up the Humber rivers, the rivers of the Wash, and up the Thames, in the middle decades of the fifth century, looking for their new homes.

SELECT BIBLIOGRAPHY

CLARK, GRAHAME, *Archæology and Society* (1930).
CLARK, GRAHAME, *Prehistoric England* (1940).
COLLINGWOOD, R. G., and MYRES, J. N. L., *Roman Britain and the English Settlements* (1936).
CRAWFORD, O. G. S., *Man and His Past* (1921).
CURWEN, E. C., *Air Photography and the Evolution of the Corn Field* (2nd ed. 1938).
CURWEN, E. C., *The Archæology of Sussex* (1937).
Field Archæology (H.M.S.O., revised ed. 1951).
FOX, SIR CYRIL, *The Archæology of the Cambridge Region* (2nd ed. 1948).
HENCKEN, H. O'N., *The Archæology of Cornwall and Scilly* (1932).
MARGARY, I. D., *Roman Ways in the Weald* (1948).
Ordnance Survey Map of Roman Britain (2nd ed. 1931 in course of revision).

II

The English Settlement

Villages and their Fields

THE Anglo-Saxon settlement was spread over some twenty generations between about 450 and 1066. During this time England became a land of villages. Historians used to draw a contrast between the small, scattered settlements—hamlets and single farmsteads—of the north and west, where Celtic life continued, and the more or less compact and nucleated villages of central, eastern, and southern England, where the Old English swept all before them and built and planted afresh. But this picture is much too simple and does not square with the facts. Even in Cornwall and Devon, in the far south-west, the large compact village can be found all over the map and is found at the time of the Norman Conquest; and hamlets and isolated farmsteads of great antiquity can be found dotted about the midland and the eastern counties.

The village can be found everywhere in England. In certain parts (in the Midlands, above all) it is the predominant—and at times the only—form of settlement, while in the northern and western counties we find a thoroughly mixed pattern of settlement, of villages, hamlets, and single farmsteads. Here the village is only one form of settlement among several, all of considerable antiquity.

Compact villages, of varying size, are to be found in all counties, dating for the most part from Anglo-Saxon times. Everywhere they were accompanied originally by the open-field system. It used to be thought that open fields had never been imposed upon the landscape in the peripheral regions of England—in Kent and Essex, Devon and Cornwall, Lancashire and the north-west. In fact they were introduced into all these regions, but they disappeared from them long before the period of parliamentary enclosures in the eighteenth century. Indeed, they had gone even before the Tudor enclosures of the sixteenth century, so long ago that it was rashly assumed that they had never existed. It seems likely—though we know too little to generalize—that in these peripheral counties the open fields were being enclosed into the hedged fields that we know today during the course of the thirteenth and fourteenth centuries, at a time when records of the process are hard to come by.

Nor is much known of the nature of the open-field system in the Anglo-Saxon period. In its simplest form it probably consisted of two large fields—one on each side of the village, and often called the East Field and the West Field, or the North Field and the South Field. Each field covered perhaps a few score acres to begin with, but every decade and generation added to their area by clearing the woodland and other wild ground around their circumference. It took many centuries for villages to reach the limits of their territory, and for the fields to reach their maximum extent. Not until the end of the thirteenth century, or the beginning of the fourteenth, was this generally achieved.

PLATE 8

The village of Haxey in the Isle of Axholme (Lincolnshire) still retains a large extent of its medieval open fields, and gives some idea of the original appearance of the English landscape under open field cultivation.

Most people are now familiar with the fact that the unit of cultivation was the *strip*, which varied in area, and in length and breadth, according to the nature of the soil and the lie of the land. The standard or "normal" size of one acre—

220 yards long by 22 yards wide—was only rarely found in most parts of England. Strips of half an acre or even one-third of an acre were probably the most usual. A bundle or parcel of strips, all running in the same direction, made up what was known as a *furlong* (or *cultura* in contemporary documents), so that the field (or *campus*)—the largest unit of all—was made up of scores of furlongs of varying shapes and sizes, and hence of several hundred strips. A map will make the picture clearer than a good deal of description. (Fig. 3.)

PLATE 9

Combe Martin on the North Devon coast: a street-village which originated about a mile inland and has since grown down the bottom of the valley (combe) to the seashore. The field-pattern, especially on the right-hand side of the valley, makes it clear that the village once had open fields laid out in strips. These have been enclosed with hedges, probably in medieval times.

There may have been some Anglo-Saxon villages with three fields instead of two. When the records became numerous and more informative about village fields, in the last decades of the twelfth century, we find both two-field and three-field villages. It is possible that the three-field system evolved out of the two-field, as we know happened in some places in medieval times.

This is no place to describe in detail the agricultural arrangements of the open-field system. So far as the open fields are concerned, we can see the kind of land-

FIG. 3.—WEST FIELD AND WESTWOOD COMMON, AT LAXTON (NOTTINGHAMSHIRE), IN 1635

The common lies to the west of the arable field. The individual strips are grouped in blocks (furlongs), clearly seen on the map. The broad green balks or occupation roads are also very conspicuous.

Reproduced by permission from C. S. and C. S. Orwin, The Open Fields.

scape they produced in a few places to this day—at Haxey in the Isle of Axholme (Plate 8), at Laxton in Nottinghamshire, or at Braunton in North Devon. It also survives in many parts of the Midlands where the arable strips of the open fields were fossilized, so to speak, under grass when the extensive sheep and cattle pastures were created between the fifteenth and seventeenth centuries. (Plate 10.)

The up-and-down ploughing of the long narrow strips, with a certain type of plough, threw the soil towards the centre of the strip, so producing a high ridge. Each strip was separated from its neighbour by a double furrow (in some districts by an unploughed grass balk), so that the ancient pattern of the medieval and Saxon open fields is perpetuated by the ridge-and-furrow which is so conspicuous an element in the Midland landscape today. One sees particularly widespread and interesting patterns of ridge-and-furrow from the train on the former Great Central line in the country to the south of Rugby. Much of this ridge-and-furrow disappeared with the intensive ploughing-up of pastures during the Second World War, but a good deal remains. This should be mapped and photographed from the air while there is yet time. In certain places it is very likely that one has the complete lay-out of a medieval open-field system. The more we can discover of these arrangements the better, for "strip-maps" are relatively uncommon and there is much yet to be discovered about the agrarian arrangements even of the recent past. Not all ridge-and-furrow is of this antiquity; some is of comparatively recent origin and of no historical significance. We need the local historians and topographers to distinguish carefully between the two types.

The Anglo-Saxons covered the whole of England with their villages, much more thickly in some parts than others. In Leicestershire and Lincolnshire, for example, the villages were often less than a couple of miles apart, and the Scandinavian settlement later added to the "congestion"; but in Devon and Cornwall they were half a dozen miles or so apart, especially to the west of the Exe, probably because Celtic hamlets and farmsteads survived in not inconsiderable numbers and occupied much of the intervening country.

Villages were not new to England at the coming of the Anglo-Saxons. A considerable number, as we have seen, had existed in Romano-British times, but most of these were probably deserted by the fourth or the fifth century. It yet remains to be proved that there is any village in England which has been continuously inhabited since Celtic times. Most of our villages are certainly on new sites—along the river-valleys for the most part, which earlier village-dwellers had ignored—selected by the Old English, the Danes, and the Norwegians, between the fifth century and the eleventh. Yet there are, here and there, certain exciting clues which suggest that a few villages may have been continuously inhabited since pre-Saxon times. Though such villages may be only a small minority, they are all the more worth pursuing.

Hill-top villages are particularly suggestive of a great antiquity. High up on the edge of Cranborne Chase, on the borders of Dorset and Wiltshire, stands a village with the good old Saxon name of Ashmore; but it has probably been continuously lived in since Romano-British times. Not only does it stand on a hill-top, in country that is thickly strewn with evidences of early man, including several Romano-British villages, but it is built around a big embanked pond which gives the village its Saxon name—ash-mere, "the pond of the ash tree." Crawford,

PLATE 10

Midland "ridge and furrow" at Crimscote in Warwickshire. Undoubtedly we have here the ridged strips of the open arable fields, which were converted to grass at some distant date. It is clear that the popular explanation of ridge and furrow as the result of drainage requirements breaks down in a view like this. We have here a fossilized medieval field-pattern. Note how scrub is again invading the landscape with the neglect of farming between the two recent wars.

in a highly interesting essay on Ponds,[1] shows that these embanked ponds go back in some instances to the beginning of the Christian era or a little earlier, and that the upland villages which take their names from such ancient ponds or *meres* "have either been continuously occupied since pre-Saxon times, or . . . were

[1]*Archæology in the Field*, 123-31.

Ashmore

Water Column

St. Nicholas's Church

(Rectory)

FIG. 4.—PLAN OF ASHMORE IN NORTH DORSET

The large embanked pond (114) was the ancient nucleus of the village, which takes its Saxon name from it: the pond of the ash tree. The village lies on the highest point of upland country, on the edge of Cranborne Chase, which is thickly studded with native villages and other remains of the Romano-British period. Ashmore may well be a Romano-British village which has survived without a break to the present day. The parish church lies some distance from the pond, on the outskirts of the village, as we might expect if it is so much later in date than the village.

Reproduced by permission from the 25-inch map of the Ordnance Survey.

re-occupied, after abandonment for a period, by early Saxon settlers." Buttermere (in Wiltshire) is another such village.

Crawford also shows that when the Old English settlers occupied the valleys and marked out their boundaries, certain upland areas were left untouched and native (Romano-British) villages went on untroubled. Where the uplands took the form of narrow ridges, the settlements in two adjoining valleys had a common frontier down the middle of the intervening ridge of downland; and the ancient upland villages, where they still survived, were squeezed out of existence. But Ashmore lies in one of those upland areas too far from the valleys to be touched. Its Saxon name may be misleading: that may well have been bestowed by the Old English down in the lowlands, for the great majority of place-names must, from their nature, have originated with neighbours and not with the inhabitants themselves. We know, for example, because we happen to have the necessary early records, that in Somerset certain Celtic place-names were changed by the newcomers. In a charter of 1065 relating to the village of Biddisham near Axbridge, we are specifically told that its proper name is *Tarnuc*, an earlier Celtic name. Similarly, the Celtic *Lantokai* ("the church of St. Cai") is now the prosaic Leigh near Glastonbury.[1] The Saxon name of Ashmore, then, is no argument against its possessing a pre-Saxon antiquity.

Seebohm, in his neglected and under-valued book *The English Village Community*, has a dozen fascinating pages on Local Evidence of Continuity between Roman and English Villages. He gives several examples of possible continuity in the Hitchin district, in north Hertfordshire, of which it will be sufficient to cite one. At Litlington, near Ashwell, "the church and manor house . . . lie near together on the west side of the village, and in the adjoining field and gardens the walls and pavements of a Roman villa were found many years ago. At a little distance from it, nearer to the Ashwell Street, a Roman *ustrinum* and cemetery were found, surrounded by four walls, and yielding coins of Hadrian (to) . . . Magnentius."

At Woodchester in Gloucestershire, the parish church, the mansion-house, and a Roman villa all lie close together; and there are other very suggestive sites in the Cotswold region which was rich in villa sites and to some extent in Romano-British village sites also. Ditchley in north Oxfordshire has produced a villa site that continued in use possibly into the fifth century. At Eynsham, about six miles to the south, the evidence for continuity of occupation on a native village site is very suggestive. Here various finds of pottery and coins show occupation from the first century A.D. to the fourth; and in the year 571, Eynsham was one of the places captured by the Anglo-Saxons as a result of the battle of Bedford. Quite clearly it was a living village at that date. There are not a few places in southern England where the evidence for continuity of life calls for a new examination.

In Cornwall, the Old English conquerors in the eighth century seem to have

[1]Turner, "Some Aspects of Celtic Survival in Somerset," *Proc. Somersetshire Arch. and Nat. Hist. Soc.*, xcvii (1953), 148-51.

taken over places with Celtic names and to have transformed them into large Teutonic villages. They certainly seem to have introduced their open-field agriculture in such places.[1] The east Cornish village of Callington bore the Old Cornish name of *Celliwic* ("village by a grove") to which the English added *tun* when they took over. Kilkhampton, in the north of the county, and Helston, in the west, are other examples of villages with Old Cornish names, where a Saxon termination was added at a later date and Saxon open fields were introduced. Such villages as these have conceivably had a continuous existence since Romano-British times.

Hamlets

Even for the Old English, the village and the open field was not the only form of human settlement. "No single type of settlement," says Sir Frank Stenton, "can ever have prevailed throughout the whole, even of southern England. On heavy lands, and, indeed, wherever there was a prospect of a steady return to co-operative agriculture, ceorls tended to live together in villages. But as late as the eighth century life for perhaps a quarter of the English people was a struggle for existence against unprofitable soil and a scrubland vegetation which would spread again over cultivated fields on any slackening of effort. It was by individual enterprise that these poor lands had been brought into cultivation, and innumerable isolated farmsteads bearing Anglo-Saxon names remain as memorials of the process."

Such an isolated farmstead of Saxon origin may be seen at Queen Hoo Hall, in Hertfordshire, among the winding lanes three miles east of Welwyn. This is recorded in a Saxon charter of *c.* 1060 as *Quenildehaga*, signifying "the enclosure of a woman named Cwenhild," clearly a farm with separately hedged fields that formed no part of the open fields of the older village of Tewin from which its first founder had probably come. There are other farms, not far away, such as Roxford (in the parish of Hertingfordbury) and Epcombe, which Domesday Book shows were cultivated on their own, quite outside the co-operative agriculture of the village fields. The counties of Devon and Cornwall are full of such isolated farmsteads, founded in small clearings in the woods, and recorded in Anglo-Saxon charters or at the latest in Domesday Book.

The clearance of the woodland was, indeed, the greatest single form of change in the natural landscape, especially in the early stages of the Old English settlement before there was any thought of draining the water-logged fens and marshes or the estuarine flats, or of reclaiming the high, stone-strewn moorlands. The Old English have left us with almost no word at all about the kind of landscape they found on arrival, that they set out to reclaim from the natural wilderness. They had no eye for scenery, any more than other hard-working farmers of later centuries. But the "lives" of the Celtic saints, missionizing in the south-west

[1]See W. G. V. Balchin, *Cornwall*, in this series.

of England between the fifth and eighth centuries, and founding small monastic communities in isolated places, give us some idea of the work that was involved. In the life of St. Brioc, the fifth-century Welsh saint who travelled through Cornwall and Brittany, we read that the brethren "gird themselves to work, they cut down trees, root up bushes, tear up brambles and tangled thorns, and soon convert a dense wood into an open clearing. . . . Some cut down timber and trim it

PLATE 11

Westcott Barton in Marwood parish, North Devon. This isolated farmstead is recorded in Domesday Book and is of Saxon origin, founded beside a stream and far from any village. Its fields were small, hedged enclosures from the beginning, but some hedges have evidently been destroyed in recent years to give larger fields.

with axes, others planed planks for the walls of their houses, many prepared the ceilings and roofs, some turned up the sod with hoes. . . ." This is one side of the picture, of zealous men joyfully clearing the ground for their monastic home; but the lonely pioneer without the burning zeal of an intense faith must have felt more like lamenting in the words given to Adam in the ancient Cornish drama *The Beginning of the World*:[1]

[1]Quoted by Pounds in "The Ancient Woodland of Cornwall," *Old Cornwall* (Dec. 1942), 523-4.

> "Strong are the roots of the briars,
> So that my arms are broken
> Working at them again and again."

The smaller trees, bushes, and undergrowth were cleared by the axe, the mattock, and the bill-hook, but no family or village community could have survived long enough without crops if this were the only way of clearing the ground. There is evidence that the forests were set on fire and rapid clearances effected in that manner. A number of place-names testify to this. Swithland, a Leicestershire village on the edge of Charnwood Forest, means "the land cleared by burning"; and this is the meaning of the place-name Sweden, often found in the northern counties. Barnet was a considerable district on the wooded borders of Hertfordshire and Middlesex where the ground was similarly cleared by burning, and Brentwood in Essex is "the burnt wood." Brindley in Cheshire is "the burnt clearing."

There is evidence that neolithic man cleared woodland by burning: layers of charcoal occur at neolithic level in the bogs of Denmark. All the English examples quoted above are late in date (twelfth and thirteenth centuries), showing that this method of clearance was being employed in medieval England; but some of the laws of the Anglo-Saxon kings show that it was a recognized method in pre-Conquest times. Among the laws of Ine (688-94) is one penalizing anyone who destroys another man's trees by fire: "he shall pay sixty shillings because fire is a thief."

The axe was probably the most important method of clearance, for the large and small timber was needed for a multitude of purposes. Timber played the part played by steel, concrete, and coal in the modern economy, in the building of houses, ships, and churches; in the making of farming implements, household tools, and in repair-work of all kinds; and in supplying domestic fuel. Fire must have been regarded generally as a rather desperate expedient, to be employed in a frontier-economy and not after the establishment of a settled community. A third powerful agent in the rapid clearance of the forests was the grazing of animals, who by consuming the seedling trees in large numbers as they roamed in the woodlands round their homesteads prevented the natural regeneration of the forest, and the replacement of its losses from old age, and eventually reduced it to more or less open clearings of the nature of park-land. This process may be seen at work today round the frontier-homesteads of northern Norway.

The Shape of Villages

The axe, fire, and animals combined to reduce the dense and continuous woodlands of Anglo-Saxon England. By the middle of the tenth century, says Sir Frank Stenton, charters prove 'the existence of innumerable villages, each known by a permanent name and maintained by a territory of which the boundaries could be described in minute detail." Nearly every village on the map of England today—except in certain industrial districts—existed by the eleventh century and is described in Domesday Book. Some go back in date to the fifth and sixth centuries, as we know from the clues afforded by their place-names or from the archæological evidence of heathen cemeteries; many more are recorded in the surviving charters of the seventh to the tenth centuries. The work of colonization went on generation after generation, century after century, and it is impossible to give even an approximate date to the foundation of most villages. Even a place called Newton ("the new *tun*") may be recorded in Domesday Book, though we might be fairly safe in assuming that it was then of comparatively recent origin and possibly dated from the tenth or the early eleventh century.

As he goes around England, the observant traveller will notice the variety of plan, of general shape, in all villages that have not been swamped by twentieth-century building, and this is brought out, too, on the earliest detailed maps of villages that we possess, those made in the late sixteenth century and the early seventeenth. There are three great types into one of which most villages fall: the village grouped around a central green or square, the village strung out along a single street, and the village which—though noticeably a conglomeration of houses—consists of dwellings planted down almost haphazard, with no evident relationship to each other or to any visible nucleus. There are innumerable examples of all three types, but it is sufficient to cite such examples as Finching-field (Essex) or Easington (Durham) among the "green-villages"; Long Melford (Suffolk) and Henley-in-Arden (Warwickshire) among the "street-villages"; and Middle Barton (Oxfordshire) as an example of the "fragmented village." It is possible, of course, to distinguish well-marked varieties even within some of these types. The "green-villages" of county Durham, for example, have been studied in detail and classified by Mr. H. Thorpe, and Mr. Conzen has done likewise for the whole of north-eastern England. There are mixed types also, possibly the result of later changes, and there is finally a comparatively small number of planned villages (mostly of eighteenth-century date) such as Milton Abbas in Dorset or Blanchland in Northumberland.

The variety of plan among the villages of England, besides affording one of the most delightful characteristics of the countryside, is profoundly interesting—and tantalizing—to the historian of the landscape. It is interesting because he realizes that this variety of forms almost certainly reflects very early cultural or historical differences, and it is tantalizing for two reasons. First, because we cannot be sure that the present plan of a village is not the result of successive changes that had been completed before the earliest maps are available: we cannot be sure we know what the *original* shape was in many instances. And secondly, even if we are sure of the original shape of a village, we are not yet in a position to say—for the subject has been so little studied in this country—what the various shapes and plans mean in terms of social history.

4

Though the village green is popularly supposed to be the essential attribute of the rural scene anywhere in England, it is in fact found predominantly in the Lowland Zone of eastern England and rarely in the Highland Zone to the west. It is particularly characteristic of north-eastern England, where a typical green-village has been described in these words: "The homesteads form a compact block bordering the green and their frontages face on to it so that in some cases, as at Heighington and Easington, the flanks of the greens have been taken in as front gardens for some of the houses. Of the dwellings fronting the green, many are still

PLATE 12

Finchingfield, Essex: an ancient village built around a large green, with the parish church overlooking the whole site. Green-villages are a distinct type of village but their precise significance is still not known. Finchingfield was "the *feld* of *Finc* or his people," the *feld* being a piece of open land in otherwise densely forested country. The green may have served the original purpose of a refuge and temporary pasture for all the village livestock in the event of attack in the early days of the settlement. There are numerous *-field* place-names in this part of Essex.

farmsteads, complete with farmyards and outbuildings, all strikingly divorced from their fields; their status within the village differs markedly from peripheral dwellings in that grazing rights for cattle, sheep, and horses (pigs are usually excluded), as well as for the homely goose, are restricted to homesteads which face the green. . . . The backs of the houses and farmsteads usually lead on to a 'Back Lane,' which may be continuous around the settlement and which often separates them from newer houses. . . . This back lane, which reflects the shape of

FIG. 5.—PLAN OF THORVERTON IN EAST DEVON

Thorverton is a village of Saxon foundation, first settled in all probability in the seventh century. The original nucleus was the large rectangular open space beside the stream, with the significant name of The Bury (from the Saxon word *burh*, meaning "a fortified place"). The reference must be to the Saxon earthwork or other fortification which formed the original nucleus, as there is not the slightest trace of any Roman or pre-Roman fort here. This significant name is also found on a similar site in the neighbouring village of Silverton, founded at the same date. The parish chuch lies at one end of the *burh*, again a very characteristic position. The original large space has been halved in area by the encroachment of domestic building on its eastern side, probably in medieval or sub-medieval times.

Reproduced by permission from the 25-inch map of the Ordnance Survey.

the village green, has clearly developed from the link-up of old cart-roads and drove-roads leading from the ancient common fields and pastures to the out-buildings of the farmsteads."[1] The green almost invariably contains two features which are contemporary (or almost contemporary) with it: a well (usually now covered by a small stone building and disused) which represents the primaeval

FIG. 6.

Middle Barton in Oxfordshire is a settlement without any nucleus or discernible plan. Houses lie scattered at all angles to each other and usually detached on their own little plots of land. Some are evidently eighteenth-century cottage encroachments on the roadside, but most probably occupy medieval sites. The village is first recorded by name in 1316, but the water mill (marked A on the map) was in existence in 1279 and this was possibly the origin of the village. It lay within the manor of Steeple Barton and probably grew up on the common pasture on the western edge of the manor. The roads and lanes of the village suggest an origin in paths and tracks across open land.

water-supply without which the community could not have come into being at all, and the church, which stands on the green or to one side of it. In later centuries, the school and the smithy were sometimes permitted on the green, but no other building was allowed.

Although village greens are rare on the western side of England, it seems likely that the compact villages built around the perimeter of a large square or rectangle,

[1]Thorpe, 160-1.

such as may be found in Devon and elsewhere, represent the same type as the "green-village" of eastern England. The plan of Ugborough in south Devon or of Bradworthy in west Devon suggests this clearly. In many other Devonshire villages the open square or rectangle has been partly built over at a later date and the original plan obscured (as at Thorverton, Fig. 5), just as hundreds of original "green-villages" have lost their greens at some more or less distant date, or at the parliamentary enclosure.

It seems likely that these villages built around the perimeter of a large green or a square represent enclosures for defensive purposes, like the native villages of some East African tribes today. Here the huts are grouped around the perimeter of a circular pound, with narrow openings between them which are closed at night by thorn-fences and which it is an obligation upon the householder to keep in repair. Into these pounds the livestock are driven at night for fear of the lions. In the villages of Saxon England, the necessity for protection from wolves in forested country may have led to the same plan being adopted, though any obligation to keep in repair the entrances to the green or square dissolved long ago with the disappearance of the larger predatory animals. Still, the ancient plan remains, with the church, the public well, and the lanes and roads leading into the central space from all points of the compass; and such names as Stockton may well commemorate the original stockade of wooden posts that surrounded the original settlement.

Though some of these green- or square-villages go back to the early days of the Old English settlement, we cannot assume from this defensive shape that they are necessarily the oldest plan. A life of St. Cuthbert (c. 634-87) gives us one of the rare descriptions of an early village, an unidentified place that was in danger of being burnt. It is apparent from the account that this seventh-century village was strung out in an east-west direction along a single street. Some "street-villages" are therefore of great antiquity; though many of them can be shown, on the other hand, to have developed along a busy main road in early medieval times, and not before.

As for those villages that are neither grouped around a central space nor along a street, where the houses are dotted about singly or in pairs, and joined together by a network of lanes and paths, we shall probably be right in seeing them as the result of individual squatting on the common pasture or in a clearing in thickly wooded country. Such squatters had no concerted plan and no leader with a small community around him, as in those numerous early villages the name of which embodies some Old English personal name. They acted individually and built wherever they had cleared a sufficient space, though always in close proximity to their neighbours. They were not building isolated farmsteads in the depths of the woods, but a loosely-framed village covering a considerable area (Fig. 6). Possibly this type of village is later in date than those created as a whole by a community led by one man, as at Peatling in Leicestershire, which means

"Peotlas's people" and suggests a concerted effort in clearance and building. A great number of the village-names ending in -ing, -ingham, and -ington, which are numerous all over southern and eastern England, fall into this class, and are among the earliest villages to be founded. Certainly this is true of the -ings and the -inghams.

In Lincolnshire, the green-village is uncommon, but Mr. M. W. Barley observes that "often the village plan is rectangular, and the area enclosed by the lanes, and given up now to cottages, farmhouses, and the home paddocks, was originally the first furlong of arable laboriously cleared and ploughed by anxious and toiling pioneers." There are scores of Lincolnshire villages with this rectangular lay-out of which Mr. Barley cites Mareham le Fen, Goulceby in the Wolds, and Scotton, as good examples. In these open-field villages, dependent on a co-operative agriculture from the start, room was found in the back lanes for another cottage whenever required, and the ancestral village slowly swelled in size. In the Fens, on the other hand, there was no open-field agriculture, and young men dispersed into the marshes and made new hamlets and farmsteads on their own from late Saxon times onwards. So the pattern of settlement is different: the ancestral village lies on the silt ridge, but roads run out from it in all directions to its daughter hamlets and its lonely farms down towards the sea. The map of the Fenland parishes is dotted with their names and laced together by winding roads, while the map of the open-field parishes shows the ancient village at or near the centre, with few or no names outside it, only empty fields. Such farmsteads as there are in these parishes, and they are always few if there are any at all, date from the parliamentary enclosure of the parish in the eighteenth century.

Many English villages have suffered considerable changes in plan since they were first founded, and it requires some practice to see the Anglo-Saxon bones beneath the later growth. But one can still come across remote villages where one feels oneself in the presence of remote antiquity, a parental type, such as Bygrave, two miles to the north-east of Baldock in Hertfordshire (Fig. 14). The late William Page called it "one of the most interesting survivors of a primitive self-contained settlement in England." It stands in the midst of the 1,620 acres of its territory, just off the Icknield Way which forms the entire southern frontier of the parish. The site of the manor-house and the church, which stand on the highest ground in the parish, is enclosed by a moat, and the minute village lies along the street to the west. There is not a single outlying farm in the parish, which looks exactly the same on the map of 1950 as it did on the first edition of the Ordnance Survey map in 1834. It is first recorded in a Saxon charter of 973—"the place by the ditch"—and it retains all the essential characteristics of a small community founded a thousand years ago. Even the Saxon open fields of Bygrave disappeared within living memory. There are more of these primaeval villages left than we might imagine, and it is one of the pleasures of the traveller on foot in England to come across one he had not known before.

Some Anglo-Saxon Estate Boundaries

The villages have undergone great changes in appearance since they were founded by the Anglo-Saxons, but there is at least one feature in the countryside which is of Saxon origin and often remains more or less intact. I refer to the boundary banks of large Anglo-Saxon estates, which one learns to recognize by laboriously tracing the points named in the surviving charters. This exercise gives one a truer and more detailed knowledge of the English countryside than any other pursuit, not excluding fox-hunting. By the time one has scrambled over hedges, leapt across boggy streams in deep woods, traversed narrow green lanes all but blocked with brambles and the luxuriant vegetation of wet summers, not to mention walked along high airy ridges on a day of tumultuous blue-and-white skies with magnificent views of deep country all round—by the time one has done this, armed with a copy of a Saxon charter and the $2\frac{1}{2}$-inch maps, the topography of some few miles of the English landscape is indelibly printed on the mind and heart. And at the same time, one has the constant intellectual exercise of fitting the frequently-obscure landmarks of the charter to the ground one is traversing, and the mental excitement of making some unmistakable identification and of revealing to oneself the age of some ordinary feature of the scene—a ditch, a hedge, a piece of marsh, a pond, or what you will.

Between 925 and 939 King Athelstan gave to the abbey of St. Mary and St. Peter at Exeter one "mansa" at Monkton (*Munecatun*), an estate of about four thousand acres about six miles NNW. of the city, in the beautiful New Red Sandstone country rising to the Raddon Hills. The whole of the southern boundary, some three miles long, is marked by an ancient road ("herepath") from the Exe to the Creedy, about which there can be no doubt; and a small stream demarcates the entire western boundary. The eastern boundary of the estate also presents no problem for the greater part of its length (Plate 13); but it is when one comes to work out the northern and the north-eastern boundary on the ground that one makes discoveries.

This is no place to speak of the details of the northern boundary, which has several points of interest. But perhaps the most interesting of all is the high earthen bank (called the *dic* in the charter). On the map a narrow lane, quite unfit for wheeled traffic, winds around the end of the Raddon ridge. There is nothing about it to suggest great antiquity or any special interest; but one's attention is drawn to it, as mine was for years, by the fact that it obviously serves no modern purpose. In fact it is the north-eastern boundary of this tenth-century estate and, when one sees it, it runs like a rampart-walk cut half-way up the side of a high, steep bank (Plates 14, 15).

Even if one did not know of the existence of a Saxon estate here, and were merely walking along it for the pleasure of exploring a new piece of country, one could not fail to notice the construction and course of this bank. It is the charter which

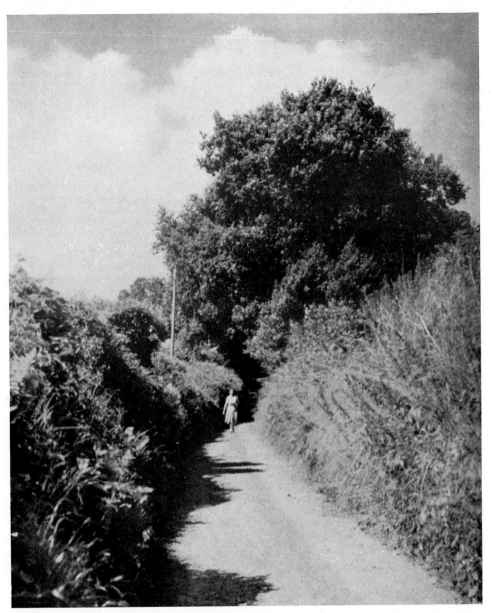

PLATE 13

A sunken lane in East Devon: Armourwood Lane, near Thorverton. It originated as a
boundary (probably in the seventh century) between the royal estate of Silverton (left)
and the Exeter Abbey estate (right). A double ditch was dug out by slave-labour, and
the earth thrown up to form hedgebanks on each side. The "two-fold ditch" thus becomes
a sunken lane running as far as the Saxon boundary required.

reveals, with the aid of painstaking field-work, that the bank is the boundary of an estate which goes back to the early tenth century, and conceivably back to the seventh century when Exeter Abbey was founded. The fact that the estate was called Monkton when Athelstan granted it to the abbey in 925-39 suggests that his charter was a confirmation of a grant of land already called after the monks of Exeter, and originally given to the abbey at its foundation.[1]

A casual exploration one evening near Somerton, in the heart of Somerset, revealed a similar construction, undoubtedly a boundary-bank of an estate for which no charter survives. his may be seen by taking the lane that runs around the north and north-western side of Bradley Hill, $1\frac{1}{2}$ miles north-west of Somerton. This lane is a sort of rampart-walk along the top of a high bank, similar to that already described; and the estate boundary clearly follows the line of ground a few feet above the edge of the levels, then mostly water-logged and useless.

Somerton was a royal estate; so, too, was Monkton before it was given to Exeter abbey. It may be that these massive ramparts, for such they are at times, could only be constructed by kings and magnates with the command of unlimited slave-labour, and therefore that where they are found they represent the boundaries of the more important estates. Here, too, a great deal of fascinating field-work awaits the historically-minded explorer of the English landscape. One would naturally work most profitably from specific Anglo-Saxon charters, but if one felt like a casual evening walk any piece of narrow lane which appears from the $2\frac{1}{2}$-inch or 6-inch map to have no particular objective—especially if it is followed by a parish boundary, always a sign of antiquity—is worth looking at carefully. One may draw a blank, but there is so much of this field-history waiting to be discovered in England that one is bound to be fortunate sometimes.

A remarkable survival of a Saxon landmark may be found at Alton Priors, on the northern edge of the Vale of Pewsey in Wiltshire.[2] In the year 825 King Egbert granted to the church of St. Peter and St. Paul at Winchester an estate at Alton, covering the greater part of the present parish. At one point the boundary ran, so the charter tells us, "to a stone in Woncumb in the lower part (of which) on the upper side is a hole." This stone, a sarsen with a hole right through it, was found by the party working out the bounds of the charter, still where the Saxon "surveyors" saw it more than eleven centuries ago.

The Scandinavian Settlement

From the late ninth century onwards the Scandinavian conquest of a good deal of England resulted in a great number of new villages being founded. How many we do not know, for though many hundreds bear pure Scandinavian names (those names ending in -by are the most easily recognizable), we have reason to

[1]Too much weight cannot be put on this evidence, however, for the extant charter is itself a later reconstructed text.

[2]I owe this information to Mr. G. M. Young, to whom the original discovery was largely due.

PLATES 14 AND 15

Saxon boundary bank in East Devon: the continuation of the sunken-lane boundary shown in Plate 13. Plate 14 shows the upper half of the massive bank which bounded the seventh-century Monkton estate belonging to Exeter Abbey. The sunken lane has here become an open path running half-way up the side of the great bank. Plate 15 shows the remainder of the bank (called the *dic* or dike in a tenth-century charter) below the path. Here the monastic estate marched along the lands of a private landowner, probably the Cada who gave his name to the adjoining parishes of Cadbury and Cadeleigh and to a stream called Kidlake, now a farm-name. Many of the great Saxon boundary-banks still remain to be identified.

know that sometimes—and perhaps in many instances—the newcomers took over an Old English village and gave it a new name. Thus Wigston in Leicestershire was called "Viking's *tun*," after some local Danish leader, and might be supposed to be a foundation of the Scandinavian period. But at the close of the eighteenth century an Anglo-Saxon cemetery of the heathen period was discovered just outside the present village. There can be no doubt from the contents of this that Wigston had existed, under another name, for nearly three hundred years before Viking and his men appeared on the scene. We know, too, that Derby formerly bore the Old English name of Northworthy, indicating a settlement founded in the Old English period.

Nevertheless, the demobilized Danish soldiers, bringing over their families, also founded a great number of new villages in country which still lay uncleared and untilled by the Anglo-Saxons. In some parts of eastern England they greatly outnumbered the native English. The Scandinavian partition and settlement of Yorkshire began in 876; that of the East Midlands (Mercia) in the following year. By 919 Mercia had been reconquered for the English, so that Scandinavian settlements in this part of England can be dated for the most part between 877 and 919; but north of the Humber a Scandinavian kingdom lasted much longer. And in the tenth century there came waves of Norwegians who settled in the north-western counties of England and left characteristic traces of their presence in the place-names of this region—*e.g.*, the numerous *thwaites* of Cumberland and Westmorland.

This is not, however, a history of England. Here we are concerned with the changes brought about in the landscape by this fresh wave of settlers, and these seem to be mainly two: first, a great intensification of the work of forest-clearance in districts still relatively untouched by Old English settlers, and the establishment of new village-communities; and second, the establishment of isolated hamlets and farmsteads away from the villages, some of them the result, apparently, of the drainage of marsh and fen-land.

As to the first, we do not know whether the Scandinavian settlers brought with them any peculiar and distinctive village-type. There is nothing we can recognize in those parts of eastern England that were intensively Scandinavianized, that suggests that the Danes of the ninth and tenth centuries built villages to any plan fundamentally different from those built by the Old English. This failure to recognize any distinction today may, of course, be due to the modifying changes effected in villages during the course of the past thousand years, changes which may have gradually obliterated any original differences of plan. It may be that when we come to excavate villages of Danish foundation that were abandoned at an early date (*e.g.*, Revesby in Lincolnshire), before important changes of plan had taken place, we shall learn more about this subject; but in the landscape as we see it today there is certainly nothing that stands out as a distinctively Scandinavian contribution. Nor did the Scandinavian settlers introduce any new field-system. In the open-field parts of England they, too, established open fields of their own; and in those districts that did not lend themselves to such large-scale co-operative agriculture they established hamlets or farmsteads with small fields enclosed and worked like the farmers' fields of today, just as the Old English had done in similar country.

Domesday Book shows scattered hamlets and homesteads, in the broad plains of eastern England, founded by Scandinavian settlers. Stallingborough, on the edge of the Lincolnshire marshland, near Grimsby, consisted of a central village and three scattered homesteads occupied by five sokemen (of Danish descent) and three villeins. There were only one to three households in each settlement, and the eight households had only one plough between them. Many other examples of isolated homesteads may be found in the Lincolnshire marshland, some of which date back to the ninth and tenth centuries, and others to the eleventh. Here was "a very different economy from that of the ancient open fields. The inhabitants lived not in village streets but in dispersed dwellings, supporting themselves on their small enclosures of meadow and marsh."[1] The very scattered settlement of many Norfolk parishes goes back, in part at least, to the intensive Danish partitioning of the land in this period. At an early date we find in these parishes homesteads well away from any village, and small compact farms quite unlike those of the open-field regions; and later we find the phenomenon of two churches (or even three) within one vill and sometimes within one churchyard. This is undoubtedly a reflection of the peculiar social structure and social history of the region, the precise effects of which still need working out.

[1]Stenton, D. M., *English Society in the Early Middle Ages* (Pelican edition), 125.

SELECT BIBLIOGRAPHY

BARLEY, M. W., *Lincolnshire and the Fens* (1952).
COLLINGWOOD, R. G., and MYRES, J. N. L., *Roman Britain and the English Settlements* (1936).
CRAWFORD, O. G. S., *Archæology in the Field* (1953).
FINBERG, H. P. R., *The Early Charters of Devon and Cornwall* (1953).
GRAY, H. L., *English Field Systems* (1915).
HENCKEN, H. O'NEIL, *The Archæology of Cornwall and Scilly* (1932).
HOSKINS, W. G., and FINBERG, H. P. R., *Devonshire Studies* (1952).
PAGE, W., "The Origins and Forms of Hertfordshire Towns and Villages," *Archæologia*, LXIX (1917-18).
SEEBOHM, F., *The English Village Community* (1926 ed.).
STENTON, D. M., *English Society in the Early Middle Ages* (Pelican ed., 1951).
STENTON, F., *Anglo-Saxon England* (1943).
THORPE, H., "The Green Villages of County Durham," *Institute of British Geographers* (1951).

III

The Colonization of Medieval England

The Landscape in 1086

THOUGH Domesday Book is so full of factual information, much of which still awaits excavation from its pages, it does not tell us directly how much of each county had been colonized and populated, and how much was still "waste" of one sort and another. But we can obtain a fairly good idea of the extent to which England had been colonized during the six hundred years since the first Old English landings by looking at the Domesday population of different parts of the country. The total population of the country was possibly about $1\frac{1}{4}$ million, of whom about one in ten lived in the "boroughs." Only six counties had more than fifty thousand people each. The most populous county in England was Norfolk, with some ninety-five thousand people, rather fewer than the city of Oxford today. Lincolnshire had about ninety thousand people, Suffolk and Devon about seventy thousand each. Essex and Somerset each had between fifty and sixty thousand people. A group of four southern counties—Kent, Hampshire, Sussex, and Wiltshire—had between forty and fifty thousand people each. Yorkshire, which had suffered great devastation since the Norman Conquest, had considerably fewer than thirty thousand people all told, about the same number as modern Redcar or half as many as modern Wakefield. Over the whole of northern England it is doubtful whether there were, on an average, more than about four persons to the square mile. Even in the east Midlands, one of the more populous parts of Norman England, the whole of Northamptonshire contained fewer people than modern Kettering, Leicestershire had about as many as modern Coalville, and Nottinghamshire—least colonized of all in this region—had only twenty thousand people altogether, fewer than the little borough of Newark today.

East Anglia was the most thickly settled part of England at the end of the eleventh century, with an average of between forty and fifty people to the square mile. But there were wide variations even here from district to district. In Norfolk, for example, the density of population ranged from about eighteen to the square mile in the western Marshland and twenty in the Breckland, to eighty or more in the coastal parishes north of Yarmouth and the inland parishes to the south of Norwich. The parishes in the latter districts are remarkably small, as we should expect with this high early density of population, whereas in the Marshland, Fenland, and Breckland—all down the western side of the county—they each run to several thousand acres. Feltwell, down in the Fens, runs to more than fourteen thousand acres, Methwold to over thirteen thousand; but some parishes to the

61

south-east of Norwich, such as Sisland and Ashby St. Mary, have fewer than five hundred acres and many have less than a thousand.

The counties of Lincolnshire and Essex had about thirty-five people to the square mile on an average, but again with a very wide variation from district to district. Only two parts of England at this date had an average of more than thirty people to the square mile: a large block of eastern England from Lincolnshire down to Essex, and another block of three counties in the south Midlands—Oxfordshire, Wiltshire, and Berkshire. Somewhere between these two extremes, of four persons per square mile in the north and rather more than forty in the east, lay all the other counties of England. Even after six hundred years of colonization much of England was still only thinly settled.

Though most English villages had made their appearance by the time of the Norman Conquest, and indeed many others which have since perished, vast areas remained in their natural state, awaiting the sound of a human voice. In many regions, like the extensive forest of Andred in Kent and Sussex (*Andredes Weald*) or the great Midland forests, the primaeval woods were still "shedding and renewing their leaves with no human eye to notice, or human heart to regret or welcome the change." Elsewhere, along the Sussex and Kentish coast, in the deep Fens of eastern England, in the Somerset Levels, and in patches all over the lowlands, much of the landscape was populated only by great wading birds. Inland, especially in the far west and north, there still remained millions of acres of stony moorland haunted only by the cries of the animal creation, where the eagle and the raven circled undisturbed. The villages of Earnwood in Shropshire and Yarnscombe in Devon commemorate a former "eagles' wood" and "eagles' valley"; while far up in the West Riding of Yorkshire the limestone crags above Littondale provided eyries for these noble birds, and in due course the Old English village of Arncliffe took its name from the "eagles' cliff." Over some inner fastnesses there reigned, except for the wind and the rain, an utter silence. Carrington's description of the central waste of Dartmoor (Plate 1) in the early nineteenth century would have been true of most of the higher moors of Norman England:

> Nothing that has life
> Is visible;—no solitary flock
> At will wide ranging through the silent Moor,
> Breaks the deep-felt monotony; and all
> Is motionless, save where the giant shades,
> Flung by a passing cloud, glide slowly o'er
> The gray and gloomy wild.

Since Saxon times the clearance of the natural woodlands had been the greatest single change in the landscape; by the time of Domesday the attack on the moorlands was just beginning and that on the marshland and the fenland was well advanced. In Devon, for example, where there was much high moorland, a close examination of Domesday Book reveals that late Saxon farmers had reached a height of about nine hundred feet on the western and wetter edge of Dartmoor, and of twelve hundred feet on the drier eastern side. On Exmoor one or two farmers had also reached a height of twelve hundred feet above the sea. These isolated farms were the spearheads of the attack: one can sometimes see fields on such frontiers shaped precisely like this, thrusting a blunt point into the waste. But in general the frontier of cultivation was probably much lower than this. How high it had been drawn on the Yorkshire moors and on those of north-western England we have yet to discover.

In south-eastern England, where there was much marsh, there is evidence that it was being used for pasturage as early as the seventh century. In the year 697, for example, Wihtred, king of Kent, gave to the monastery at Lyminge pasture for three hundred sheep in Romney Marsh. Sir Frank Stenton observes that "the local names of the Kentish weald and marsh are, in general, of an ancient type, and prove that the intricacies of these regions had been familiar from a very early time." The Romans indeed had settled on parts of Romney Marsh and shown what could be done to reclaim valuable pasture-land. The water-table was lowered by the making of ditches, and banks were constructed to keep out the sea. Such ditching and embanking was costly and possible only on a piecemeal scale. It gives us therefore relatively small enclosed fields, instead of the large-scale open fields, in which the ditches not only serve as drains but also as the boundaries of the newly-reclaimed land.

The "inning" or reclaiming of the Pevensey Levels in Sussex dates in part from pre-Conquest times. A charter of 772 by which king Offa gave land at Bexhill to the see of Selsey refers to a number of ditches in the levels, some already of great age and therefore possibly Roman. In Somerset, Glastonbury abbey had begun the draining of the water-logged "moors" by the tenth century, and there is some reason to believe that the great Dunstan, when he was abbot about the middle of the century, had been responsible for much work of this kind. A certain bridge and a ditch were still named after him in the thirteenth century. Down in mid-Somerset the foundation of Muchelney abbey before the end of the seventh century probably initiated drainage of the wet "moors" in this district, and we find it still going on centuries later.

In the levels of east Yorkshire, a number of place-names in Holderness and near the alluvial Derwent suggest widespread drainage activities before 1066, for example the village-names of Catfoss, Fangfoss, Wilberfoss and Fosham. In Devon, where there was not much marsh except in local patches, a village-name like Powderham (*polder-ham*) reveals successful reclamation of marsh before the Norman Conquest. All over England, in patches both large and small, one finds this evidence of the successful attack on fen and marsh begun well back in Saxon times. Many of the embankments of the Fenland proper, most notably the so-called Roman Bank near the Wash, will prove upon detailed examination of the evidence to be of Anglo-Saxon origin, or the work of Scandinavian settlers (Fig 7). Even so, a vast amount remained to be done. Though Offa's charter speaks

FIG. 7.—THE EARLY COLONIZATION OF THE LINCOLNSHIRE MARSHLAND

The early Anglo-Saxon villages (and North Thoresby, which is Danish in origin) are marked thus: ●. The probable course of the Sea Dike constructed by these villages before the Norman Conquest is indicated by a broken line. Daughter-villages founded on the Dike are shown thus: ○ and the earliest reference to them is indicated by a date in brackets. The marshland between the parent villages and the Dike had been reclaimed from the sea by the eleventh century for the most part; and the earliest settlements on the Dike were probably of huts occupied in the summer months only (as is suggested by the name Somercotes, "summer cottages or huts"). Beyond the Dike lie no villages but only single isolated farms of varying dates from medieval times onwards. The parent villages were all founded between twenty and forty feet above sea-level.

already of ditches in the Pevensey Levels, Domesday Book shows us that three hundred years later the tide-water still flowed freely over most of the Sussex marshes, and so it was everywhere else near the sea. Though the beginnings had been made so early, we have always to remember that (in the words of Eric Gill) "it was a hand-made world throughout, a slow world, a world without power, a world in which all things were made one by one . . . a world dependent upon human muscular power and the muscular power of draught animals." Unless we keep this continually in mind, and think ourselves back imaginatively into such a hand-made world, we shall never understand the immeasureably slow processes by which the English landscape, down to the nineteenth century, came into being, and much of the beauty and fascination of its detail will for ever escape us.

It is not entirely true to say that it was a world without power. The water-mill had appeared in England by the eighth century and spread steadily all over eastern England and the Midlands during the next three hundred years. About six thousand mills are recorded in Domesday Book. In Lincolnshire about one village in three possessed a mill, in Norfolk and Suffolk about the same. But as one went westwards the number of water-mills fell rapidly, despite the greater number of suitable streams. In the west and north the ancient method of the hand-quern was still practised. Thus Somerset had 371 mills, but Devon only 98, and Cornwall only six.

Such water-mills were very small, generating perhaps the same horsepower as a small car today, and were driven by streams which now look as though they could hardly propel a minnow, so clogged have they become with rushes and weeds. Nearly all rivers were originally much wider than they are today. A few mills recorded in Domesday Book are still working, but they are rare in all parts. With the modern development of large-scale milling in the coastal ports the great majority of local mills have ceased to work. Many had ceased work in earlier centuries, with the conversion of old arable lands to pasture, and their very sites are now difficult to locate. One sometimes comes across a little water-mill lying derelict far from any habitation, and realizes yet again the hand-made scale of that early world. These derelict mills, though they may now contain nothing of great antiquity, stand upon ancient sites that often go back to Saxon times. Once a site had been selected and a stream diverted or dammed, it would tend to continue in use until the end of local corn-milling. All the mills recorded in Domesday Book are water-mills for grinding corn. Neither the windmill nor the fulling mill for stamping cloth by water-driven hammers had yet made its appearance in England. They appear simultaneously towards the end of the twelfth century.

Besides the water-mill, another building had made its appearance on the scene by the time of the Norman Conquest—the country church. From the sixth century onwards, even a little earlier perhaps in some places, Christian churches had been built. By 1086 there were several hundreds in existence, possibly a few thousand, for it is quite certain that Domesday Book (which had no particular concern with churches) does not attempt to record all those that existed at that date. In the regions where good building stones were available, some of these churches were stone-built and large (as at Brixworth and Earls Barton in Northamptonshire), but over most of England they were inconspicuous little log-huts, roofed with thatch, which have long ago been replaced, except at Greenstead in Essex. The church was usually as inconspicuous in the scene as the water-mill. Towers were exceptional, and that very characteristic English view of the church spire rising from the tufted trees or piercing the quiet autumn skies in a wide view had yet to be seen. The earliest spires were built at the end of the twelfth century or the beginning of the thirteenth, and we find them first, as we should expect, in the great limestone belt of Northamptonshire and its adjacent counties.

Nearly every village we know today had appeared on the scene by 1086. The chief exceptions are the villages of the north and Midlands that were created by the Industrial Revolution, but here and there in the still densely wooded districts of England a few villages had to wait for their foundation until the twelfth or thirteenth century. Around nearly every village stretched its open fields, either two or three in number, each covering a few hundred acres, but hardly anywhere had these fields reached the frontiers of the village territory. If one walked half a mile, a mile at the most, out from the village, one came to the edge of the wild, to a wide stretch of moory or boggy ground that formed a temporary barrier, or the massed tree-trunks of the primaeval woods still awaiting the axe. Every village had its own frontiers, probably as yet ill defined in upland country and the subject of disputes with neighbouring communities when they began meeting in no man's land; and at the time of Domesday perhaps half the land of the village territory (the ecclesiastical parish to be) still remained to be rescued from the natural wilderness.

Over a good deal of England, especially in the west and north (but sometimes in the heart of the Midlands also), one found few villages but a scattering of hamlets and single farmsteads in remote clearings, settlements so remote that they betrayed their presence only by the smell of wood-smoke among the trees. Around the larger hamlets, open fields may have been laid out like those of a village but on a smaller scale. One finds records of these miniature open-field systems in Devon and in Oxfordshire, and no doubt they were to be seen in all counties. But often the hamlets, like the single farmsteads, were surrounded by small fields, usually of very irregular shape and enclosed by massive earthen banks that betrayed their piecemeal reclamation, acre by acre, by pioneering households rather than the large-scale clearing operations of the village lands. Fields were small, often barely an acre in extent, because of the nature of the tools with which they were created and because the need for more land was desperate. Every acre was brought into use as quickly as possible.

Small fields of irregular shape were, and are, characteristic of the more difficult regions of England, especially those with slopes too steep for the plough or those where the surface was thickly strewn with stones. In such rocky districts boulders were often so huge that it was not worth while to shift them, and they were incorporated in the line of the hedge-bank to save trouble and to render them harmless.

Frequently the extreme irregularity of the course of an early hedgebank was due to its going around or taking in a large tree or a massive boulder in this way. One finds this illustrated best of all in the granite regions of south-western England, but it is generally true of all regions where the rock lies near or on the surface.

Elsewhere, the shape of fields depended very largely on the kind of plough that was customarily used in the region. In south-eastern England it has been shown that the plough with a fixed mould-board produces long, narrow strips. These, grouped in parcels or *furlongs*, formed the basis of the open-field system as it is generally understood. On the other hand, the one-way plough, with shifting ear or turn-wrest device, could produce either strips or square plots, and either of these shapes could be associated with open-field agriculture. Kent shows both types of "field" at an early date.

The prevalence of square plots in Kent, perhaps more convenient for grazing cattle, meant that it was easier to consolidate and to enclose plots with hedges so as to produce what we regard as the typical modern pattern. Hence the very early enclosures of Kent, where the open fields probably disappeared well before the end of the Middle Ages.[1] The same considerations may well apply to the early enclosure of the open fields in Devon, which we know was taking place in the thirteenth and fourteenth centuries, and where we find hints of squarish plots as well as of elongated strips on the maps. There is still a great deal we do not know about field-shapes and their origins in different parts of England, and only the patient work of local scholars will enable us to add to our knowledge.

The landscape of 1086 was not entirely rural. The town had made its appearance—or re-appearance in some instances—in a rudimentary form. Some towns of Roman foundation had struggled through the Dark Ages to a new life, or had been revived on the same site after a period of desolation, and the Saxons had added more towns, especially in the ninth and tenth centuries. Such "towns" were small and hardly distinguishable from villages, except that they might have around them (or partly around them) an earthen rampart such as we can still see at Wareham in Dorset or at Lydford in Devon. Only five towns had more than a thousand burgesses in 1086: London, Norwich, York, Lincoln, and Winchester. At the other end of the scale, many Domesday boroughs had minute populations: St. Albans and Pershore, which had grown up at the gates of monasteries, had only forty-six and twenty-eight burgesses respectively. St. Albans had been founded about the year 950 by abbot Wulsin, but even after four or five generations it had fewer than 150 to 200 people. Elsewhere in Hertfordshire, Westminster abbey had founded a borough at Ashwell before 1066. Only fourteen burgesses are recorded here in 1086, and no recognizably urban life ever developed here. Stanstead Abbots, on the Lea, was even smaller and soon faded out as a borough.

[1]Michael Nightingale, "Ploughing and Field-Shape," *Antiquity*, xxvii (1953), 20-6; and "Some Evidence for Open Field Agriculture in Kent" (unpublished Oxford thesis, 1952).

PLATE 16

Launceston castle and town. The castle was built soon after 1066 by the Norman Count of
Mortain, on a hill known as Dunheved, as the military key to the Cornish peninsula.
From the canons of St. Stephen, in a neighbouring village, he filched a weekly market
and established it at his castle by 1086. This is the beginning of the town of Launceston,
the dependent origin of which at the foot of the castle is clearly brought out in the
photograph.

All over England we find these little towns planted in a landscape that was predominantly green country. Some, like Exeter, still had their impressive Roman walls, and a cathedral within, but most were mere collections of huts and houses surrounded by an earthen bank, and many were destined to fade out altogether during the course of the next century or so. A few towns were brand-new at the time of Domesday: Newbury in Berkshire is first heard of about the year 1080, and Okehampton in Devon had but four burgesses and a market at the time of Domesday—evidently newly born. And all over England towns that are historic today were as yet empty sites. Newcastle, Hull, and Liverpool in the north; Boston and Kings Lynn in the east; Portsmouth and Salisbury in the south; Plymouth and Ludlow in the west. In Midland and eastern England scores of little market towns were still unborn—Woodstock, Market Harborough, and Newmarket—and scores of others were still mere agricultural villages, like Stratford-upon-Avon and Burton-upon-Trent.

With an average of only about twenty-five people to the square mile, England at the end of the eleventh century was greatly under-populated. Thousands of square miles were still untouched by plough or beast, thousands more only half used in a shifting cultivation of out-field. The rich natural resources of mineral wealth had hardly been scratched. Great tracts of forest, of moor and heath, marsh and fen, lay awaiting reclamation by pioneers. England was still in an early colonial stage of development, and it is in this light—of pioneers, frontiers, and forests—that we must look at the tremendous activity of the eight or nine generations between the making of Domesday Book and the coming of the Black Death, which put a decisive end to the first great wave of medieval colonization.

The Clearing of the Woodlands

Much of England was still thickly wooded, even in districts that had long been settled. Generally it was a thick oak and ash forest, especially on the clays that were to be found in most parts of the country, but on the chalk and limestone uplands (or rather on the extensive patches of clay that capped them in places) the beech woods extended for miles. In the lowlands the elm, the maple, and the lime were all familiar trees, and on the hills, where the forests thinned out, the silver birch grew as it does today. Most of the trees we know were familiar to our Saxon and medieval ancestors, but there were two important differences from today. The first was that the oak was so much more common in medieval England: there were tens of thousands to be seen in places where we now see a few hundreds. And secondly, one of our very characteristic trees, especially around upland farmsteads—the burnished sycamore so familiar to Wordsworth and Matthew Arnold—was nowhere to be seen. It was not introduced into England until the closing years of the sixteenth century.

From rising ground England must have seemed one great forest before the fifteenth century, an almost unbroken sea of tree-tops with a thin blue spiral of smoke rising here and there at long intervals. Even after twenty generations of hacking at the waste, the frontiers of cultivation were rarely far away from the homesteads. At Lawling, in the eastern marshes of Essex, we have a place-name of an archaic type suggesting very early settlement by the Old English, possibly as far back as the fifth century. Nevertheless, we find extensive woods eight hundred years later. A survey made in 1310 shows that more than six hundred acres of woodland had been cleared in recent assarts (a word derived from the Old French *essarter*, "to grub up trees"), and there were still more than five hundred acres left untouched. Essex as a whole was a heavily wooded county in the eleventh century, even more so in the west than in the east. In the west we find villages with woods capable of feeding a thousand or two thousand swine.

Most of this woodland was cleared and turned into arable land or pasture by individual peasants in the twelfth and thirteenth centuries, who thereby created new fields and new farms out of the waste. But sometimes we hear of new villages being founded in this way. In the deep woods of the Midland clays, we hear of Woodhouse Eaves in Leicestershire for the first time between 1209 and 1235. The name means "the houses in the wood." Numerous Woodhouses appear in the Nottinghamshire forests in the same period. So, too, does Woodhouse, now a suburb of Leeds, which we first hear of in the year 1208, and Woodhouse, now a suburb of Sheffield, first recorded between 1200 and 1218. Scores of English place-names, from Yorkshire down to Devon, reveal the importance of this post-Conquest clearance of woodland, most of them first recorded in the twelfth or thirteenth century—the Woodcotts, Woodmancotes, Woodhalls, and the like. Numerous Newlands and Newhalls date from the same period. These all became villages, or at least parishes with their own church serving a community of scattered farmsteads and cottages, but thousands of other woodland clearings were never more than single isolated farmsteads, such as all those in Devon whose name embodies the element "wood" or "beare" (from the Old English word *bearu*, "a wood"). Such a farm is Woodland, on the steep and still-wooded sides of the Torridge valley near Great Torrington, which we first hear of as *La Wode-lond* in the year 1302. It had probably come into existence only a few years before this. One could find scores, if not hundreds, of similar examples of this type of colonization in south-western England in this period.

The *Red Book of Worcester* shows us forest-clearance on the western slopes of the Cotswolds, near Cheltenham. Bishop Roger of Worcester (1164-79) had granted a tract of woodland at Bishops Cleeve to one Girold for an annual rent of one mark, and we are told that Girold had succeeded in adding no less than 170 acres to his holding, though some of the woodland still remained to be cleared. Here the cleared land was not enclosed in separate little hedged fields, but was added to the existing open fields of the village for purposes of communal cultivation, half to one field, half to the other. Not far away, however, the name of Woodmancote, first recorded in the *Book of Fees* in 1220, suggests that a new hamlet had also been founded. At Lawling, in the survey of 1310 already referred to, it seems clear that separate little fields were being created. We read, for example, that John de Wycumbe has a certain holding called *Heggelond* for which he pays a rent of 4s. 1d. a year, and elsewhere within the manor he has a parcel of land "newly assarted, lying within his enclosures" for which he pays only a penny a year at Michaelmas. The difference in rent possibly arises to some extent from a difference in acreage,

PLATE 17

The Norman church at Fingest in the Chilterns (Bucks). The heavily wooded Chiltern Hills were colonized comparatively late. Several villages (or parishes) make their appearance in the twelfth century. The building of a church sets a spiritual seal upon the creation of a new community of scattered farms with no real centre until that event. Fingest is first recorded by name in 1163, a date contemporary with the fabric of the church. Many such solitary Norman churches are to be found in the more densely forested parts of England or on the moorland edges.

about which we are given no information, but in the main it probably springs from the fact that Hedgeland was an older enclosure and now under profitable cultivation, while the new assart in *Danegris* had yet to be brought into full use as farmland.

Elsewhere in the forested parts of England we find both types of landscape coming into being: old villages enlarging their open fields, and new hamlets and

PLATE 18

A landscape of scattered farms near Exeter, Devon. This is a piece of hilly country on the shallow infertile soils of the Culm Measures at Whitestone, to the north-west of Exeter. All
the numerous isolated farmsteads in this view date from the eleventh to thirteenth
centuries and are generally reached by narrow, winding lanes. An ancient through-road
runs across the bottom half of the picture and the farm-lanes run off it. The fields are
mostly small and irregular in shape, cleared direct from the natural woodland. A great
deal of woodland remains to this day, representing the tattered remnants of a once-
continuous covering.

farmsteads being created at the centre of islands of small irregular fields enclosed by earthen hedgebanks.

Much of England was "forest" in a more technical sense in the centuries following the Norman Conquest, that is country set aside as royal game preserves and subject to special law—the forest law. The Anglo-Saxon kings had had their parks for hunting, large tracts of natural woodland and open country which were surrounded by a fence or a bank and ditch and jealously guarded against poachers and trespassers. Such a royal preserve was Woodstock, near Oxford, which we first hear of about the year 1000, though it may well go back to Alfred's time. It was not difficult to find considerable tracts of uninhabited country in Saxon England, but the Norman kings were not content with this. They introduced their forest and onerous forest laws into settled and cultivated country, and extended them to a great part of England. The making of the New Forest by William the Conqueror, which involved the destruction of a number of villages and many farms, is the best known example of this process, but other forests were much larger. The whole of Essex lay under forest law, and the whole of the Midlands from Stamford bridge in Lincolnshire south-westwards to Oxford Bridge, a distance of eighty miles. By the thirteenth century a great belt of forest extended from the Thames by Windsor through Berkshire and Hampshire to the south coast.

The royal forest reached its greatest extent under Henry II, when it may have covered as much as one-third of the whole country. It had the effect, because of its severe penalties against poaching and trespass, and the fact that it was periodically hunted over, of greatly hindering the farming of occupied lands and of impeding the colonization of new land, but we must not exaggerate its importance in these respects. It was probably no more irritating to settled farmers than the equally crude behaviour of the hunting squires in our own day, with their trampling of crops, and breaking down of fences, and the depredations of their sacred game. Similarly, the existence of forest law over wild, unsettled country did not entirely stop peasants from making clearances in places and paying a fine for doing so. The Pipe Rolls of this period are full of references to such fines for making assarts in the king's forest, but these are to be regarded rather as payments for licences to do so. Medieval men were as licence-ridden as we are, and they were accustomed to paying for every licence. Once the assart was made and the fine or licence-money paid, the peasant was left alone to make what he could of the new land, which, however, still remained subject to forest law with all its irritations and penalties.

In the year 1184-5, for example, we read of Richard Fortescue, a small landowner in South Devon, paying a fine of one mark for "waste of forest," almost certainly the result of clearing and enclosing new fields out of the woodland. But in the same record we find one Jacob of Mountsorrel (a Leicestershire place-name) fined no less than £12 3s. 8d. for his activities in the royal forest, the equivalent

FIG. 8.—SAXON VILLAGES AND MEDIEVAL DISPERSION IN HERTFORDSHIRE

In the river valleys lie the Saxon villages of Hadham, Widford, Sawbridgeworth, and Harlow (Essex). Between them lay a forested upland of heavy clays which was opened up and colonized in the twelfth and thirteenth centuries. The tangle of narrow lanes and paths winding from one isolated farmstead to another, the score or more of farms named after medieval owners or occupiers, the numerous "Greens," and the still-frequent remnants of woodland, are all deeply characteristic of country enclosed direct from former forest. Notice, too, the "lost" villages of Thorley and Gilston, where only the church and a "hall" survive in each instance. Gilston itself is a late settlement (twelfth century), and Thorley ("thorn clearing") was probably settled late in the Saxon period.

Reproduced by permission from the 1-inch map of the Ordnance Survey.

of possibly twelve or fifteen hundred pounds today. It is highly likely in this instance that Jacob had been attracted all the way from Leicestershire to Devon by the tin boom of these years—in which the Jews probably played a prominent part—and that he had been prospecting on a considerable scale in the royal forest. Indeed, the search for minerals—chiefly coal, tin, and lead—in the twelfth and thirteenth centuries all over the upland regions of England must have led directly to the opening up by prospectors of country so difficult that it might otherwise have waited for decades or generations for settlers.

Nevertheless, the existence of royal game preserves on this scale must have discouraged new settlement and made existing farming difficult, and the steady disafforestation of large areas by Richard I and John, in return for lump sums of ready money, gave a strong impetus to new colonization in the waste lands. That it was felt to be a heavy burden is borne out by the size of the payments made by the working population to be free of it. The men of Devon paid John no less than five thousand marks in 1204 to have the whole county, except Dartmoor and Exmoor, disafforested. In terms of modern money this is somewhere between £300,000 and £400,000.

Less burdensome and extensive were the private parks which were the game preserves of certain feudal magnates. In many instances these represent the beginings of the country house parks as we know them today. Thus Knowsley, now the largest park in the north of England, is first heard of in 1292 when we are told that Sir Robert de Latham had "a wood which is called a park." The word *park* meant originally no more than "an enclosure." It is used in this sense in several languages, and also in many field-names especially in south-western England. Knowsley begins as a piece of natural woodland enclosed from a larger area by means of a live hedge or a bank and ditch. Thirty years later it is described as "a park with herbage." It is evidently evolving into more open country in places, but there is a long way to go before it becomes a park as we visualize the word.

Similarly, the beginnings of Hatfield Park in Hertfordshire have to be sought in the thirteenth-century woodland. Hertfordshire was naturally a densely-wooded country, and the manor of Hatfield had been given by King Edgar (959-75) to the monks of Ely in order to secure ample wood for their building activities. By the middle of the thirteenth century two parks had been enclosed out of the manorial woodland, one of them—the Great Park—containing about a thousand acres, the other about 350 acres. Not until the nineteenth century were these two ancient parks united to form the present Hatfield Park. The well-known park at Ashridge, on the northern slopes of the Chiltern Hills, is also first heard of in the thirteenth century, though large additions were made to it, as to many other notable parks, at a later date. Bradgate Park, in Leicestershire, still largely in a natural state of bracken, rocks, and water, existed in the year 1247 when Roger de Somery made it over, "with the deer-leaps then made in it," to the Earl of Winchester in return for hunting rights in the Earl's forest all around.

Where a medieval park was enclosed by means of a bank and ditch it is possible to follow this boundary for great distances and even, in some cases, to restore the complete original boundary to the map. Mr. O. G. S. Crawford demonstrates this of the large twelfth-century park at New Buckenham in Norfolk and at Hampstead Marshall near Newbury, in Berkshire, where the original boundary-bank can be traced for several miles.[1] The bank along the south side of John of Gaunt's deer-park in King's Somborne (Hampshire) is still twelve feet high, with a ditch on the outside, and many others of these medieval boundary-banks are massive earthworks, rivalling in size (as Mr. Crawford says) such defensive earth-works as Offa's Dyke and Wansdyke. But not all are as impressive as this, and the explorer of these forgotten boundaries must be prepared to look for much smaller banks and ditches at times. The reconstruction of medieval parks and their boundaries is one of the many useful tasks awaiting the field-worker with patience and a good local knowledge.

Marsh, Fen, and Moor

There are certain sheets of the one-inch Ordnance Survey maps which one can sit down with and read like a book for an hour on end, with growing pleasure and imaginative excitement. One dwells upon the infinite variety of the place-names (and yet there is a characteristic flavour for each region of England), the delicate nerve-like complexity of roads and lanes, the siting of the villages and hamlets, the romantic moated farmsteads in deep country, the churches standing alone in the fields, the patterns made by the contours or by the way the parish boundaries fit into one another. One dissects such a map mentally, piece by piece, and in doing so learns a good deal of local history, whether or not one knows the country itself.

Such an exciting map is that of the country around the Wash, particularly the country on the western and southern sides—the Lincolnshire and Norfolk Marsh-land. One can no more do justice to this beautiful map in a few lines than pro-gramme notes can convey the quality of a symphony. The very names like Bicker Haven and Fleet Haven, now many miles inland; or Moulton Seas End and Surfleet Seas End and Seadyke Farm, all far back today from the shore-line; the so-called Roman Bank twisting across the open levels, and the chapels far out on the salt marshes—all these matters of observation set the mind working at once about the past history of this piece of country. One observes also the intricate tangle of the road and lane pattern between Boston and Wainfleet, along the western side of the Wash, in marked contrast to the great open spaces of the Fen behind where the roads are few and straight, or to the Marsh in front where they fade out altogether and give us a landscape of nothing but scores of drains running straight ahead to the mud-flats and the sea and sky beyond. The belt of tangled roads and lanes is only a mile or two wide for the greater part of its length, and is

[1]Crawford, *Archæology in the Field*, 189-96.

thickly sprinkled with dispersed farmsteads and a few hamlets. At intervals of
every few miles one finds a considerable village. And one notices one other remarkable thing—that the main road from Boston to Wainfleet is as full of bends
and corners as any of the little lanes that lie on either side of it: it must be the most
difficult main road in England for motorists. It runs roughly parallel, so far as
anything is parallel to anything else in this irregular landscape, to what the map
calls the Roman Bank and the Old Sea Bank, and roughly parallel also to a string
of lanes. By now we are convinced that this piece of country, like that along the
southern side of the Wash which it so much resembles, has had an exceptional
history: and so indeed it has. It is a landscape of a few ancient villages and of
centuries of reclamation from the marsh on one side and the fen on the other; a
landscape created largely between the seventh century and the seventeenth, where
many of the winding lanes represent successive frontiers in the conquest of the salt
marshes from the sea.

The first settlements in this landscape were the nucleated villages. Although
the one-inch map does not show it, these all lie along a belt of silt which itself lay
between the fen and the marsh and several feet above both. On this dry, firm
foundation the first Old English settlers made their homes, possibly in the seventh
century and not earlier. There is not a single early place-name in all this region
between Steeping, on the edge of the Wolds, and Spalding, far up the Welland,
and not a single cemetery of the heathen period.

Into this thinly peopled and somewhat unattractive landscape came the
Danish conquerors, soldier-settlers of the tenth century for the most part, as
evidenced in village-names like Skirbeck and Wrangle. But most of the village-
names are English. The narrow band of silt was embanked both against the fen
behind and the sea ahead. As the population grew, the pressure on the available
land became acute, and we begin to hear of banks being constructed further out
in the fen and marsh in order to bring in new land.

Despite the name *Roman Bank*, which appears in half a dozen places on the map
of this district, there is no evidence that the Romans carried out any embanking
in this region around the Wash. Much of what is called the Roman Bank is known
to be as late in date as the sixteenth or seventeenth century, especially that section
to the east of the Boston-Wainfleet road. But the old bank, so far as it can be
traced now, is certainly pre-Conquest in date, and its line is probably represented
by that of the main road from Wainfleet as far as Benington. When we regard this
road as originally the causeway along the top of an ancient sea-bank, and as the
result of a gigantic piecemeal effort by hand-labour, we begin to understand the
extraordinary number of corners and curves in its course. Beyond Boston (which
did not then exist) the bank swept miles inland to run around Bicker Haven,
which was at that time open sea. This haven is known to have silted up soon after
the Norman Conquest, so giving us a terminal date for the construction of the
bank; and the fact that certain Domesday villages lie upon it (*e.g.*, Wrangle)

clinches the argument for a pre-Norman date. Beyond that we cannot go at present.

The marshland villages were still few and small at the end of the eleventh century,[1] the marshland and fen hardly touched. It is between about 1150 and 1300 that we get abundant evidence of the construction of banks and ditches in both Fen and Marsh.

Rainfall may have been more moderate then. At any rate the Crowland abbey chronicle speaks of the fen drying up in this period, so that it was not difficult to make fen-banks on a large scale and to take in wide tracts of new arable land. To the south of the Wash, the men of Holbeach, Whaplode, and Fleet were hard at work from about 1160 onwards. We hear of the Saturday Dike by about 1160-70, Hassock Dike by 1190-5, Asgardike in 1203-6, and the Common Dike in 1241. All these dikes represented successive advances into the Fens, so that in the space of eighty years no less than fifty square miles were added to the arable and pasture of these townships. Of this some seventeen or eighteen square miles were added by the last great intake between 1206 and 1241.[2]

This fen-reclamation was carried out by whole communities, mainly by the hundreds or double-hundreds of the Danelaw, and the newly won land was divided into bovates, each of which carried with it the obligation to keep a certain length of the dikes and ditches in repair. In the village of Walsoken, for example, every acre of land repaired four feet of sea-bank in the marshes, and one foot of Podike in the fen. At West Walton every acre repaired six feet two inches of sea-bank and one foot of Podike. What might happen if a single man neglected this duty was illustrated on 19 January 1439. One Thomas Flower, despite the warning of the dike-reeve, failed to repair his section of the Wisbeach fendike, the flood-waters pouring down from the Midlands broke through, and in a short time between twelve and thirteen thousand acres of land were under water. On another fenland manor in 1331 we are told that nearly a thousand acres were under water; and at Terrington and West Walton in 1316 "a great part of the lands are submerged in the sea."

Simultaneously with the embanking in the Fens, there was an advance from the village towards the sea. The action of the tides around the southern end of the Wash especially was raising up the salt marshes, so that there came a point at which they could be enclosed and protected from the tides by a sea-bank. Salt marsh became fresh marsh after a few seasons, and some of the fresh marsh eventually became fertile arable. We get therefore a series of sea-banks of different dates between the villages and the sea today. For example the men of Holbeach and Whaplode built a town dike outside the Roman Bank in the year 1286.

Many of these dikes were high and wide enough to carry a road. When the

[1] See the population maps in Darby, *Domesday Geography*, i, 52, 116.
[2] I am indebted to Mr. H. Hallam of Spalding for the substance of this paragraph. See the Select Bibliography at the end of this chapter.

Old Podike fell into disrepair and a new dike was to be raised by all the townships of Marshland and by Wiggenhall, we are told it was to be five or six feet high, eighteen feet wide at the base, and twelve feet wide at the top. Elsewhere we read that the dikes between the townships of a certain hundred were to be sixteen feet high to keep the waters of one vill from another vill. Many of these ancient fen-dikes and sea-banks carry secondary roads today and this helps to explain their peculiarities, both their frequent and abrupt bends and the fact that they often extend for several miles in what is obviously a continuous line despite the frequent

PLATE 19

The Somerset Levels at Godney, near Glastonbury. Godney means "Goda's island" and is recorded in a charter dated 971. The island referred to is probably the rocky outcrop in the background of the view, which rose out of a Saxon landscape of swamps and lagoons. These swamps were mostly drained between the tenth and fourteenth centuries by the marshland abbeys, producing the sort of country we see here: a narrow drain or *rhine* fringed with stumpy pollarded osiers, broad rich pastures, and the lumpy "island." Some of these lumpy islands were terraced for vineyards even in late Saxon times, and the terraces may still be seen in places.

changes of direction. In north Lincolnshire, near Grimsby, we are told in a survey of 1595 that what was then the main (and only) street of the hamlet of Marsh Chapel was in former times the old sea-bank. As early as the twelfth century we find villages and hamlets strung along this bank, which can be traced on the map from Tetney down to Saltfleet (Fig. 7). One or two of the villages on the bank existed at the time of the Norman Conquest, so that here again we have a communal reclamation of marshland going back to pre-Conquest times.

Not only do we find this reclamation of marsh and fen going on throughout

Lincolnshire and the adjacent counties, carried out by monastic houses in some cases, by feudal magnates in others, by whole villages in other places, and no doubt by individual peasants at times, but we find similar activity in all the marshland regions of England—in the Somerset Levels (where the abbeys of Glastonbury, Muchelney and Athelney were busy), in the Kentish marshes (where Canterbury Cathedral Priory was foremost from the twelfth century to the late fifteenth), and in Holderness. The reclamation of marsh and fen brought hundreds of square miles of new land into cultivation, and produced a characteristic landscape of willow-lined ditches, rich green pastures that carried thousands of sheep, and scattered farmsteads. We can generally distinguish the work of the medieval centuries by the irregular pattern it makes on the map: winding ditches, frequent abrupt bends in banks and consequently in the roads upon them, a thick powdering of dispersed settlement, all in contrast to the long, ruler-straight lines of later drainage and the wide, empty spaces between infrequent farmsteads.

The reclaimed pastures of the marshlands were not the only ones to carry large flocks of sheep. There is evidence from the eighth century onwards to suggest that the chalk and limestone downlands had much the same aspect as they have today of open and rolling sheep-pastures. The nuns of Holy Trinity abbey at Caen had a flock of seventeen hundred sheep grazing on Minchinhampton common in the Cotswolds early in the twelfth century; and in the south Wiltshire village of South Damerham and its hamlet of Martin over four thousand sheep were grazing on the chalk downs in 1225. We do not know when the pastures of the limestone and chalk downlands were first exploited in Old English times, for Domesday Book gives us no information about livestock in these parts, but casual evidence from Saxon charters suggests that the value of these upland pastures was well known at that time. When I visited recently some outlying fields of my own Oxfordshire parish, on the oolitic limestone, to discover the whereabouts of *Rammadene*—the rams' valley—mentioned in a charter of 958, there on the open sunny slopes were hundreds of sheep grazing, precisely as they must have grazed a thousand years ago when their numbers gave a name to the little dry valley. It was an immemorial scene. We cannot doubt, I think, that the landscape of the Cotswold uplands and the Wiltshire downlands was even in late Saxon times much as we know it today. The numerous Shiptons and Shipstons in the Cotswold country are further testimony to the existence of large flocks of sheep on the uplands at the time of Domesday and earlier. Shipston-on-Stour owes its name to a sheep-wash which existed here in the eighth century. Shipton-under-Wychwood is also recorded in a charter of the eighth century, and Shipton-on-Cherwell in the first years of the eleventh. Indeed, the discovery of a considerable fulling establishment in the Roman villa at Chedworth, a few miles south-east of Cheltenham, takes large-scale sheep-farming on the Cotswolds back to the third or the fourth century.

In the medieval period the monasteries, above all the Cistercian houses from the early twelfth century onwards, were responsible for many changes in the landscape: the large-scale drainage of marsh and fen, the clearance of woodland, and the extension of sheep-farming on their ranch-like granges, especially in the Yorkshire Dales and in Wales. Usually they settled in a wilderness and brought it into cultivation, but occasionally the Cistercians had to create an artificial wilderness for themselves by wiping out settled villages and farms. In the Midlands, Combe Abbey destroyed the hamlet of Upper Smite in 1150, and Garendon Abbey wiped out the village of Dishley and made a grange of it where, centuries later, Robert Bakewell carried out his revolutionary experiments in stock-breeding. In Lincoln-shire, Revesby Abbey in 1142 reduced three small villages to ruins so effectively that their very sites are now hard to discover.

Many monastic granges were created for arable farming, especially in lowland areas like the Vale of York, but most of them were created for sheep-farming on a large scale, above all on the chalk and limestone uplands of Yorkshire and Lincolnshire. Without doubt the monastic sheep formed the largest single flocks, but the peasant flocks, taken all together, often greatly outnumbered them, as the evidence from south Wiltshire shows. In many places the peasant had been exploiting the upland pastures before the monasteries appeared on the scene.

On the true moorlands, the monastic contribution was less evident. The transformation of moorland into little pastoral farms was mainly the work of peasant households, sometimes working as a single household, sometimes appar-ently in small groups, so that we get either a single farmstead or a small cluster of three or four—a hamlet. We notice this in the re-colonization of Dartmoor from the middle of the thirteenth century onwards, after an almost total abandonment since the Iron Age. Of the thirty-five "ancient tenements" of Dartmoor, some, like Riddon, consisted of a single farm; others, like Babeny and Pizwell, each consisted of three farmsteads grouped together on one site. The remains of some of these medieval farmsteads, built of enduring granite, can still be seen on Dartmoor, as at Yardworthy, Challacombe, and Cholwich Town (Plate 20). In most instances it was the individual peasant household that laboured among the bracken and the rocks to make a new farm, such as Fernacre ("bracken land"), far up the De Lank valley on Bodmin Moor, or Wortha in St. Neots parish, which we first hear of in 1241, and numerous other farmsteads in all the parishes adjoining the Cornish moorlands.

In the north of England the frontier of cultivation was similarly being pushed higher up the hillsides. Along the western slopes of Cross Fell we hear of the small village of Milburn for the first time in the year 1200; and the late Norman work in the parish church supports the view that it was the result of moorland reclamation in the twelfth century. Not far away we see pioneers at work well into the thirteenth century, as on the moors of south-western England: Kirkland is not heard of until about 1230, Murton ("moor *tun*") in 1288, and Dufton in 1289. All these are hamlets, but the single farmstead is also found, like Brackenthwaite ("bracken

FIG. 9.—MEDIEVAL FIELD PATTERN IN DEVON

The area shown on the map lies on the south-western edge of Dartmoor. Willsworthy ("Wifel's farm") is recorded in Domesday Book and is a farmstead of late Saxon origin. There was a small amount of arable in 1086, and a large extent of pasture (two leagues long by one league in width). The farm was worked by four slaves for Alured the Breton, who took over from Siward, the Saxon owner, in 1066. Standon ("stone hill") is first recorded in 1242. The fields around this farm were probably first made from the rough moorland pasture recorded in Domesday, at some date in the twelfth century, and are typical of piecemeal enclosure direct from the waste—very small and very irregular in shape. Nattor Farm is first recorded in 1340. No early reference to Lanehead has been found, but it is almost certainly of medieval origin like all the outlying farms in this district. The medieval frontier of cultivation is well brought out on this map.

Reproduced by permission from the 6-inch map of the Ordnance Survey.

clearing") and Outhwaite. Beyond a certain height, however, the high moorland was not worth reclamation. It was incapable of supporting even the hard life of a medieval peasant family, and it was left to the curlews and the mountain sheep. Even so, it was not a No Man's Land. It became the subject of dispute when villagers in adjoining dales met on the high watershed with their flocks and accused each other of trespass over an invisible line in the rough pastures. The tenants of Fountains abbey on the Kilnsey Moors, above Wharfedale, and those

PLATE 20

A medieval moorland farmstead: Cholwich Town, Devon. Cholwich, which means "the coldest farm," lies on the south-western edge of Dartmoor, and is first recorded about 1200-20. The moorstone farmstead shown above dates mostly from about 1500, but the remains of the earliest peasant farmstead on this site still survive in the lower yard.

of Salley abbey on the Arncliffe and Litton Moors to the west, were at loggerheads until, in the year 1279, a boundary was marked out with great stones, each stone marked with a cross. On Malham Moor the abbeys of Fountains, Bolton, and Salley were erecting miles of limestone walls to clear up boundary disputes. Such walls have doubtless been repaired many times since then, but they are still substantially walls of medieval origin, representing the climax of the colonization movement high up among the cotton-grass and the cold mists.

Buildings in the Landscape

By the eve of the Black Death the population of England was about three times that of Domesday. It is impossible to be very precise about such statements at

PLATE 21

The head of Wasdale in Cumberland showing the frontier of cultivation and the characteristic field pattern of medieval colonization—winding lanes and tiny irregular fields: a hand-made landscape.

this period, but it has been estimated that at the peak, just before the first outbreak of the Black Death (1348), there may have been nearly four million people in all.   Hundreds of thousands of acres of new land had been won from the waste and the water, and settled, though still thinly, in the ten generations that had elapsed since the Norman Conquest. Many new towns had appeared, a number of new villages, and some thousands of hamlets and isolated farmsteads had been brought into being. There were now far more buildings to be seen in the landscape than ever before.

In certain parts of the country, monastic buildings—some of them on a grand scale—were a common sight. There were in England as a whole between five and six hundred monasteries. In Yorkshire alone there were sixty-six, in Lincolnshire fifty-one. Somerset, Kent, and Gloucestershire were similarly rich in great abbeys and priories. The abbey churches of some of them resembled cathedrals, set in the depths of the countryside (Plate 22) or towering above a medieval market-place.

Much more numerous than the monasteries, and generally less grand, were the parish churches, of which several thousands had been built since the Conquest, most of them perhaps in the hundred years between 1150 and 1250. It was in this period that the division of England into ecclesiastical parishes was completed (at least until the rapid expansion of the northern and midland towns during the Industrial Revolution) and the parish church arose as a visible symbol and centre of a new community. Many of these parish churches were small and unpretentious structures, a simple nave and chancel built of rubble masonry from a local stone-pit, built with peasant labour and peasant materials as at Honeychurch in deepest Devon. Sometimes the lord of the manor paid for most of the fabric, and the result is a handsome and more sophisticated village church, like Stoke Golding (Leics.). But not all peasants were poor by the early fourteenth century. There were certain parts of England with a considerable population of wealthy peasants, as for example the Marshland and Fenland parishes of south Lincolnshire and western Norfolk, and here we find a splendid constellation of parish churches without a break for mile after mile. Many of these superb churches have spires, which first appear in the early years of the thirteenth century; and so we get what is often regarded as a typical English scene: church spires rising from clumps of trees or piercing the Fenland skies all around the horizon. The spire is in fact particularly characteristic of a broad belt of country running diagonally across England from Lincoln down to the north coast of Somerset, along and near the belt of fine oolitic building stones. Elsewhere, towers considerably outnumber spires, but it is not entirely a matter of geology.

In the rich little county of Rutland, which had about twelve or thirteen thousand people at the most, there were more than fifty medieval churches, one to every 250 people. Most of the Rutland churches are handsome, some of them are large and strikingly beautiful (Plate 23). In the neighbouring county of Lincolnshire, Cobbett reckoned that one could count a hundred parish churches within a six-mile radius of Horncastle. Parishes in such parts of England as this were generally very small: some near Norwich, as we have seen, had fewer than

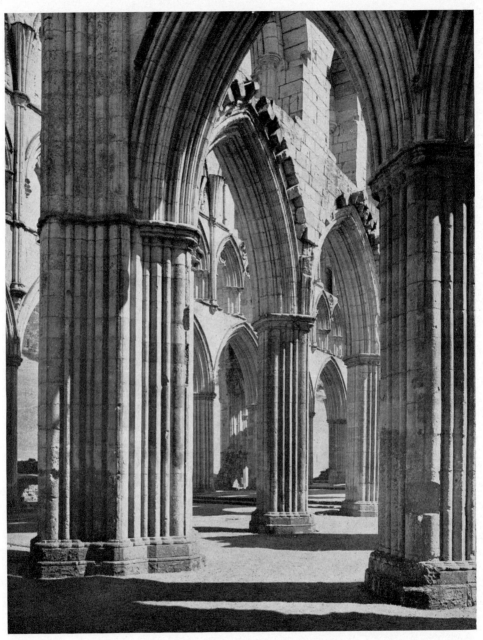

PLATE 22

Rievaulx Abbey (the choir): one of the most beautiful of the Cistercian abbeys of Yorkshire.
Rievaulx was founded in Ryedale in 1132. Like all the other abbeys of the same foundation it colonized the wilderness around, and later in its outlying granges. Arable farms
were created in the valleys and extensive sheep-walks on the limestone hills above.

PLATE 23

Ketton, Rutland. As the farmlands and sheep-pastures of Eastern England reached their
first great period of prosperity during the thirteenth century, one of the consequences
was the rebuilding of parish churches on a grander scale. The Early English churches of
Rutland and Northamptonshire are particularly notable. Here is the suave beauty of
Ketton tower and spire, unsurpassed even in its own countryside.

five hundred acres. But up in the moorland parts of Yorkshire and Lancashire medieval churches were few and far between, and parishes ran to enormous sizes. The old parish of Halifax ran to nearly seventy-six thousand acres; in Lancashire the mother-parish of Whalley was, even in the nineteenth century, still about thirty miles in length and fifteen miles wide. It had included, in medieval times, nearly fifty townships.

Two new kinds of mill made their appearance almost simultaneously towards the end of the twelfth century—the windmill and the fulling-mill. The earliest windmills are recorded in the reign of Richard I, after which they spread rapidly in southern and eastern England above all. Greenwood and Pringle's survey of Essex in the early nineteenth century marks 212 mills in the county, while the earliest large-scale map of Kent shows seventy-eight and that for Sussex shows sixty-six. Windmills are still a conspicuous feature of the landscape in these counties, but the vast majority have long since ceased to work and stand or lie in various stages of dereliction. As for fulling-mills, which we first hear of about the year 1185, they were more highly localized and have all disappeared without a trace, though here and there a derelict corn-mill represents a former fulling-mill.

Towns were a more important and enduring element in the landscape. It is remarkable how many English towns have come into existence since the Norman Conquest, most of them as a result of "the fever of borough creation" in the twelfth and thirteenth centuries. All classes of landowners shared in this fever of speculation —the King himself, bishops and abbots, lay magnates, and even small local landowners. It was Henry II who founded the town of Woodstock in Oxfordshire, at the gates of the royal park, and its dependent origin is revealed to this day in the fact that this pleasant and thriving little town is still technically a chapelry of the mother-church at Bladon, an inconspicuous village a mile off. It was Richard I who founded the town of Portsmouth in the year 1194, to take the place of the more ancient town of Porchester, now becoming silted up; and it was King John who gave to the growing village of Liverpool in 1207 its first charter setting up a borough.

Great ecclesiastics were prominent among the borough-founders. Plymouth was the creation of the priors of Plympton in the middle years of the thirteenth century; the abbot of Eynsham in 1215 laid out a piece of his demesne, on the edge of the old village, as building-plots for his new burgesses. At Stratford-upon-Avon the bishop of Worcester in 1196 similarly laid out, on the edge of the Saxon village (now called Old Town), a piece of his demesne covering 109 acres. This was marked out in building-plots twelve perches in length and three and a half in breadth (roughly one-third of an acre each) and six streets were planned, three running parallel with the river and three at right angles to it, a piece of elementary town planning such as one finds on a far larger scale in the bishop of Salisbury's creation of New Sarum a few years later (Fig. 10). Stratford, like Salisbury, was an immediate success. A survey made in 1252 records "some two hundred and forty

FIG. 10.—THE MEDIEVAL PLAN OF SALISBURY

Salisbury (New Sarum) retains its original gridiron plan, laid out in 1220–25. The bishops of Sarum possessed rich meadow lands beside the Avon, two miles to the south of Old Sarum, and upon these Bishop Richard le Poore laid out a city to the north of his new cathedral. Straight streets, with streams running down them, cut the site into rectangles or chequers. Inside each chequer the individual house-plots were also marked out, with a standard size of seven perches by three, each plot paying a ground rent of twelve pence yearly to the bishop. A large market-place was laid out, with a gild hall on one side and the chief parish church on the other. Though the burgage tenements or house-plots have long ago lost their perfect symmetry, the original street-plan survives, for the later city grew on the western and eastern sides and left the thirteenth-century nucleus intact.

Reproduced by permission from the 6-inch map of the Ordnance Survey.

burgage tenements, besides about fifty plots of land, various shops, stalls, and other holdings." An area of 109 acres with three houses to the acre would have held about three hundred houses, allowing for the streets and other open spaces, so that within two generations probably all the available area at Stratford had been taken up and built upon. Great lay lords also created boroughs, like the Grenvilles at Bideford or the Berkeleys at various places in Gloucestershire, with varying degrees of success.

Some of these boroughs were created on entirely new sites, others were an enhancement in status of an agricultural village. Some grew successfully into market-towns; many failed to develop any urban characteristics, for a royal or a seignorial charter was not in itself any guarantee that people and trade would follow. About one-half the boroughs set up in Devon failed to come to anything, and about the same proportion in Cornwall. Some of the new towns were laid out on a simple grid-iron plan from the beginning, like Salisbury, Stratford, Ludlow, and Eynsham; but the great majority were just left to grow anyhow within the specified area.[1]

The towns of medieval England were, by the early fourteenth century, a common feature in the rural landscape (most of them remained small and half-rural in any event) and their successful growth between the twelfth and fourteenth centuries affected the nature of communications throughout the country.

The creation of hundreds of little market-towns, each serving a radius of three to five miles, perhaps up to ten miles in the remoter parts, brought into existence, or perhaps we should say solidified, a great number of main roads for the first time, and led to the erection of hundreds of bridges. These main roads joined town to town, and some became of national importance.

Various roads called *Port-street* in pre-Conquest charters constituted early through-roads from one town to another, and there are many such roads in the southern half of England. Even so, the period between 1066 and 1348 saw hundreds more come into existence, mostly by the linking together of already ancient inter-village paths, and where necessary filling in gaps in the direct line by treading out a new stretch. Simultaneously, we find most of our ancient bridges appearing for the first time in the records.

The importance of bridges had been well recognized in Saxon times, when their repair was regarded as among the "three necessary duties" of all landowners. A certain number of English bridges go back to Saxon (and even Roman) times, but over most of the country fords or primitive plank bridges were the usual means of crossing rivers. Stone bridges were sufficiently rare in the twelfth and thirteenth centuries to be recorded as such in charters of the period. They were naturally commoner where good building stone was available, as along the oolitic limestone belt. In counties such as Devon, where suitable stone was unobtainable, even important bridges like those at Barnstaple and Bideford were built of timber when

[1]See also Chapter IX on "The Landscape of Towns."

they were first erected in the closing years of the thirteenth century. The twelfth-century bridge at Exeter was of timber, but had been replaced by a stone bridge before the middle of the thirteenth century.

Most bridges that are well known today first appear in these years of growing internal trade and prosperity. The Trent was bridged at Nottingham as early as 924, but this was the only crossing, other·than by ferry, until one arrived at the upper reaches. We hear of Wichnor bridges in the reign of Henry III, of the bridge at Burton-upon-Trent in 1175, and, a few miles below, of the important Swarkeston bridge (of which much still remains to be seen) in 1204. Kelham bridge, near Newark, is first heard of in 1225; and Muskham bridge, the lowest medieval bridge over the river, was a going concern in the year 1301, when it was known as "hay bridge"—that is, one capable of bearing a load of hay. Thus nearly all the important bridges over the Trent came into existence in the twelfth and thirteenth centuries, and we should find that the same is true of most of the larger English rivers.

Castles made their appearance in England in the late eleventh century. Before long nearly every important town had one towering over it, considerable numbers of houses being demolished to make room for it in many old towns. In many places where a great castle was built on a strong and strategic site an entirely new town grew up beside it, to supply its daily needs and to enjoy its protection. Such towns were Ludlow, Launceston (Plate 16), Newcastle-on-Tyne, and Devizes, among others. Castles were to be found all over England, by the early fourteenth century, but were by no means uniformly distributed. Thus Kent had about forty castles; the large county of Devon had only eight.

SELECT BIBLIOGRAPHY

CRAWFORD, O. G. S., *Archæology in the Field* (1953), chapters 18, 19.
DARBY, H. C., *The Domesday Geography of Eastern England* (1952).
DARBY, H. C., *The Medieval Fenland* (1940).
FINBERG, H. P. R., *Tavistock Abbey* (1951), chapter II.
GRAY, H. L., *English Field Systems* (1915).
HALLAM, H. E., *The New Lands of Elloe* (1954).
HELM, P. J., "The Somerset Levels in the Middle Ages," *Journal British Archæological Association,* 1949.
HOSKINS, W. G., and FINBERG, H. P. R., *Devonshire Studies* (1952), essays on "The Open Field in Devon," "The Making of the Agrarian Landscape," and "Three Studies in Family History."
MILLER, E., *The Abbey and Bishopric of Ely* (1951).
NEILSON, N., *A Terrier of Fleet, Lincolnshire* (1920).
PAGE, W., "The Origins and Forms of Hertfordshire Towns and Villages," *Archæologia,* vol. 69 (1917-18).
POWER, EILEEN, *The Medieval English Wool Trade* (1941), chapter II.
RAISTRICK, A., *The Story of the Pennine Walls* (2nd ed. 1952).
SAVAGE, SIR WILLIAM, *The Making of Our Towns* (1952), chapters 6, 7.
SMITH, R. A. L., *Canterbury Cathedral Priory* (1943), chapter 11.

IV

The Black Death and After

The Abandonment of Villages

DESPITE the great colonization movement of the twelfth and thirteenth centuries, England still contained many wild and secret places when the bubonic plague smote the country for the first time in the late summer of 1348, an event which had profound consequences in many ways, including the bringing about of considerable changes in the landscape. Successive outbreaks of the plague reduced the population of the country by somewhere between one-third and one-half. This put an end to the "land-hunger" of the thirteenth century, which had led pioneers higher into the moorlands and farther into the woods and heaths. The pressure of population eased off, and there followed a retreat from the marginal lands. The infertile farms were abandoned in favour of the more rewarding farms elsewhere. Instead of peasants seeking land, landlords now sought for tenants.

The retreat from the marginal lands was most evident in the sandy Breckland of south-western Norfolk and north-western Suffolk, and on the thinner soils of the Lincolnshire heaths and wolds. The Breckland had been only sparsely peopled at the end of the eleventh century. Domesday Book indicates that it provided a livelihood for only twenty to twenty-five people to the square mile as against seventy to eighty elsewhere in East Anglia. The region stands out noticeably as one carrying a considerable sheep population. Probably some of the Domesday sheep-pastures were colonized and settled as arable villages in subsequent generations, as we know happened at Aunby on the west Lincolnshire heaths. An abstract of a title deed dated 10th September 1626 says that "the village of Aunby was first constituted from the ancient use of Pasture for sheep, Beasts, and a warren of Conyes [rabbits], with a shepherd's and a warrener's lodge only thereon, to be broken up for corne, and used in tillage and building of houses fitt for husbandry and other necessaries there convenient." It appears that the neighbouring village of Holywell originated in the same way, for we are told that the inhabitants of the two places "were first planters, tenants, and occupiers thereof." Probably the original "planters" of the two villages came from the ancient mother-village of Castle Bytham some time in the latter part of the twelfth century. We hear of Holywell for the first time in 1190, and of Aunby in 1219. Aunby is a pure Scandinavian name: it is "Outhen's by or farm." The history of Aunby's origin tells us incidentally that not all villages with Scandinavian names go back to the days of the Danish Conquest in the ninth and tenth centuries. Danish personal names were in common use throughout the twelfth century in Lincolnshire and other parts of the Danelaw, so that Outhen or Authun could well have given his name to a village founded during the reign of Henry II or a little later. Aunby had only a short life: it seems to have been abandoned during the fifteenth century and is now only a solitary farm beside a stream. Two miles away over the heath is the deserted village of Pickworth, where a single arch remains of the medieval church. Pickworth, too, is last heard of as a village in the fifteenth century.

There are more than thirteen hundred deserted villages in England. The sites of most of them are to be found in the Midlands, and the eastern half of England— the Lowland Zone. In the East Riding of Yorkshire about a hundred sites are known, in Lincolnshire nearly a hundred and fifty, in Norfolk a hundred and thirty. Back in the Midlands, there are about two hundred and fifty deserted village sites in the three counties of Warwickshire, Leicestershire, and Northampton-shire. The number of sites falls appreciably as we go north and west into the upland regions of England, but that is probably because villages are much fewer in these regions, and here we have the harder task of locating abandoned hamlets and single farmsteads. For example, Crowndale Farm, the reputed birthplace of Sir Francis Drake just outside the Devonshire market-town of Tavistock, had been a hamlet with seven farmsteads in 1336. Sixty years later it had been re-duced to one holding and its corn-mill lay derelict; and it has survived as one farm down to the present day.

The Black Death, though it wiped out possibly as many as one and a half million people altogether within thirty years, was not the immediate cause of this large-scale extermination of villages and hamlets. Some villages, it is true, were completely depopulated and never re-settled, such as Tilgarsley in Oxford-shire, Middle Carlton in west Lincolnshire, and Ambion in west Leicestershire, over the empty site of which in 1485 the battle of Bosworth Field was fought. Occasionally a village was emptied by plague and re-settled on a new site some little way off. This happened at Combe in Oxfordshire and possibly at Steeple Barton, a few miles away. In both instances the survivors returned, not to the original village, but to one of its hamlets, leaving the old site forlorn and rat-ridden.

The making of the New Forest in the eleventh century, and of many of the Cistercian granges in the twelfth, had already brought about a number of early desertions of villages. In addition to these deliberate erasures of villages, it seems that some villages, settled late in difficult, unrewarding country, were decaying and on the point of collapse even before the Black Death. Asterleigh, a twelfth-century clearing on the edge of Wychwood Forest in Oxfordshire, acquired a parish church and parochial rights by the early thirteenth century; but by 1316 it was united with the neighbouring parish of Kiddington for reasons of poverty. England is full of sizeable villages, founded back in Saxon and Scandinavian times, which have survived to this day; but there were also many hundreds of villages like Asterleigh, or like Maidenwell on the Lincolnshire Wolds, which struggled

along on marginal lands, blessed with a parish church but unable to keep it
going, and to such places as this the plague dealt a further and ultimately fatal
blow.

The vast mortality of the successive epidemics led to the piecemeal abandon-

FIG. 11.—THE DESERTED VILLAGES OF LEICESTERSHIRE

Several of the sites in the west of the country are the result of early conversion into monastic
granges. In the eastern half of the country, the concentration of sites on the Liassic clay
uplands is very noticeable. The western edge of the Liassic clays is indicated on the map
by the thick black line. Most of the sites on these clays were deserted in the period 1450–
1600.

ment of villages and hamlets on marginal land. On and around the edges of the Breckland there are no fewer than twenty-eight deserted villages. Most of them were small and poor, and the desertions were gradual, extending over two, three, or four generations, so that most instances of final abandonment occur during the fifteenth century. There are four ruined churches within four miles of Colkirk, in the North Norfolk country, small chapels built by the pioneers of the High Middle Ages and abandoned to the weather before the Middle Ages ended.[1] Ruined churches abound on the Wolds of Lincolnshire, as at Calceby (Plate 24). The one-inch map of Lincolnshire reveals over and over again where these lost villages are to be sought for. It abounds in examples of united parishes such as

PLATE 24

The ruined Norman church of Calceby, Lincolnshire: the site of the abandoned village lies on the other side of the hillock on which the church stood. It was first founded by the Danes in the ninth or tenth century upon the thin unrewarding chalk soils of the Wolds, and abandoned some time during the Middle Ages.

Lenton, Keisby, and Osgodby or Careby, Aunby, and Holywell (both on sheet 123). In such instances it will generally be found that one place survives as an ecclesiastical centre and the other two are each represented by a solitary farmstead.

If one visits such a site, the evidences of the former village may generally be found in a field adjoining the farmstead which perpetuates the old name. Often the fragments of a small medieval church meet the eye and identify the site at once, but more often even these have entirely disappeared and the only visible signs are the grassy banks which cover the rubble foundations of the peasant farmsteads, and the shallow depressions between them that mark the line of the

[1]Saltmarsh, "Plague and Economic Decline," *Cambridge Historical Journal,* 1941.

former streets and lanes (Plate 25). It is best to visit these sites in the six months between autumn and spring, before the new grass and the nettles have half obliterated the markings on the ground.

The final stages of the abandonment were very often hastened by landlords, both laymen and monastic houses. The dwindling population was insufficient to maintain the traditional arable husbandry of the desmesne. Pastoral farming

Crown Copyright Reserved

PLATE 25

The site of the deserted village of Lower Ditchford (Warwickshire), between Moreton-in-Marsh and Shipston-on-Stour. The village probably disappeared some time in the middle decades of the fifteenth century, and nothing remains but the ground plan—a more irregular plan than usual. The ridge-and-furrow, marking the former open-field arable, is also well revealed in this view.

required only a fraction of the labour needed by arable. Where a landlord had absolute ownership of most of the soil he evicted the remnants of the village population in order to convert the open arable fields into large enclosures of pasture for cattle and sheep, the village houses were demolished—an easy business, for above their rubble foundations they mostly had mud walls—and men, women, and children departed in tears to find a new livelihood elsewhere. The landscape in such parishes and districts changed completely. The strips disappeared under the grass (though they are perpetuated all over the Midlands in the rolling ridges), the vast and hedgeless open fields gave way to hedged enclosures—usually still very large by modern standards—and more than a thousand villages and hamlets were wiped off the scene. Their site was marked only by a solitary farm-stead or a shepherd's cottage.

New Colonization

But the century and a half that followed the first outbreak of the Black Death was not entirely a picture of retreat, decay, and melancholy. There is some reason to suppose that the profound economic decline that marked these genera-tions was at its worst in the Midlands, where equally the prosperity of the thir-teenth century had been at its highest. In the west and north, where life was harder and more primitive, settlement more scattered among the hills, and estates perhaps generally smaller, life seems to have gone on much the same as before, once the worst of the epidemics was over. Indeed, in south-western England we see plenty of evidence of moderate growth rather than decline, and of modest prosperity among some social classes at least.

In some parts of England new land was still being brought into cultivation from the wilderness, though on nothing like the scale of thirteenth-century colonization. In the thick woods of Buckinghamshire and Hertfordshire, and perhaps in the Sussex Weald also, new fields were being added to existing farm-steads; and the priors of Canterbury were still engaged in making reclamations in the marshlands of eastern and south-western Kent. Prior Thomas Goldston (1449-68) spent £1,200 during his rule—some £80,000 in modern values—on the "inning" of Appledore Marsh, and Prior William Petham (1471-2) spent a further £300 on reclaiming six hundred acres of marsh. At Monkton, in the Isle of Thanet, there were also considerable reclamations of marsh by the priory.

A few new settlements came into existence in the fifteenth century—the fishing villages. We first hear of Staithes, the fishing-village on the north Yorkshire coast, in 1415. The name means "landing place." It was the landing-place for the older villages of Seaton or Hinderwell, a mere cleft in a mighty cliff-wall, of no interest until the fishing industry developed along the coast. Similarly, we first hear of the south Cornish village of Mevagissey in the year 1410, and on the north coast both New Quay and Bude are first recorded in the fifteenth century. There may have been a few cottages at any of these places before this time, but not enough to attract a separate name. It is when they suddenly begin to grow that we hear of them by name; and they probably owe their growth to some marked development in the offshore fishing industry which enabled whole villages to gain a livelihood by it. The industry may have become organized on a more or less capitalistic basis instead of the casual fishing for individual needs which had gone on from time immemorial. At any rate it paid someone to build quays and breakwaters at suitable points in order to create artificial harbours on otherwise dangerous coasts.

The best example of this type of village comes from the late sixteenth century when the north Devon village of Clovelly (Plate 27) was given a breakwater or quay by the squire, George Cary. Clovelly had been an obscure agricultural parish until this time, turning its back on the sea in which it had no interest. But

PLATE 26

An almost medieval scene in Polperro (Cornwall). Polperro is first recorded in 1303, somewhat earlier than the other well-known fishing villages, and probably developed from the start as a fishing village on an almost land-locked harbour.

all was changed by the building of the massive stone pier, which created the only safe harbour on this merciless coast between Appledore in Devon and Boscastle in Cornwall. In his will, dated 9th August 1601, George Cary says: "I have of late erected a pier or key in the sea and river of Severne upon the sea-shore, near low water of the said seas, within or near about one half mile of my said capital messuage of Clovelly, and also divers houses, cellars, warehouses, and other edifices, as well under as in the cliff and on the salt shores of Clovelly aforesaid, and also near above the cliff there, which standeth and hath cost me about £2,000 and which place was of none or very small benefit before my said exertions and buildings." It is rarely that we get such an authentic picture of the creation of a new village, for until this date Clovelly had merely been a parish of scattered farms and cottages on the plateau. The squire built cottages up the narrow valley on either side of a tumbling stream—the only practicable way down to the sea-shore—and fish-cellars and warehouses below the cliffs. The watercourse was

PLATE 27

Clovelly (Devon) owes its origin as a fishing village to its Elizabethan squire. There was no natural harbour in this tremendous cliff-wall, but he built the granite pier seen here and so created a small anchorage. The village grew up the hillside along the banks of a stream, now diverted.

later diverted into a cascade to fall into the sea elsewhere, and its dry bed converted into a series of terraces or broad steps paved with cobbles. The village scene as we know it was then complete.

New Buildings

The years between 1350 and 1500 saw a great number of new buildings added to the landscape. Hundreds of parish churches were rebuilt or enlarged, more so in some parts of England than others. Hundreds of little private oratories or chapels appeared during the fifteenth century, most of them attached to remote houses, but some built at a lonely cross-roads to serve an area far from a parish

PLATE 28

Fotheringhay church, Northamptonshire, built by the royal Dukes of York. The lantern-tower, nave, and aisles are the work of William Horwode, a Stamford freemason, who contracted to build them in 1434. The splendid choir, completed by 1415, was unroofed and destroyed in the sixteenth century, so giving the church its present unbalanced appearance. Fotheringhay was built at a time when practically all other church-building in the Midlands had ceased.

church. More castles were built, and finally more bridges were built or rebuilt of stone in these generations.

There is very little evidence of new church-building in the Midlands, where the agricultural depression was most general and acute, except in special cases like Fotheringhay which was magnificently conceived by the royal dukes of York between about 1400 and 1440, and added something superlative and civilizing to the peasant landscape (Plate 28).

In south-western England a great number of churches were entirely rebuilt or enlarged, so that Perpendicular Gothic is the characteristic and almost monotonous style of the region. Most of them were given beautiful gilded and coloured roodscreens running the entire width of the church. Torbryan in Devon is an outstanding example of early fifteenth-century craftsmanship in wood and stone, but there were scores of others until the Low Church vandals got to work in the eighteenth century and the Victorian "restorers" in the nineteenth.

Not all parishes had the funds to rebuild or even enlarge their churches. The little building at Honeychurch in Devon was given a plain tower and three new bells in the fifteenth century, the chancel arch and roofs were renewed and some new windows put in, but substantially the twelfth-century church was left untouched. There was no need to enlarge the fabric in this sequestered hamlet. Some simply-carved oak benches were provided, probably the first seating the little church had ever had, and everything settled down again for the next five hundred years.

Even Honeychurch, remote and small as it was, managed to add a tower to its church and to follow the prevailing fashion. Towers sprang up everywhere in the countryside and in the towns, some of them magnificent. The towers of Somerset, Suffolk, and Yorkshire are especially notable and numerous. Those of Devon and Cornwall are very numerous—there are hardly a dozen medieval spires in the two counties—but with rare exceptions that are usually copied from elsewhere, they are not beautiful or striking. Most are plain and dull (Plate 29). It was partly the lack of suitable building stone, though not entirely, for even granite could be made to produce grand towers like those at Widecombe-in-the-Moor and Moreton-hampstead. Some of the finest towers among the parish churches are the product of local industrial prosperity in the years down to 1550. Widecombe tower is traditionally said (and probably rightly) to have been built at the cost of the tinners of the parish; Lavenham tower in Suffolk was built at the cost of two generations of the Spring family, the wealthiest clothiers of their age. Indeed, the clothiers and wool merchants often paid for the complete rebuilding of their parish churches, as witness the fine church at Steeple Ashton in Wiltshire, built at the cost of two local clothiers, Walter Lucas and Robert Long, between 1480 and 1500. And the Cotswold "wool churches" are too well known to require any further comment.

In some parts of England, where parishes were large and houses scattered, private oratories or chapels began to appear in considerable numbers in the fourteenth and fifteenth centuries. Landowners, large and small, applied to the bishop for licence to have such chapels, mainly on the ground that their houses

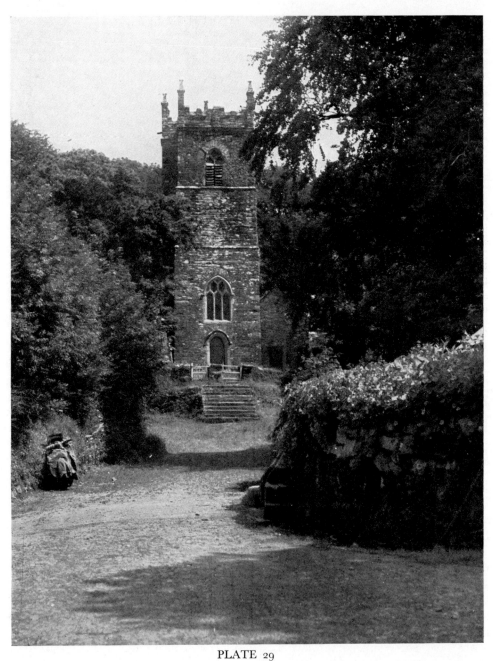

PLATE 29

Michaelstow church, Cornwall: a complete rebuilding of an older church in the fifteenth century, in the plain and simple style common to the poorer country parishes.

were too far from the parish church to make access possible during the winter months. These private chapels were particularly numerous in the south-western counties, where at least two or three hundred existed in pre-Reformation days. Sometimes the chapel or oratory was a room in the squire's or franklin's house, but often it stood as a separate building such as the still-perfect medieval chapel at Trecarrel, four miles south of Launceston. Trecarrel, the ancient home of a family who took their name from their dwelling, lay about a mile and a half from

PLATE 30

The private medieval chapel or oratory at Trecarrel, near Launceston. The medieval mansion-house of the Trecarrels still stands near by. The chapel, dedicated to St. Mary Magdalene, was first licensed by the Bishop of Exeter in 1405, but the present structure was built of granite in the early sixteenth century by the Sir Henry Trecarrel who rebuilt Launceston church. Very few private oratories of this kind survive intact, though many ruined examples can be found in south-western England.

the parish church of Lezant, quite far enough in the deep mud of a Cornish winter. Robert Trecarrel and his wife and mother therefore petitioned the bishop to have a chapel within their "mansion" and on 8th May 1405 the necessary licence was granted. The present structure, which stands detached from the surviving medieval hall and other buildings, represents a rebuilding in granite of about a hundred years later, probably by the Sir Henry Trecarrel who rebuilt Launceston church between 1511 and 1524.

Some of these chapels stood by the roadside in lonely places, like No Man's Chapel which in the fifteenth century stood at a cross-roads where three parishes met, to the north of Exeter. Mostly, however, they lay inside the house or in the yard outside, as they were not intended for public worship. Licences were usually granted only for the landowner and his own household, and even then were subject to further conditions such as attendance at the mother-church upon all the great feasts.

Most of the houses for which these private chapels were licensed have become farm-houses with the passage of time, and have been rebuilt since the Reformation so that all trace of the chapel has been lost. But in scores of instances in south-western England one may yet find considerable traces of the medieval chapel in one of the out-buildings, in a hay-loft or a small barn. At Bury Barton, in the Devonshire parish of Lapford, the chapel of St. James, licensed by Bishop Lacy in 1434, still stands by the roadside, very largely intact and in use as a barn. In other houses which have been rescued from the exigencies of day-to-day farming—such as Fardel and Bradley, also in Devon—the fifteenth-century chapels are quite complete and are occasionally used for their proper purpose. Where, however, they have fallen into ruin or been desecrated, traceried windows, or buttressed walls, or a dimly-seen cradle roof, reveal their original purpose.

Such private chapels or oratories are not to be confused with the parochial chapels which sprang up in the vast parishes of northern England. These were designed for public worship in some village or hamlet far from the mother-church, as in the enormous parishes of Halifax and Whalley, and they were parish churches in all but name. Sometimes certain rights, such as that of baptism or burial, were carefully reserved to the mother-church, but in the great moorland parishes even these rights generally had to be conceded to distant chapelries. Very often, the relationship of mother- and daughter-churches gives us a valuable clue to the nature of early colonization of which we have no other record. The mother-church stands in the parental village, from which pioneers went out to colonize in the woods, moors, and marshes, and to found new villages and hamlets that ultimately got a dependent chapelry of their own. This is not so obviously true in the northern moorland parishes where this simple relationship is obscured by the sheer size of the parish, but it is generally true to the south of the Trent. Mother-churches indicate the primary settlements of a district and by mapping them we can get some sort of picture of settlement before the Norman Conquest, at a period when records are few and scattered.

The late fourteenth and the fifteenth centuries also saw the building or re-building of a great number of bridges in stone. Some of our most handsome bridges date from this time. Most of the important English bridges originated in the twelfth and thirteenth centuries. With the great growth of road traffic these early bridges proved too narrow or too unsafe, and were replaced by stone structures. The bridges over the Ouse at Huntingdon and St. Ives are particularly

notable examples of this period of rebuilding, and East Farleigh bridge over the
Medway is another very fine medieval stone bridge. In the north of England, the
splendid Devil's Bridge over the Lune at Kirkby Lonsdale probably dates from
the fifteenth century, and the remarkable bridge over the Till at Twizel (Northumberland) certainly existed by the early sixteenth. Leland saw it about 1540
and describes it, just as it is today, as "of stone one bow, but greate and stronge."

Some beautiful medieval bridges survive in Devon, especially over the Tamar.

PLATE 31

Medieval bridge at Wadebridge, Cornwall: built about 1468-70 and widened in 1847.
Wadebridge started as a ford over the Camel estuary, and was simply called *Wade*, from
the Old English word for a ford. This medieval bridge is still, in the words of Carew
(1602), "the longest, strongest, and fairest that the Shire can muster."

Greyston bridge (built about 1439) is perfectly preserved. A little downstream is
Horse Bridge, built in 1437, and below that again is New Bridge, a noble bridge
of white granite, built by Sir Piers Edgcumbe, a neighbouring landowner, about
1530. In north Devon, the famous Bideford bridge—twenty-four pointed arches
in stone—replaced a timber bridge some time after 1460, and is still one of the
most striking medieval bridges left in England.

Cornwall contains a number of interesting medieval bridges, though some of the best—such as Looe bridge (1411-36)—were destroyed in the nineteenth century. At Wadebridge in north Cornwall there had been for centuries a ford over the Camel, here widening towards the sea; but about 1468-70 a stone bridge was built (Plate 31), much like that at Bideford with which it is contemporary. Abingdon bridge, over the Thames, replaced an old ford in 1416, and considerably enhanced the importance of the town.

Not all the medieval bridges were on important roads or across noble rivers. One can find little medieval bridges tucked away in the upper reaches of English rivers, especially in the remoter counties like Cornwall. Such are Panters Bridge

PLATE 32

Bolton Castle, overlooking Wensleydale in Yorkshire. Richard le Scrope received a licence to crenellate it in 1379. Leland says it took eighteen years to build.

at Warleggan, which carried the old road from Bodmin to Liskeard, or Treverbyn bridge over the Fowey at St. Neot, both perfect fifteenth-century bridges. But in the more sophisticated and busier parts of England these ancient little bridges, so full of charm if not of beauty, have been replaced by brick, iron, or concrete and one passes by with averted eyes.

New churches, new chapels, new bridges, new quays: the fifteenth century saw the sparkle or the golden warmth of new-cut stone almost everywhere up and down the country, though less in the Midlands than elsewhere. And rich and powerful men were still building themselves castles. In Yorkshire, the lordly Scropes erected Bolton Castle (Plate 32), in the last quarter of the fourteenth century, with its four massive angle-towers looking southwards across Wensley-dale. Raby, in county Durham, is of the same period, the most perfect of the northern castles. The great castle of Berkeley, in Gloucestershire, was also re-modelled in the fourteenth century.

> Berk'ley's towers appear in martial pride,
> Menacing all round the champaign wide.

With the revival of anarchy and private warfare in the fifteenth century, great men built themselves new castles, or, more strictly, fortified houses, of which the keep at Ashby de la Zouch in Leicestershire, built by William lord Hastings about 1475-80, is one of the most remarkable. Not far away he built himself a fortified house of brick, within a moat, at Kirby Muxloe. Somewhat earlier, William, first baron Herbert, had built the castle at Raglan in Monmouthshire, now one of the noblest ruins in England.

Many castles were built of brick in the fifteenth century. Tattershall in Lincoln-shire (begun about 1434) and Hurstmonceaux in Sussex (about 1460) are perhaps the finest of these, and did much to spread the use of brick in English building. It was not indeed an entirely new material, for examples of thirteenth-century brickwork can be found in East Anglia, that of Little Wenham Hall in Suffolk (c. 1260-80) being the best known. The building of Eton College called for two and a half million bricks between 1442 and 1452. Most of the early bricks were imported from Flanders, but those for Kirby Muxloe Castle (1480-4) were made on the spot and pointed the way to the builders of country houses in the succeeding generations. Brick was only employed where suitable building stone was difficult to obtain, and its use was restricted to large houses for a good while to come. Not until the end of the seventeenth century did it become a common building material for the houses of ordinary people.

SELECT BIBLIOGRAPHY

ATKINSON, T. D., *Local Style in English Architecture* (1947).

BERESFORD, M. W., "The Deserted Villages of Warwickshire," *Trans. Birmingham Archæological Society*, vol. 66 (1950).

BERESFORD, M. W., "The Lost Villages of Yorkshire," *Yorkshire Archæological Journal*, Parts 148, 149, 150 (1951-3).

BERESFORD, M. W., *The Lost Villages of England* (1954).

HENDERSON, C., and COATES, H., *Old Cornish Bridges and Streams* (1928).

HENDERSON, C., and JERVOISE, E., *Old Devon Bridges* (1938).

HOSKINS, W. G., "The Deserted Villages of Leicestershire," in *Essays in Leicestershire History* (1950).

HOSKINS, W. G., *The Heritage of Leicestershire* (1946), for Ashby de la Zouch and Kirby Muxloe castles.

HOSKINS, W. G., *Devonshire Studies* (1952), essay on "The Wealth of Medieval Devon."

JERVOISE, E., *The Ancient Bridges of the South of England* (1930).

JERVOISE, E., *The Ancient Bridges of the North of England* (1931).

JERVOISE, E., *The Ancient Bridges of Mid and Eastern England* (1932).

MESSENT, C. J. W., *The Ruined Churches of Norfolk* (1931).

TOY, S., *The Castles of England* (1953).

V

Tudor to Georgian England

The Landscape in 1500

THE most striking single aspect of the English landscape at the beginning of the sixteenth century was that there were about three sheep to every human being. There were only two and a half to three million people in the whole country, and possibly eight million sheep. After a thousand years of settlement and hard labour, England was still a colonial economy with too few people to civilize the whole landscape (or even that part of it capable of improvement), too few to develop the rich mineral resources, which were as yet hardly scratched, too few to develop any large-scale industry. "The population of this island," wrote an Italian visitor about the year 1500, "does not appear to me to bear any proportion to her fertility and riches." England was a green and quiet agricultural country in which miles of deep forest alternated with thousand-acre "fields" of barley, beans, or wheat, or with variegated heaths and bleak moors, and little pasture closes.

At the end of the seventeenth century, Gregory King estimated that about a half of England and Wales was under cultivation as arable, pasture, or meadow. He thought there were three million acres of woods and coppices, and another three million acres of "Forests, parks, and commons." The woods and coppices were worth on an average nearly as much as the arable (5s. an acre as against 5s. 6d.), and the forests, park and commons he valued at an average rent of 3s. 8d. an acre. Then there were, he reckoned, no fewer than ten million acres of "heaths, moors, mountains, and barren land," worth on an average one shilling an acre for sheep feed. Pasture and meadow were the most valuable, being worth generally 8s. 8d. an acre. These are all averages: there were wide variations between the good and bad lands of each type. But the figures serve to show in a rough and ready way the relationship between the different uses to which land was put in the 1680s, and the approximate extent of each category. It is possible that King over-estimated the amount of waste land; but we have no better figures than his either for the seventeenth century or the sixteenth.

At the beginning of the sixteenth century the extent of the woodlands was considerably greater than in Gregory King's day, for there had been immense destruction of timber in the intervening period. Timber alone served the purposes of coal, steel, and concrete today—as a fuel, as material for ship-building, and house-building and for many other constructional purposes, and for an infinite variety of repair work. When we read that one Durham man alone was said in 1629 to have felled more than thirty thousand oaks in his lifetime, and reflect that similar destruction was going on in all the iron-working districts of England—in the Weald, the Forest of Dean, round Birmingham and Sheffield, and in the Clee Hills—we can envisage something of the extent of woodland lost between 1500 and 1688.

Nor were the iron-workers the only destroyers of the woods. The revolutionary improvements in farming in the sixteenth and seventeenth centuries led to large tracts of woodland being grubbed up for corn and cattle. In 1553 William Cholmeley spoke of "the unsatiable desyre of pasture for sheep and cattel" which had resulted in much permanent destruction of woodland during the preceding thirty years. Blith, in *The English Improver*, a hundred years later, spoke of woodlands all over the West Midlands, and also in Derbyshire and Yorkshire, "which now enclosed are grown as gallant cornfields as be in England." The historian of Nottinghamshire (1641) had seen "numberless numbers of goodly oaks" replaced during his lifetime by sheep and oxen "grazing upon a Carpet Green."[1]

If Gregory King's estimate for 1688 is about right, there must have been at least four million acres of woodland in England at the beginning of the sixteenth century, and all hardwoods at that. The forests of Epping and Arden, Sherwood, Dean and Wychwood, and a score of others famous in their own countryside, were a living reality. Smaller woods abounded all over England, though they were fewer in the Midlands than elsewhere. Few boys lived beyond easy walking distance of thick woodland, or of wild and spacious heaths, where they could work off freely the animal energies that in the twentieth century lead too many of them in the foul and joyless towns into the juvenile courts. There was plenty of scope for poachers of fish and game, and plenty of fresh air and space for everybody, and silence if they wanted it. No industrial smoke, nothing faster on the roads than a horse, no incessant noises from the sky: only three million people all told, spread thinly about the country. The largest provincial town (Norwich) could be described as "either a City in an Orchard, or an Orchard in a City, so equally are Houses and Trees blended in it"—how infinitely more pleasant a place England then was for the majority of her people!

People took their own wild places for granted. There are no contemporary descriptions of the woods, the heaths and the moors as scenery. The taste for "scenery" had yet to develop, and the few travellers who mention the wild places do so only in terms of distaste, for such country produced nothing useful and was inclined to be dangerous for strangers. Chaucer, however, makes a casual and pleasant reference, most unexpected in a medieval writer:

> His dwelling was full fair upon an heath
> With green trees shadowed was his place,

an allusion that Clare would have appreciated.

The most usual attitude to wild places was that of Defoe in the eighteenth

[1] Darby, "The Clearing of the English Woodlands," *Geography*, xxxvi (1951).

century. His description of the crossing of Blackstone Edge, the high moorland between Rochdale and Halifax, even in the middle of August, has almost the scale and feeling of a crossing of the Andes today. After running into a blinding snow-storm "near the top of the mountain," losing sight of all the tracks, and finding themselves on the edge of "a frightful precipice," they began to talk seriously of returning to Rochdale: "but just then one of our men called out to us, and said, he was upon the top of the hill, and could see over into Yorkshire . . ." There are, however, two more solid pages about mountains, precipices, wind and snow, and apprehensions of all kinds, before they struggle into Halifax.

As for the heaths, here is his description of Bagshot Heath in Surrey:

> Here is a vast tract of land, some of it within seventeen or eighteen miles of the capital city; which is not only poor, but even quite steril, given up to barrenness, horrid and frightful to look on, not only good for little, but good for nothing; much of it is a sandy desert, and one may frequently be put in mind here of Arabia Deserta, where the winds raise the sands, so as to overwhelm whole caravans of travellers, cattle and people together; for in passing this heath in a windy day, I was so far in danger of smothering with the clouds of sand, which were raised by the storm, that I cou'd neither keep it out of my mouth, nose or eyes: and when the wind was over, the sand appear'd spread over the adjacent fields of the forest some miles distant, so as that it ruins the very soil. This sand indeed is check'd by the heath, or heather, which grows in it, and which is the common product of barren land, even in the very Highlands of Scotland; but the ground is otherwise so poor and barren, that the product of it feeds no creatures, but some very small sheep, who feed chiefly on the said heather, and but very few of these, nor are there any villages, worth mentioning, and but few houses or people for many miles far and wide; this desert lyes extended so much, that some say, there is not less than a hundred thousand acres of this barren land that lyes all together, reaching out every way in the three counties of Surrey, Hampshire and Berkshire; besides a great quantity of land, almost as bad as that between Godalming and Petersfield, on the road to Portsmouth, including some hills, call'd the Hind Head and others.

The heaths and commons often extended for a dozen miles or more, with hardly a habitation upon them, and only rough and narrow tracks crossing them, so that travellers feared the sudden onset of bad weather or the premature falling of darkness. There were more than a hundred thousand acres of wastes in Hampshire even at the end of the eighteenth century (excluding the Downs), and sixty thousand in Berkshire. As for the moors, three-quarters of Westmorland was still uncultivated in 1793, and in Devon there were more than three hundred thousand acres wild and untamed.

On the other hand, some parts of England were highly cultivated and fruitful at the beginning of the sixteenth century. Leland observed how the aspect of the country changed for the better as soon as one crossed the Trent, coming away from the northern parts. All over the lowlands of Central England the ancient and hedgeless open fields stretched to the horizon, but in the regions towards the west, and towards the east and south-east, the typical landscape was one of small, hedged fields, as we know them today, of scattered farmsteads, and winding lanes and paths joining farm to farm. In the south-east of England, Kent and Essex were probably wholly enclosed; so, too, were the eastern halves of Suffolk and Surrey. In the south-west, the open fields of Cornwall, Devon, and Somerset were mere remnants of what they had once been. In Henry VIII's time, Leland observed that "most part of all Somersetshire is in hedgerows enclosed." What little open field remained was largely enclosed, as in Devon and Cornwall, during the sixteenth century. The counties along the Welsh Border, too, were nearly all enclosed by Leland's time, extending well up into Lancashire; and considerable areas of the North Riding and of Northumberland were similarly devoid of open field.

In all these peripheral regions, a great deal of land had been enclosed into small hedged fields direct from the original woodland. There never had been open fields in these districts. But in all these counties, too, there had been open fields in some parts, around the Old English villages, and these also had been transformed into smaller, hedged fields like those reclaimed direct from the waste in later times (Fig. 12). Why were counties like Kent, Essex, and Devon enclosed so early? One reason may be that the existence of so much farmland cultivated in separate small enclosures, with all the evident advantages this had over the communal management of the open arable fields, led the open-field farmers, persuaded by the evidence of their own eyes, to agree to the enclosure and re-arrangement of their strips at a very early date—some centuries before the open-field farmers of central England were so persuaded. Another reason undoubtedly was the abundance of pasture in these counties. A shortage of pasture made a wholesale enclosure more difficult, if not impossible, because common rights and the right to pasture animals on the open-field stubbles were jealously safeguarded and preserved. No change in the *status quo* was likely to be agreed by the multitude of peasant-farmers in these circumstances. Where pasture was abundant, as in the *denes* of the Weald of Kent and Sussex, or in the woodlands of Essex and East Suffolk, or near the Devon and Cornish moors, there was no such obstacle to change, and the great change to small fields held in severalty was duly accomplished.

We do not know precisely how this important change in the landscape was accomplished, nor even when; though if the Devonshire evidence is typical it seems to have begun in the thirteenth century, and to have continued into the fourteenth and fifteenth.[1] By Elizabethan times there was very little open field left anywhere in Devon.

Sometimes it appears that single strips or perhaps pairs of strips were enclosed,

[1] See Hoskins and Finberg, *Devonshire Studies*, esp. 277-8.

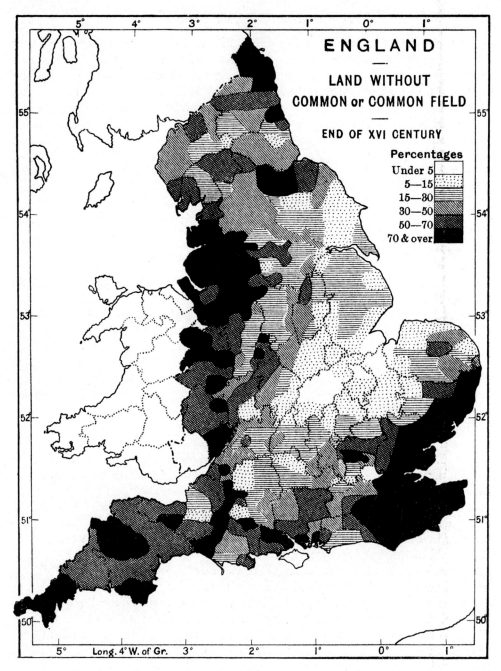

ENGLAND
—
LAND WITHOUT
COMMON or COMMON FIELD
—
END OF XVI CENTURY

Percentages
Under 5
5—15
15—80
30—50
50—70
70 & over

FIG. 12.—LAND WITHOUT OPEN FIELD OR COMMONS AT THE END OF THE SIXTEENTH CENTURY
Reproduced by permission from Gonner, *Common Land and Inclosure.*

by a hedgebank, so giving a pattern as it were of "fossilised open field" which is still preserved in some parishes. Sometimes, however, it is clear that a whole furlong or block of land was enclosed in a single piece of perhaps thirty or forty acres. Probably such comparatively large enclosures were separate parcels of the lord's demesne land, either always of that size and separateness or built up by purchases and exchange of other men's strips.

We can see the creation of this new kind of landscape clearly on the Tavistock Abbey estates in Devon:

It begins with a consolidation of holdings, brought about by purchase and exchange. Then a trench is dug to mark the limits of the holder's land, and the soil removed from it is thrown up into a mound on the inner side of the ditch. (A lease of Furze Close at Woodovis in 1465 specifies that the ditch shall be four feet wide and four feet deep; and the same dimensions are given at Leigh in 1398.) The mound is planted with a quickset hedge, and grows in course of time by the addition of soil thrown up whenever the ditch is cleared. No feature of the Devon landscape is more characteristic than these vast banks, crowned with oak, ash, hazel, or other coppice wood growing to a height of twenty feet or more and forming an impenetrable screen. Wasteful as they are of space and soil, they have the merit of permanence and they provide cattle with the shelter that is badly needed in so boisterous a climate. Marshall suggests that coppice fences may have been designed at first to make good the loss of fuel attendant upon forest clearance. He adds: "Many farms have no other woodland, nor supply of fuel, than what their fences furnish; yet are amply supplied with this; besides, perhaps, an overplus of poles, cord wood, faggots, and the bark of oak, for sale."[1]

Each of these enclosures was called locally a *park*, but the process of change did not end there. Areas of twenty to forty acres were generally found to be too large for good farming, especially in a pastoral region like Devon. They did not give the best control of grazing, and in upland and windy country they did not give adequate shelter for livestock. They were therefore reduced in size by making more hedgebanks. Two fields at Bowrish, near Tavistock, of twelve and twenty acres respectively, were each divided into three at some date after 1491, and remain as six fields to this day. Another enclosure of about thirty-two acres was divided into three after 1416; and it seems likely that subdivision may have been carried much farther than that until the original enclosures were reduced again to something hardly bigger than open-field parcels, difficult to distinguish on the map from the piecemeal enclosures taken in direct from the waste. The significant difference was probably that the direct enclosures from woodland and moorland were irregular in shape, while those that resulted from the later subdivision of enclosed "parks" usually had more or less straight hedges.

[1]Finberg, *Tavistock Abbey*, 50.

The creation of tiny fields could also result from the division of an estate among co-heirs. When Lord Dynham died in 1501, for example, the small manor of Wreyland near Lustleigh (Devon) was divided, like the rest of his lands, between his four sisters, and each farm on the manor was cut up into four parts. Later, one of these quarter-shares was halved, so producing two eighth parts. "Whenever a tenement was divided, each fraction had to be equipped with a fair share of every sort of land—garden, orchard, meadow, arable, pasture, wood and heath—so that it generally was formed of several patches of ground at some distance from each other."[1] The result was a fantastically small set of fields—many of them only an acre or so in size, some as little as half an acre. All these hidden factors, so to speak, have gone to the making of the landscape in different parts of England. The facts of topography, soils, and climate explain much, but beyond them lie purely historical facts like the laws of property and inheritance. The peculiar field-patterns and other features of the Kent and Norfolk landscapes can probably only be explained in the last resort by the social and legal history that lie behind them; and they still await their interpreter. Here, as in Devon, we have, for the greater part, landscapes of dispersed farmsteads and hamlets, enclosed fields, winding lanes, and large hedgebanks.

At the beginning of the sixteenth century, the towns were still relatively unimportant as features in the landscape. They were small, neat, and contained. Even where suburbs extended outside the medieval walls, they were not large; and within the walls there was a great deal of open well-tree'd ground, large gardens, and orchards. The city of Exeter, capital city of a large province, contained within its walls only ninety-three acres of ground, and of this fully one-quarter, possibly as much as a third, was not built upon. Considerable suburbs lay outside the East Gate and the West Gate: possibly a fifth of the total population lived outside the walls. But one could have walked around the entire circuit of the city walls in half an hour, or could have reached the open country from the centre of the city in any direction in fifteen minutes. And this was equally true of such cities as Norwich, Bristol, York, Salisbury, and Coventry, the largest in the provinces. Even London, with its sixty or seventy thousand people, was soon left behind if one had a mind to see green fields and natural heaths.

The Enclosure of the Midland Fields

The open-field system took its classic form, and had its deepest roots, in the Midlands. Here the great majority of villages lived and worked within the frame of a two-field or a three-field system, though in a few places a somewhat greater number of fields were making their appearance by subdivision. But even in the Midlands the ancient landscape was not everywhere left untouched. We have already observed the creation of large arable or pastoral granges by the Cistercian houses in the twelfth and thirteenth centuries; and the decay and abandonment

[1]Torr, *Wreyland Documents*, xxv, 155.

of villages, in the two subsequent centuries, to be replaced by large enclosed pastures for cattle and sheep (Plate 33). The earlier stages of this second movement were mainly the result of a passive decay of village life and arable husbandry, following a prolonged decline of population; but in the later stages it was actively assisted by the more progressive landlords who could not wait for Nature to complete her leisurely work.

At Wormleighton, in the deep country where Warwickshire and Northamptonshire meet, William Cope, Cofferer of the Household to Henry VII, evicted the occupiers of twelve farms and three cottages in the October of 1498. He enclosed 240 acres of arable with hedges and ditches, and converted the new fields to sheep and cattle pastures, displacing sixty persons all told. Sir Edward Raleigh, another

PLATE 33

The site of the deserted village of Ingarsby, Leicestershire. Ingarsby, founded by the Danes in the ninth or tenth century, came into the sole possession of Leicester Abbey by the fifteenth, and was enclosed and converted to sheep and cattle pastures in the year 1469. Here we have a completely medieval scene: cattle grazing over the grass-covered foundations of the deserted village.

landowner in the same parish, destroyed six other farms in the same way. Eight years later, Squire Cope sold the manor to John Spencer, a neighbouring squire, who soon afterwards began the building of "a fair Manor House." The house was completed and there he was keeping up a good estate "with sixty Persons of his Family," when in 1517 he was arraigned before Wolsey's commission of enquiry into depopulating enclosures. Despite the fact that Cope had enclosed the manor several years before Spencer bought it, the latter was ordered to pull down the new hedges and to restore the lands to tillage.

His petition against this order is an interesting document for the light it throws upon the changes in the local landscape consequent upon enclosure. He described what he had done for his adopted parish since he came:

First in building and maintaining of the church and bought all ornaments, as cross, books, cope, vestments, chalice, and censers, for all the church gear that was within the church at the time when husbandmen were there inhabited was not worth £6, for they had never service by note. For they were so poor and lived so poorly that they had no books to sing services on in the church. And where they never had but one priest, I have had and intend to have two or three. And also he hath builded and inhabited four houses. And men, women, and children dwelling in them. And so, what with his own house, and the other four houses, there is within twenty persons as much people as was in the town before.

And where there is no wood nor timber growing within twelve or fourteen miles of the same lordship, the said John Spencer hath there set trees and sown acorns for timber and wood, and double ditched and set with all manner of wood both in the hedgerows, and also betwixt the hedges adjoining to the old hedges that William Cope made before in the said lordship, whereupon now groweth much wood which is already grown to the profit of all them that should dwell in the said lordship, as also in the country adjoining thereunto. For in those parts there is no wood, so that the poor men of the country are fain to burn the straw that their cattle should live by. Therefore it were a great loss to destroy these hedges, for it is a greater commodity than either corn or grass in these parts. . . .

He hath no other pasture left him now in his country (i.e., his own part of Warwickshire) but the same. Which if (it) now should be put in tillage . . . it should be to his utter undoing, for his living is and hath been by the breed of cattle in his pastures, for he is neither buyer nor seller in common markets as other graziers be, but liveth by his own breed of the same pastures, and sold it when it was fat to the City of London, and other places yearly, as good cheap in all this five or six years past as he did in other years. . . . He hath bred and fed within the said lordship, which was never good for corn, as the country will testify, more cattle this six years than was bred in the lordship when the town (i.e., village or township) was inhabited in twenty years before, or shall be in twenty years after it shall be inhabited.

The petition was apparently of no avail, for three years later (1522) he was peremptorily ordered to restore all his lands at Wormleighton to tillage by Candlemas next (February 2), to destroy his hedges and ditches by the same date, and apparently to rebuild all the houses that had been destroyed by William Cope. An agitated second petition went up from Wormleighton to London, begging for more time, at least, in which to restore the status quo, with what result we do not know. Whatever happened the Spencers were not ruined by this ill-fortune; they acquired more land in the pastoral uplands of Northamptonshire and installed themselves at Althorp, whence they founded two noble families—the Earls Spencer of Althorp and the Spencer-Churchills, Dukes of Marlborough.

John Spencer's defence—apart from the fact that he himself had not committed the crime of depopulation—was a very reasonable one. The destruction of timber had gone on so recklessly for centuries in the Midlands, and there was so little room for replacing it in the open-field landscape, that he was performing a valuable service to the entire neighbourhood in planting so vigorously in the new hedgerows. And further, the replacement of tillage by grass was, in these heavy Liassic claylands, a step forward in the long process of finding out what each type and quality of land was best suited for, of looking beyond the ancient pattern of mixed open-field husbandry to more profitable and varied ways of using land. By the end of the sixteenth century there was, if not a continuous belt of grassland on the Liassic uplands of Northamptonshire and Leicestershire, at least something very near it, and tens of thousands of cattle and sheep grazed over what had been the arable lands of the medieval peasantry. And instead of a hundred peasants, the typical figure was that of John Isham. "The astute merchant turned squire, perambulating his newly-made enclosures at Lamport in 1586, lovingly counted his sheep and jotted down the totals in his account book. Piously he added, 'God bless them all'."

Where such landlords, lay or monastic, owned the whole or greater part of the manorial soil, the eviction of the open-field farmers was easy enough. At the end of the farming year, immediately after the corn-harvest, they were ordered to go; their farmsteads were demolished; and the multitudinous strips of the open fields were laid down to grass. The two or three arable fields were replaced by a number of large pastures, enclosed by a hawthorn hedge and a ditch.

It seems likely that the enclosed pastures so created were of great size. Indeed for all we know no new hedge may have been made at first; each of the original open fields may have been converted to pasture just as it lay. Thus the one thousand acres of pasture in the south Leicestershire manor of Pulteney were contained in 1547 in two great closes—Middle Field and High Field. The Middle Field in the depopulated parish of Knaptoft, not many miles away, contained no less than six hundred acres of pasture in 1525. At Whatborough, in east Leicestershire, the original enclosure made by Launde priory in 1494 covered rather more than four hundred acres, but when the lordship was surveyed and mapped in 1586 this ranch-like pasture had been broken up by hedgerows into a number of smaller fields, though they were still large by modern standards. At Galby, in Leicestershire, a lease of 1640 shows two yeoman-graziers renting a pasture covering one hundred and twenty acres. One could find similar examples of vast pasture closes in all the Midland counties where the Tudor encloser had been at work. Defoe, in the reign of Anne, saw a single enclosed field of pasture in the Vale of Aylesbury that was let to a grazier for a rent of £1,400 a year. He does not state the acreage, but it must have been enormous.

These great pastures, undulating away almost to the horizon, were possibly the first exuberant experiment in large-scale sheep and cattle farming by men with little practical experience of a new kind of farming, and it was not long before the disadvantages of these enormous fields were revealed—lack of shelter in the Midland winters, especially on the uplands, and the impossibility of achieving close grazing over such a large unfenced area. As time went on, new hedges were made inside the original fences, and smaller fields created; but even then some of them were still large and betray themselves today by their size. In Knaptoft, for example, the Great Close still covers nearly eighty-eight acres. Many of these large fields were reduced during the late eighteenth century when graziers like Bakewell found by experience that enclosures as small as ten to twelve acres were the right size for the most economical grazing of pastures, but some hundred-acre fields remain to this day in the green uplands of central England.

Probably the largest enclosures were to be found where the landlord owned the entire parish and could do as he liked. But in many parishes there were other freeholders besides the squire, and however small they were their agreement was necessary before this kind of enclosure could be carried through. Their lands lay intermixed with the squire's in the open fields, and he could not move far without coming up against them; and they also possessed rights of common pasture over the entire open fields after harvest which he could not arbitrarily take away or in any way diminish. In such parishes, therefore, the squire was obliged to obtain their consent to enclosure and to offer them a tempting bargain. So we have, from Elizabethan times onwards, hundreds of examples of parishes being enclosed by agreement, and where the lesser freeholders had not been bought out before the change they received two or three enclosed fields as their share in lieu of the hundreds of strips they may have thrown into the pool for redistribution. Hence many fields of Tudor or Stuart origin are not of great size, for they represent the allotment to small freeholders. There is no mark that one knows of whereby hedges of this period can be distinguished on the ground. They are probably less massive than hedgebanks of medieval origin and possibly carry less great timber, and they are certainly more substantial than the rather flimsy hawthorn hedge-rows that were planted as a result of the parliamentary enclosure movement of the eighteenth century. But our best evidence for their date lies in this instance in the written documents.

The enclosing activities of the Tudor squires generally diminished during the middle decades of the sixteenth century, but the spread of enclosure by agreement among all the freeholders led to a renewed wave of change from the last quarter of the century, continuing down to the outbreak of the Civil War. After 1660 the government ceased to oppose enclosure by private landlords, as it had done ever since the early years of Henry VIII's reign. Its efforts had, it is true, been largely ineffectual, but down to 1640 they had acted as a brake on wholesale agrarian change. The new government of landlords at the Restoration was of a different mind, and all over open-field England parishes were transformed from a medieval to a modern landscape. In Durham, for instance, "the common fields of townships were for the most part enclosed soon after the Restoration," according to Joseph Granger, who reported on the county to the Board of Agriculture in 1794. North-west Wiltshire—the great dairying country—was being enclosed about the same time, and in Leicestershire the movement was particularly active in the 1660s and succeeding decades. We hear more in contemporary sources about the iniquities of the Tudor enclosers, but it is likely that there are more miles of seventeenth-century hedges in the Midlands than sixteenth. It may be surprising to some who look upon the Midland landscape as the undoubted product of the parliamentary enclosure movement to know that even in Northamptonshire one-half of the county had been enclosed and transformed to a modern landscape before the first private enclosure act; and in the adjacent county of Leicestershire three in every five fields had been created before the parliamentary period. English hedges are of all dates—Celtic, Saxon and Danish, medieval, Tudor, Stuart, Georgian, even Victorian in places. It is a complex pattern with a complicated history, and generalizations do not do it justice. All the pleasure and the truth lie in the details, as Stendhal remarked in another connection.[1]

The Flowering of Rural England

The total effect of the depopulating enclosures of the fifteenth and sixteenth centuries, devastating though they were in certain small districts, where three or four adjoining villages and hamlets might be wiped off the face of the landscape, must not be exaggerated. Thus in the small county of Leicestershire some sixty villages and hamlets disappeared, mainly between about 1450 and 1600 (earlier rather than later). This represents about one settlement in every six of the medieval total. A number of other villages and hamlets shrank considerably in size, like Cold Newton and Illston-on-the-Hill, and one finds them today as a little huddle of houses at the head of a "main street" which passes through a field-gate and becomes a grassy track between the mounds of the lost farmsteads and cottages. What happened in Leicestershire is typical of nearly all the counties in the Lowland Zone of England. Many places vanished; others shrivelled in the economic blizzard; but most survived into the warm and expansive age of Eliza-beth I and flowered forth as never before. All over England, except in the four most northerly counties, we find abundant visual evidence of a great age of re-building in the two generations between about 1570 and 1640. The wave of country house building, from Henry VIII's time onwards, is well enough known (and is touched upon later in this chapter); but what is less well known, though it is very evident when one's attention is drawn to it, is the remarkable surge of rebuilding and new building among all social classes except the poorest, in town and country alike.

[1]Quoted by Finberg, *The Local Historian and his Theme*, 5.

In some parts of England the squires and franklins had been rebuilding their houses throughout the fifteenth century. Devon still contains some scores of houses of this type and period, now often disguised by the improvements of a later age; and one can find examples of fifteenth-century manor-houses and farmsteads in other counties. But in 1550 most English people were still living in the rather dark, squalid, and cramped dwellings of their medieval forefathers. These were generally two-roomed houses—a hall and bower—built of a timber frame with walls of

PLATE 34

Colly Weston: Northamptonshire. Like a great number of English villages, Colly Weston was largely rebuilt in the late sixteenth century and the early seventeenth. Above is shown a typical yeoman's house of about 1620, built of the local oolitic limestone and roofed with the famous Colly Weston stone slates.

reinforced mud, the whole raised upon a rubble foundation. There were no glazed windows, and only one fireplace. The two rooms were not ceiled over, but were open to the rafters and the thatch of the roof. Few houses were built of stone, even in stone country.

By the 1560s and 1570s, the wealthier yeomen had begun to build themselves larger and better houses. Sometimes they added to and reconstructed the ancestral dwelling; often they made a clean sweep of the older house and rebuilt in free-stone where it was available. Before the end of the century the fashion for rebuilding had spread down to the lesser farmers—the husbandmen—and in some instances perhaps to the more prosperous cottagers. Cottages were generally built, however, by landlords and probably cheaply built: at any rate not a single sixteenth-century cottage appears to survive in England. What the estate-agent calls "An olde worlde cottage"—even if it is genuinely a sixteenth-century house —was originally a husbandman's farmhouse. There seem to be no true cottages left in England of an earlier date than the latter part of the seventeenth century; most are probably eighteenth-century in date.

The wave of rebuilding or enlargement of farmhouses, large and small, in the countryside grew in force down to the 1620s. It was so general that whole villages on and near the great Stone Belt, that crosses England diagonally from the Dorset to the Yorkshire coasts, seem to have been rebuilt about the same time. Colly Weston in Northamptonshire is a good instance of this (Plate 34), but there are innumerable villages of which one could say the same.

Nor was the rebuilding confined to the villages: the yeoman-farmer in his isolated dwelling was similarly moved to acquire a better house. In the upland parishes of Lancashire and in the dales of Yorkshire we find sturdy, stone-built farmsteads with their mullioned windows, and frequently a date-stone over the lintel of the front door, standing four-square to the moorland blasts.

These northern farmsteads are often sheltered by sycamore trees, which were introduced into England towards the end of the sixteenth century. Gerard, in his *Herball* (1597), says that the sycamore is "a stranger to England." The common maple, which it closely resembles, is indigenous to Great Britain, and was well known to the Anglo-Saxons. A number of place-names from Yorkshire down to Dorset (for example, Mappleton and Mappowder) are derived from the presence of this tree. The sycamore, or great maple, is a bigger tree altogether, of quick growth, and with large leaves that afford a grateful shade. It withstands sea and mountain winds better than most timber trees, and was therefore widely planted in the upland and exposed parts of England as a windbreak for farmhouses. Its abundant shade in summer was a blessing to cattle in otherwise rather treeless landscapes. And so we get a very characteristic northern scene: the low-browed farmstead of moorland stone and stone-slated roof, with a clump of burnished sycamores on the windward side:

> *A stately sycamore,*
> *That spreads, in gentle pomp, its honied shade.*

One finds the same composition in the windy uplands of West Devon. Many people profess not to like the sycamore—it seeds itself too prolifically in the garden—but some of the poets have had an affection for it, as witness both Wordsworth and Matthew Arnold.

The villages of the Midlands, whether on the Stone Belt or the claylands, show thousands of houses built in these two generations. Here the elm and the ash are the characteristic trees, planted to give shade and to add beauty to the stone or brick walls. The "black-and-white" timbered houses of the West Midland counties are almost all of this period between 1570 and 1640. Eastwards, in Leicestershire and Northamptonshire, much has been destroyed or swamped in the Victorian red brick of the industrial villages, but there is still plenty to see away from the hosiery and boot-and-shoe districts.

There is no need to elaborate the examples of this Great Rebuilding, which one finds all the way from Kent to Cornwall in the south, and over a good deal of the eastern counties. In these two generations or so, the rich variety of regional styles of building—the vernacular of the English countryside—established itself everywhere, based upon the abundant local materials that a peasant economy, a peasant culture indeed, knew how to use well and beautifully. If we are to study and record the variety of minor English building before it is too late, in both country and town, it is in these generations that we shall find our richest evidence, and to a lesser degree in the second rebuilding that flourished in the late seventeenth century and the early eighteenth.

This flowering of English peasant building in the countryside, and of minor buildings in the towns, was the product of two causes—money, and a desire for privacy and comfort. England was filling up with people, recovering vigorously from the long decline of late medieval times; the towns were growing quickly, London above all, and constituted a large food-market; industries were growing and needed in ever-increasing quantities such country products as leather and wool. Farmers had an assured market at prices that were rising rapidly from the 1540s onwards. Those who enjoyed security of tenure and relatively fixed rents and fines, whose labour was often supplied by the family, enjoyed more or less fixed costs and ever-rising selling prices. It was an age of profit-inflation for farmers as well as merchants and industrialists. There was far more money about—several contemporary writers like Harrison and Carew commented on this—and, as they do today in similar circumstances, farmers set about improving their houses.

The desire for some personal privacy, too, had percolated down from the lordly ones to the merchant and the yeoman and husbandman. This entailed more rooms devoted to particular purposes, and it led among other things to the introduction of a second floor in ordinary houses, reached by a staircase. Many a medieval house with its large, draughty hall, and other rooms open to the roof, was "modernized" in the closing decades of the sixteenth century and the early years of the seventeenth. The old rooms were ceiled over about halfway up, so creating another floor above. More fireplaces were put in (Harrison speaks in 1577 of "the multitude of chimneys lately erected"), and partitions inserted on each floor, producing possibly half a dozen or more smaller and warmer rooms in place of the two or three barn-like rooms that had served until then. More windows were inserted, and most of them were glazed for the first time. The glass industry had found a means of producing cheap glass, which was now made available to the middle class in town and country, and this meant that houses could be built with far more windows than before. Many old houses were modernized along these lines. In Devon it is common to find, upon internal inspection, a fifteenth-century house modernized and effectively disguised in this way about 1600. But far more houses were completely rebuilt, and these are a conspicuous

PLATE 35

Country Life

The manor house at Warmington, Warwickshire: the house of a successful Elizabethan yeoman who bought the manor in 1572 and built this handsome house shortly afterwards. This house is built of the warm brown ironstone found in the adjacent hills, and roofed with the stone slates from the oolitic limestone akin to those of Colly Weston (Plate 34).

feature of the oolitic limestone belt—the so-called "Cotswold Stone," though it extends right down to Dorset and up into north Yorkshire. The two generations between about 1570 and 1640 gave to the English landscape some of its most-photographed buildings. Many yeomen signalized their ascent in the social scale by building themselves new and beautiful houses, such as Richard Cooper, the successful yeoman who bought the manor of Warmington, on the borders of Warwickshire and Oxfordshire, in the year 1572, and rebuilt the manor house in

the brown ironstone from Edge Hill (Plate 35). We find his son Henry described
as "gentleman": it was a common story in these prosperous generations.

The four northern counties underwent their great rebuilding during the
eighteenth century. Possibly money was harder to come by in the wilder parts,
or not so lightly spent. One notices in the Lake District how many of the old
farmsteads were rebuilt from the 1690s onwards, about a hundred years later than
in southern England. At the same time, a good deal of the rest of England under-

PLATE 36

Henley-in-Arden, Warwickshire: not only were the English villages largely rebuilt between
1570 and 1640, but so were many of the towns. The characteristic "black-and-white"
timbered houses of the West Midlands are mostly of that prosperous and expansive
period.

went a second rebuilding or wave of new building. In the Midlands, for example,
and perhaps in East Anglia too, the graziers were prosperous in the days of
William and Mary and Anne, and built themselves many seemly houses in hand-
made brick. Much of the very attractive village of Rockingham, in Northamptonshire, appears to have been rebuilt between 1660 and 1720.

It was in this latter period of prosperity in the English countryside, when the
philanthropic impulse perhaps reached its height also, that we get so many
attractive schools and almshouses in villages and country towns. One thinks of

Peter Blundell's noble benefaction at Tiverton as an example of educational philanthropy in the earlier period: the original school of 1604 still stands on the edge of the town. At Market Harborough stands the original little grammar-school (Plate 37) founded by Robert Smyth in 1614: the same Robert Smyth who made a fortune in Elizabethan London and left money in his will to the poor of

PLATE 37

The Old Grammar School at Market Harborough, Leicestershire, founded in 1614 and endowed with £22 8s. a year. Because of the inadequacy of the endowment it was converted in the early nineteenth century into a National School. It is now disused but carefully preserved as an example of a local grammar school of the Elizabethan and Jacobean period, standing (characteristically) in the market-place and beside the church. No disintegration here: school, church and work all grouped on the same spot.

all the parishes round about his native town in whose fields he had gleaned as a boy. In the later period, one thinks of the grammar school in the remote Northamptonshire village of Clipston, built in 1667 and externally still unchanged, or of the grammar school at Guilsborough, an impressive building of ironstone with a Colly Weston slated roof (1688). At Blewbury, in Berkshire, a handsome brick-built school stands on the edge of the churchyard. It was built and founded as a charity school in 1709 by a merchant named William Malthus, and children have been taught there for nearly two hundred and fifty years.

The English village, in so far as it still remains untouched by the acid fingers of the twentieth century, with its farmsteads, cottages, school, almshouse, and perhaps a decent early chapel, is essentially the product of these two centuries between about 1570 and 1770. Before that time life had been hard and comfortless, with little or no margin to spare beyond the necessities of living: what little there was went to the adornment and beautification of the parish church. After that time we witness the break-up of the village community, the degradation of most of the rural population, and the flight into the towns. But for those two hundred years—seven human generations—rural England flowered. The exhausting labour of colonization was over, except in small patches here and there. There were now enough people for an agricultural country at least, and there was time to rest and play. The narrow margin between a hard life and death from starvation, which had haunted so many generations from the dim Saxon times onwards, had widened with the bringing into cultivation of millions more acres of land. There was no longer the need to go out at the end of a hard day's farming to hack down more trees and clear more ground: it was all done, all that was worth doing: now there was time to contemplate, and to think beyond the mere utilities of life. The Stuart or the Georgian yeoman reached for a book in the evenings, rather than for the axe or mattock of his forebears.

Country Houses and Parks

The country house, built for the pleasure of living, originates in the early sixteenth century. Before that time magnates had lived in castles, or fortified houses, or within a moat. Defence against enemies occupied much of a rich man's thought. Now, with a strong central government and judiciary, such men could relax from continual self-protection and build defenceless houses. Thornbury (Gloucestershire) was the last house to call itself a castle, built (but never finished) between 1511 and 1521; but "the building was purely domestic and the castellated details were unaffectedly ornamental."

Many country houses were built during Henry VIII's reign. Compton Wynyates (Plate 38), in a fold below the marlstone escarpment, was built on the site of the deserted village of Compton Superior. In 1510 Sir William Compton had licence to enclose two thousand acres of land, and two years later he began to make a park here. The house, one of the most attractive Tudor houses in England, was actually built of bricks brought from another deserted village—Fullbrook—where the duke of Bedford, brother of Henry V, had created a park and destroyed the village and the church a hundred years earlier. It was the brick from his castle that was used at Compton Wynyates.

East Barsham in Norfolk was built between about 1500 and 1515, and Hengrave Hall in Suffolk about 1538. In Somerset, the medieval manor house of Lytes

Cary was enlarged about 1530-3. It is impossible to catalogue all the substantial country houses built in these years: one finds them in every county of England, often disguised today by eighteenth-century enlargements and reconstructions.

PLATE 38

Compton Wynyates, Warwickshire, below the marlstone or ironstone escarpment of Edge Hill with the opulent Warwickshire plain stretching far away to the horizon. Compton Wynyates, finished by about 1520, was one of the earliest true country houses in England, and is now one of the most appealingly beautiful.

Most of the country houses built before 1550 followed the traditional medieval plan, with its emphasis on the great hall, and were haphazard in disposition; but Hengrave Hall foreshadows the new Renaissance style. It is "a stepping-stone from the medieval to the Elizabethan type." It was in the second half of the century, and particularly in the last generation, that the country house made its fullest impact on the landscape. This was pre-eminently the age of great houses, some of them indeed were palaces, and the largest of them were built by the high officers of state under Elizabeth. Both Lord Burghley, the Lord High Treasurer, and Sir Christopher Hatton, the Lord Chancellor, said that they were building on this extravagant scale in order to accommodate the Queen and her vast retinue; but there was a good deal of plain rivalry in these monstrous and really rather vulgar houses built by the new rich, often out of monastic spoils.

PLATE 39

Burghley House and Park, Northamptonshire. Burghley is an entirely Elizabethan house, built by one of the great officers of State—William Cecil, Lord High Treasurer. He began the reconstruction of a small house in 1556 and completed this palace—for such it is—in 1587. Most of the work falls into the period 1577-87. The park was landscaped, and the lake made, by Capability Brown in the late eighteenth century.

In the west, Longleat was completed by the Thynnes after a generation of building (1550-80) and Montacute (1580-1601) by Sir Edward Phelips, Queen's Serjeant and afterwards Master of the Rolls. In Northamptonshire, Cecil completed his palace of Burghley (Plate 39) in ten years of concentrated building (1577-87), and Hatton built on a still more tremendous scale at Holdenby. Holdenby, as a house, was even larger than the eighteenth-century palaces of

Blenheim and Castle Howard: its fronts were 360 ft. and 224 ft. long, as against 320 ft. and 220 ft. at Blenheim, for example. Hardly anything remains of this vast house today—only two gateways in a field and part of one side of one of its quadrangles. Not far away, Hatton was also building at Kirby Hall, a house begun in 1570 and not completed until 1632, and now the most appealing ruin perhaps in all England. And in the same county Sir Thomas Tresham was building at Rushton and Lyveden. In Derbyshire, Elizabeth, countess of Shrewsbury ("Bess of Hardwick"), began the building of Hardwick in 1576 and was still supervising the work when she died in 1607: and so it remains, a splendid example of the prosperity and vigour of the Elizabethan Age. Other great houses went up in the early years of the seventeenth century—Knole in Kent, Burton Agnes in Yorkshire, Audley End in Essex. Of the last house, completed in 1616, James I remarked, upon seeing it, that "it was too much for a King, though it might do very well for a Lord Treasurer." A good deal of this vast house was pulled down in the eighteenth century in order to make it more habitable.

A great number of smaller country houses were built between the sixteenth century and the nineteenth, and since this is not a study of architectural history but of the impact of the country house upon the landscape one need say little more about them. Palaces were built in the eighteenth century, such as Castle Howard and Blenheim, but the most characteristic scene in the countryside is the smaller Georgian mansion set in a park of modest proportions—a warmth of red brick, a flash of stucco, among luxuriant trees (Plate 40). In the eighteenth century "the sites of new country houses were chosen for aesthetic, not merely for practical reasons. They were often placed on rising ground to "command the prospect" (Plate 41). This was rendered possible by the increasing control of the wealthy over artificial supplies of water," but Cowper complained that people were induced to build on exposed hill-tops and were swept by all the winds of heaven until trees had grown up to shelter them.[1]

The building of country houses continued steadily down to the last quarter of the nineteenth century. Monstrous Gothic Revival piles arose, many of them the houses of successful industrialists and merchants. Many landowners, too, rebuilt their ancestral houses on the last wave of Victorian prosperity in farming. The very last country house to be built in England—the last that will doubtless ever be built—was Castle Drogo, built by Lutyens in Devon between 1911 and 1930 for a wealthy grocer. It is a dramatic composition in granite rising sheer from the moorland, and it makes a fitting end to the four hundred years of country-house building in England.

More important than the houses themselves, so far as the landscape was concerned, were the parks with which their owners surrounded them. The word *park* originally meant no more than a tract of ground, usually woodland, enclosed for the protection of beasts of the chase. Many of the well-known parks around

[1]Trevelyan, *English Social History*, 403.

country houses today originated in this way. Overstone Park in Northamptonshire was originally enclosed in 1255, and we hear of Exton Park (then a wood) as far back as 1185. Ashridge, Hatfield, and Knowsley parks are all first heard of in the thirteenth century. Woodstock Park (now Blenheim) is even more ancient: it was fenced around and separated from the surrounding forest of Wychwood, as a game preserve for the Anglo-Saxon kings, before the year 1000. Plot says it was created by King Alfred. The dense woodland within the enclosing fence or wall gave way to a more open scene, as grazing animals thinned out the trees and

PLATE 40

Courteenhall House and Park, Northamptonshire: a much more typically English scene than the great palaces like Burghley and Blenheim: a plain, dignified Georgian house of moderate size set in a small but well-timbered park. The house was built between 1791 and 1793 (architect, Samuel Saxon).

prevented their natural regeneration by consuming the seedlings. Many early parks were kept for deer; but in general, castles and other large houses were surrounded by a rather formless and uncouth landscape.

Parks have come and gone, commemorated only by a small name on a map. Flitteris Park, on the borders of Rutland and Leicestershire, was enclosed from the forest of Leighfield by Richard, earl of Cornwall, in the year 1250. It is marked on Saxton's map (1577) but has long since been disparked and the name survives only in a lonely farm. Not many Northamptonshire parks are older than the time of Elizabeth I. Burghley, the largest park in the county, was created as a deer park by the Lord Treasurer after he succeeded to the estate, on his father's death, in 1552. By 1562 it was apparently completed, as we read in the state papers of that year of "the deer brought to Burghley Park."

Not a few parks in England today run to a thousand or fifteen hundred acres: Woburn in Bedfordshire is twelve miles around and contains 2,400 acres. Knowsley, the largest park in the north of England, covers 2,500 acres. In the

PLATE 41

Burley-on-the-Hill, Rutland: a mansion built for the "prospect" by Daniel Finch, Earl of Winchelsea and Nottingham, between 1694 and 1702. It commands a wide view of the Vale of Catmose.

middle of Nottinghamshire lie, or lay, a famous group of great parks—Welbeck (nearly 2,300 acres), Clumber, Thoresby, and Rufford.

Such great parks are usually the result of a series of expansions from comparatively small beginnings. Apethorpe Park in Northamptonshire was enlarged in the time of James I after the king had been the guest there of Francis, Earl of Westmorland and had found the deer-park neither large enough nor sufficiently stored with covert. James directed the earl to take in and impale another 314 acres. At Althorp and Deene, in the same county, the Spencers and Brudenells were constantly adding to their deer parks by purchases and exchanges of land in the late sixteenth and early seventeenth centuries. Many expanding parks began

FIG. 13.—THE DISTRIBUTION OF PARKS IN PART OF NORTH OXFORDSHIRE

The boundaries of parks have been taken from the first edition of the Ordnance Survey map (1833). The principal changes since that date have been the creation of Barton Abbey park (which has been inserted on the map), the enlargement of Ditchley park (indicated by a broken line), and the disparking of more than a half of Heythrop (all to the north-west of the line on the map). Most of this district lies upon the oolitic limestone and has always been favoured for large houses and estates. To illustrate this point, the known sites of Roman villas—most of which were equivalent to our country houses—have been added to the map and are marked thus:+. Uncertain villa sites are marked with a query. For an even fuller picture of the Romano-British concentration in this district see Fig. 2. The parks shown here cover a wide range of date. Blenheim originated in the tenth century (perhaps a little earlier), Ditchley in 1605, Barton Abbey about 1870.

swallowing up good cornland in this period; there are frequent complaints about this development.

Parks grew yet more extensive during the eighteenth century, in the age of the territorial aristocracy. Building themselves magnificent houses, they needed (or thought they needed) more square miles of conspicuous waste to set them off. Not only village cornlands vanished inside the park walls: whole villages were destroyed and rebuilt elsewhere when they were found to stand in the way of a "prospect" or some grand scheme of landscape design. Sir Gilbert Heathcote, who created the park at Normanton in Rutland about 1764, demolished the medieval church and village to do so. The village was rebuilt elsewhere, the church rebuilt in the park.

PLATE 42

Wimpole in Cambridgeshire as it was about 1709. Kip's drawing shows the house built by Sir Thomas Chicheley about 1632, the formal gardens of that period, and the avenue which is nearly 2¾ miles in length.

At Burton Constable in Yorkshire the enlargement of the park involved the permanent destruction of the village. At Wimpole in Cambridgeshire (Plate 42) the old village stood in the way of eighteenth-century improvements and was rebuilt as a model village outside the gates of the park. The first Earl Manvers built a model village of Gothic cottages at Budby near Thoresby Park in 1807, to replace the ancient village. Perhaps the best known example is that of Milton Abbas, the little Dorset market-town which nestled for many centuries at the gates of the Benedictine monastery of Milton. The first Earl of Dorchester bought the entire site in 1752 and decided to build a great family mansion where the abbey ruins stood. The little town, now somewhat decayed, stood in the way and was demolished. In 1786-7 a model village was built on a new site nearly a mile

Easington the Seat of Nathaniel Stevens Esq

PLATE 43

Easington: a country house as it was about 1709 (after Kip) and a contrast to the order and sophistication of Wimpole. Here the big house has not yet separated itself from the country scene. There is no park, no formal gardens. Rough country roads come almost up to the house; farm buildings stand in the courtyard; sheep are dipped only a few yards from the house. Only lawns separate the house on three sides from the peasant landscape; but the beginnings of order are apparent in the relationship of the parish church to the big house and in the rows of young trees newly planted.

away. Thatched cottages were built in pairs, each pair separated by a plot of ground on which stands a chestnut tree. The church and the almshouse were also rebuilt in the new village, but the grammar school was removed to Blandford.

Three names remain to be noticed as having influenced the form of the English landscape through the great landowners. The unremitting destruction of the woodlands ever since Saxon times had produced by the seventeenth century a Timber Famine. Large tracts of countryside, especially in the Midlands, had been denuded of timber as early as Henry VIII's time, as we have seen in John Spencer's petitions of 1519 and 1522. In 1664 John Evelyn, a Surrey landowner, published his *Sylva*, a plea for afforestation, in which he was able to assert that he had induced landowners to plant many millions of trees. In the eighteenth century, especially, landowners followed his principles of arboriculture; and it is to this period that we owe a number of foreign trees that are now conspicuous in some favoured parts of the country. Many of the oaks planted under Evelyn's inspiration in the late seventeenth century came to maturity just in time for the great naval struggle with France a hundred or so years later and went to the building of the enlarged navy.

William Kent (1685-1748) is important as the real founder of landscape gardening, though his successor Lancelot Brown (1715-83)—generally known as Capability Brown—exerted a wider influence. Indeed, it is the pervasive influence of Kent, Brown and such later men as Repton, upon the laying-out of parks for the country houses, that has helped to give rise to the wholly inadequate view that the English landscape is "the man-made creation of the seventeenth and eighteenth centuries."

Kent's view of landscape gardening was a reaction against the excessively formal gardens that had surrounded the seventeenth-century houses, a formality which was further emphasized through the introduction by William III from Holland of straight vistas of water, regular avenues of trees, and trim-clipped box edges, a style exemplified in the palace gardens of Kensington. Kent's gardens were irregular and romantic, "with sudden changes of scene to ravish and surprise the beholders of temples, cascades, groves, and statues in unexpected corners." One of the most perfect examples of the new style was the park at Stowe in Buckinghamshire, which Pitt helped to create. Rousham (in Oxfordshire) remains the only untouched example of Kent's handiwork in the country.

Capability Brown worked on a grand scale at Kew and at Blenheim. In 1764 he created at Blenheim (Plate 44) the most magnificent private lake in the country by damming the little river Glyme: "there is nothing finer in Europe," says Sacheverell Sitwell. He manipulated square miles of landscape in the park, planting trees on a scale consonant with the massive Vanbrugh house.

Brown also made the lake at Burghley about 1775, wiped out the formal gardens of the earlier age, and "landscaped" the park beyond them on a grand scale (Plate 39). A guide to Burghley House, published in 1797, says: "It was the genius of the late Launcelot Brown, which, brooding over the shapeless mass, educed out of a seeming wilderness, all the order and delicious harmony which now prevail. Like the great Captain of the Israelites, he led forth his troop of sturdy plants into a seemingly barren land; where he displayed strange magic, and surprised them with miracle after miracle. Though the beauties, with which we are here struck, are more peculiarly the rural beauties of Mr. Brown, than those of Dame Nature, she seems to wear them with so simple and unaffected a grace, that it is not even the man of taste who can, at a superficial glance, discover the difference." Besides

PLATE 44

Blenheim Palace and Park, Oxfordshire. The eighteenth-century palace built for the Duke and Duchess of Marlborough by Vanbrugh between 1705 and 1722. The Park, in origin a hunting park for the Anglo-Saxon kings, contains 2,700 acres and is nine miles around. It was landscaped by Capability Brown, who made the beautiful lake in 1764 by damming the little river Glyme. The trees are planted in groups so as to form a plan of the battle of Blenheim, each battalion of soldiers being represented by a separate plantation.

creating a lake nearly a mile long, Brown moved trees of the most enormous bulk from place to place, to suit the prospect and landscape, set up a Gothic temple, made Shrubberies and new Walks. There are no "follies" at Burghley—none of the extravagances that led William Kent to plant dead trees in Kensington gardens for verisimilitude, or to erect "ruined" cottages for Earl Fortescue at Castle Hill in Devon, a folly which a more economically-minded descendant reconditioned and made habitable for some of his tenants. Sham ruins dating from this period give point to not a few hill-tops in England.

Parks continued to be made throughout the greater part of the nineteenth century, until landowners began to feel the draught of the great agricultural depression of the 1880s. One gets some idea of the number of parks of nineteenth-century origin by comparing the first edition of the Ordnance Survey map with the contemporary map. It would be interesting to know when the last private park was made in England; the last grand gesture, so to speak, of the landed aristocracy before the bell began to toll.

SELECT BIBLIOGRAPHY

CURTLER, W. H. R., *The Enclosure and Redistribution of our Land* (1920).
DEFOE, DANIEL, *A Tour through England and Wales* (Everyman ed., n.d.).
GONNER, E. C. K., *Common Land and Enclosure* (1912).
GOTCH, J. A., *The Growth of the English House* (revised ed., 1928).
HOSKINS, W. G., "The Rebuilding of Rural England, 1570-1640," *Past and Present*, No. 4 (1953).
LELAND, JOHN, *Itinerary* (ed. Smith, L. T., 1906-8).
MORRIS, CHRISTOPHER, (ed.), *The Journeys of Celia Fiennes* (1947).
PARKER, L. A., "The Agrarian Revolution at Cotesbach, 1501-1612," in *Studies in Leicestershire Agrarian History* (ed. Hoskins, W. G., 1949).
SUMMERSON, JOHN, *Architecture in Britain, 1530-1830* (1953).

VI

Parliamentary Enclosure and the Landscape

Inclosure, thou'rt a curse upon the land,
And tasteless was the wretch who thy existence plann'd.
JOHN CLARE.

A T the beginning of the eighteenth century the rural landscape of England
was still far from assuming its present likeness. Over large tracts of the
country, especially in the west and the north, and to a considerable extent in the
south-east also, the pattern of field and hedgerow, hamlet and farm, road and
lane, had established itself pretty much as we know it. But over millions of acres
between the Yorkshire and the Dorset coasts, the country scene was still largely
medieval. Farming was carried on in open fields that had not changed basically
since the thirteenth century, and beyond the arable fields and their meadows lay
great tracts of common pasture, much of it covered with gorse and furze, rising
in places to moorland and mountains.

The Extent of the Enclosure

It is impossible to say precisely how much of England still lay in open field in
1700 or thereabouts, but one can make a rough estimate. We know that enclosures
by parliamentary act and award dealt with about 4,500,000 acres of open field,
leaving aside for one moment the enclosure of the commons and other "wastes."
Gregory King had estimated in 1688 that the arable land of England and Wales
amounted to nine million acres in all. We shall not be far wrong then if we say
that in 1700 about one-half of the arable land was already enclosed in the kind of
fields that we see today, and that about one-half still lay in open field, a landscape
which survives today only in patches of a few hundred acres at Braunton (north
Devon), at Laxton (Nottinghamshire), and at Haxey and Epworth (in the Isle
of Axholme).

Gregory King also estimated that no fewer than ten million acres of England
and Wales were still "heaths, moors, mountains, and barren land," rather more
than one-quarter of the total area of the country as he reckoned it. In 1795 the
newly-formed Board of Agriculture put the "wastes" at a little under eight
million acres. It seems likely that both figures are too high. There are today some
five million acres of common, waste, and wild land in England and Wales. About
two milion acres of waste have been enclosed by act since 1700, so that we may
reasonably assume that at the beginning of the eighteenth century there were
about seven million acres of "waste" all told rather than the ten million estimated
by Gregory King.

138

The enclosure of open fields into the smaller fields that form our familiar world today, and the reclamation of the wild lands, had been going on intermittently and at a varying pace in every century. But after the Restoration the government ceased to interfere with the enclosure of open field by private landlords, and the pace of change quickened sharply. Up to about 1730 most of this enclosure was carried through by private agreements between the owners of the land in question. Very few enclosures were dealt with by act of parliament. But under George II, and above all from the 1750s onwards, enclosure by private act of parliament, working through special commissioners in each of the affected parishes, was the great instrument of change. From then onwards the transformation of the English landscape, or of a considerable part of it, went on at a revolutionary pace.

This revolution affected nearly three thousand English parishes, as near as we can tell. In many, the enclosure award of Georgian days was only the final clearing-up of remnants of open field that survived after piecemeal enclosure had been going on for generations or even centuries. Here the revolution in the landscape was a mild one. But in the great majority of the parishes it was a complete transformation, from the immemorial landscape of the open fields, with their complex pattern of narrow strips, their winding green balks or cart-roads, their headlands and grassy footpaths, into the modern chequer-board pattern of small, squarish fields, enclosed by hedgerows of hawthorn, with new roads running more or less straight and wide across the parish in all directions. It was a triumph of planning in so short a time for so complicated a matter, most of it carried through in most places within a year or two years of the passing of the act. One cannot help reflecting what would happen nowadays in a problem of similar magnitude.

It is true that the paper plans, as set out in the award made by the commissioners, did not produce all the physical changes at once, as we shall see in due course; but the transformation of the landscape was, all the same, remarkably swift. A villager who had played in the open fields as a boy, or watched the sheep in the common pastures, would have lived to see the modern landscape of his parish completed and matured, the roads all made, the hedgerow trees full grown, and new farmhouses built out in the fields where none had ever been before. Everything was different: hardly a landmark of the old parish would have remained. Perhaps here and there the old man would have found some evidences of the former world: the windmill of his younger days still standing in the corner of a new field, though now derelict and forlorn, or the traces of the former strips in the ridge-and-furrow of the new pastures, but not much else. This transformation of an ancient landscape into a modern one did not, however, affect the whole of England. In some regions the transformation had taken place much earlier, as in Kent, or Essex, or Devon, where it had taken a different form altogether, where most of the fields had been reclaimed direct from forest and moorland

FIG. 14.—The Extent of Parliamentary Enclosure
Reproduced by permission from Gonner, *Common Land and Inclosure.*

without passing through the open-field stage at all, or had been enclosed from open field at an early date.

We can indeed be fairly precise about the extent to which this parliamentary enclosure movement altered the English landscape. It affected the Midland counties most of all, and it is here more than anywhere that we find the planned landscape of Georgian times. Yet even here the actual extent to which the rural landscape was altered is considerably less than we might suppose. Of all counties the one most affected by the transformation of the open arable fields was Northamptonshire. Here just about one-half the total area was dealt with by parliamentary act and award. A block of counties adjoining it—Rutland to the north, Huntingdonshire and Bedfordshire to the east, and Oxfordshire to the south, showed nearly as great a transformation. We ought to include also the northern half of Buckinghamshire in this belt of planned country, for though parliamentary enclosure affected only one acre in three in the county as a whole it was largely concentrated in the plain to the north of the Chilterns. On the eastern side of the county, indeed, where it lay along the Bedfordshire border, one acre in every two was dealt with by the Georgian planners. Fig. 14 shows the parts of England most affected by this type of planning. Roughly speaking, it forms a great belt which sweeps round from Flamborough Head on the Yorkshire coast, down through the Midlands as far as the Dorset coast, and thence north-eastwards along the chalk uplands to the Norfolk coast. Within this stretch of country, some two hundred miles at its greatest from north to south, and 120 miles or so at its widest from west to east, an average of three acres in every ten was dealt with by parliamentary enclosure. The large counties of Warwickshire, Gloucestershire, and Wiltshire, which form a solid block to the west of this "concentrated" area, show about one acre in four dealt with by the enclosure commissioners, rising on parts of the Wiltshire chalk to one in two. Berkshire is very similar in this respect to Wiltshire: on an average about one acre in four enclosed by private act, but rising on the chalk downs to more than one in two. There is, too, a marked contrast in landscape-history between the west of the county and the east.

Outside this great tract of central England, the influence of parliamentary enclosure on the landscape dwindled rapidly in every direction. In the six northern counties of England, it had very little effect on the landscape, except in the East Riding of Yorkshire. Over large stretches of northern England not one acre in a hundred had been shaped by the Georgian planners.

It is the same all down the Welsh Border, from Cheshire down to the Severn, and thence across the Severn to the three south-western counties of Somerset, Devon, and Cornwall. The landscapes of the Welsh Border counties and of south-western England have an entirely different history from those of the Midland Plain.

In the south of England, Dorset, Hampshire, and Surrey were affected to some extent—again much more in some parts than others—but the south-eastern corner of England owes little or nothing to the enclosure commissioners. Large tracts of country in this part of England, especially in Sussex, Kent, and Essex, had anciently been thickly wooded and never brought within the open-field system. When the forest was cleared, mostly from the twelfth century onwards, the small fields were enclosed directly from the wild state. Both Essex and Kent are noted by John Hales in his *Discourse of the Common Weal* (1549) as mostly enclosed even in the middle of the sixteenth century.

East Anglia has a peculiar history also, so far as its landscape is concerned. In both Norfolk and Suffolk the eastern and western halves of the county are notice-ably different. One sees this not only on the ground, travelling through these parts, but it is also brought out clearly on the Ordnance Map. Even if one had never visited this part of England, the map would suggest that there are funda-mental differences in the way in which the landscapes of the two halves of the counties have evolved. This is particularly striking in Norfolk. In the east and centre of the county we find a close network of narrow, winding lanes, wandering from hamlet to hamlet and farm to farm, churches standing alone, isolated houses dotted all over the map, many of them called Hall or Old Hall—significant names. It is a closely-packed map with hardly a straight line or an empty space in it. The west of the county is entirely different, even to the casual glance of a motorist: far fewer lanes and by-ways, more villages, straighter roads, large, empty spaces between the villages, the whole landscape or map more "open" altogether. To put it broadly—ignoring all the smaller points of detail—one landscape has grown up piecemeal over centuries, the other is almost entirely planned on a large scale.

William Marshall, the best of the agricultural writers of his time, describes the landscape of East Norfolk as it was in 1787 in his *Rural Economy of Norfolk*. "The roads, notwithstanding King Charles was pleased to say the county of Norfolk was only fit to be cut into roads for the rest of his kingdom, are unpardonably bad; narrow, shaded, and *never mended*; they are numerous, however, especially the bridle-roads; so that a traveller, on horseback, has generally the choice of two or three ways, of nearly equal length, to the same place. . . . The inclosures are, in general, small, and the hedges high, and full of trees. This has a singular effect in travelling through the country: the eye seems ever on the verge of a forest, which is, as it were by enchantment, continually changing into inclosures and hedgerows. . . ." This is the typical landscape of ancient enclosure, as Marshall rightly observes, of fields taken in direct from woodland and waste in medieval times, such as we find in Devon, Sussex, and the other peripheral counties of England.

The Date of Parliamentary Enclosure

Before we see how the enclosure commissioners replanned the landscape of central England, and how we can identify their work today, it is necessary to say something briefly about the dating of the parliamentary enclosure movement as a whole. Practically the whole of this vast transformation was effected between 1750 and 1850, and, so far as the open fields alone were concerned, in the sixty years of George III's reign. There were only eight private acts for enclosure in the whole of England before 1714, eighteen under George I (1714-27), and 229 under George II (1727-60), most of these in the latter part of his reign.[1] The total area dealt with before 1760 could hardly have exceeded 400,000 acres, a negligible amount when one thinks of England as a whole—only just over one per cent. In the next forty years no fewer than 1,479 enclosure acts were passed, dealing with nearly $2\frac{1}{2}$ million acres. Altogether, between 1761 and 1844, there were more than 2,500 acts, dealing with rather more than four million acres of open fields. After the General Inclosure Act of 1845 there were another 164 awards which cleared up nearly 200,000 more of the remaining open field.

Besides the open arable fields, there were the extensive "wastes" of various kinds. These were mostly dealt with from 1800 onwards as the high prices of the war-years brought more and more marginal land into cultivation. More than five hundred acts had already enclosed three-quarters of a million acres of "waste" between 1760 and 1801. During the nineteenth century, another thirteen hundred acts and awards brought, or attempted to bring, another $1\frac{1}{4}$ million acres of heath and moor and commons under cultivation. Some at least of this reclamation of the "waste" by enclosure was a failure, for it was applied indiscriminately to good land and bad. Much of the extensive heath country of Lincolnshire was successfully enclosed and converted into good arable land, but between Sleaford and Lincoln, Arthur Young saw, in the 1790s, "hundreds of acres in the veriest state of waste I ever saw land, whether appropriated or unappropriated, in this kingdom. Half a dozen wild rabbits were all the stock I observed upon them with scarcely a blade or leaf of herbage to keep even these alive; doubtless through the folly or madness of the first occupiers (after appropriation) in converting them to arable farms instead of sheep walks and rabbit warrens."[2]

The New Landscape

The parliamentary enclosure movement had its most pronounced effects in the Midlands and in eastern England, in a solid block of sixteen counties. The Record Offices of these counties possess a considerable number of awards made by the commissioners, often accompanied by a map showing the new lay-out of the parish, with the fields and roads marked out pretty much as we know them today.[3] Here and there minor changes in field boundaries may have been made

[1]Tate, *Handlist of Sussex Inclosure Acts and Awards*, 8. The earliest acts were for the parish of Radipole in Dorset in 1602, and for Marden in Herefordshire in 1606.
[2]Quoted in Curtler, *The Enclosure and Redistribution of our Land*, 188-9.
[3]A map always accompanied the award originally, but in a considerable number of instances it has since been lost. Thus the Leicestershire County Record Office possesses official copies of 102 awards, but only 20 maps, a fairly typical state of affairs.

during the past 150 to 200 years, but on the whole the enclosure map lays down the present-day pattern exactly. In the same Record Offices there may exist—but in much smaller numbers—even more interesting maps which show the lay-out of the village and its open fields, with every strip separately shown, and all the other features of the fields, as they were on the eve of the enclosure. It is a completely medieval picture. Superimposed on this map of things as they were, one sometimes finds the lines drawn in by the commissioners showing where they

PLATE 45

Field-pattern created by Parliamentary Enclosure near Burrough Hill, Leicestershire: straight hedges of hawthorn interspersed with ash trees, and a farmstead built in the fields after the enclosure.

propose to create the new fields and hedges, and the new roads, public and private. One sees on such maps the new landscape actually in course of being planned, and can see how completely it was drawn afresh, regardless of almost everything that had gone before. Such maps are rare. The Leicestershire Record Office possesses only two, for the parishes of Stathern (1792) and South Croxton and Barsby (1798). The Lincoln Record Office does not possess a single map of this kind, in an otherwise rich and varied collection of records.

The Fields

By far the most conspicuous element in the new landscape were the small, hedged fields—small, that is, by comparison with the vast open fields that had preceded them, which usually ran to several hundred acres unbroken by a single hedge. As far as possible the enclosure commissioners formed square or squarish fields (Plate 45). Where we find long narrow fields they are nearly always adjacent to the village, lying behind or beside the "ancient homesteads," as they are called in the awards. These represent in most instances the crofts or separate paddocks of half an acre to an acre in size which have been hedged around since medieval times.

The new enclosures varied in size according to the size of the farms. On small farms of which there were great numbers in the Midlands and East Anglia—the holdings of the free peasantry, as we have seen—the new fields were usually five to ten acres in size. On large farms they ran up to fifty or sixty acres.[1] But in grazing country these larger fields were soon reduced to a number of smaller fields of round about ten acres apiece. Robert Bakewell (1725-95), experimenting with sheep and cattle-breeding on his farm in north Leicestershire, was convinced that "fifty acres of pasture ground divided into five enclosures will go as far in grazing cattle as sixty acres all in one piece" and his opinion was shared by other big graziers. Each ten-acre field in turn was grazed bare—"till you could whip a mouse across it"—and the cattle moved round from one field to another so that they were always eating fresh, springing grass.[2]

Not only were the new enclosures reduced to smaller fields for grazing purposes, but so were some, at least, of the older enclosures made generations or centuries earlier. Thus we find a much more uniform field-pattern, uniform as regards both size and shape, than we might have expected in the grazing counties of central England. Wherever the enclosure of the open arable fields resulted in conversion to pasture we find this regular field-pattern of straight hedges and squarish fields of roughly the same size (Plate 46). We must not overstress this uniformity, for even in the Midlands there are considerable variations, but compared with the variety of landscape elsewhere in England, the Midland pattern is markedly monotonous.

The conversion of the former arable fields to small enclosed fields of pasture had therefore two visible effects on the landscape. It tended to produce this monotonous field-pattern, and it also produced "a continuous sheet of greensward," as William Marshall observed of Leicestershire in 1790, instead of the multi-coloured patchwork of the old arable strips. These changes were particularly noticeable in the contiguous counties of Leicestershire, Northamptonshire, Warwickshire, Bedfordshire, and Buckinghamshire, and to a lesser extent in the

[1] Curtler, 164, citing the *Board of Agriculture Report*, 1808, 81.
[2] Ellis, *Leicestershire and the Quorn Hunt*, 26.

PLATE 46

Fields created by parliamentary enclosure in 1771 at Kilby (Leicestershire). The older pattern of the open fields is clearly visible from the air, not only the individual strips but also many of the furlongs. The unridged fields at the top of the plate represent the medieval meadows along the stream. The canal at the top, made in 1793, cuts through the ridges thus showing that they are older than the canal.

counties that marched with them. They were most marked on the heavy clays that overlie most of the Midlands, which produced good pastures. Where the clays gave way to the lighter soils of the Stone Belt, considerable areas of mixed farming remained. Parts of Northamptonshire did not, for this reason, go as uniformly green as Leicestershire after enclosure.

Elsewhere in England, enclosure—especially of the heaths and common pastures —had the opposite effects. This was particularly true of the vast heath-lands of western Norfolk and of Lincolnshire. According to Arthur Young "half the county of Norfolk within the memory of man yielded nothing but sheep feed," but by the end of the century was covered with fine barley, rye, and wheat. Even in East Norfolk there were localized patches of sandy heaths and commons, as at Felbrigg, a little inland from Cromer. Here, in 1781, there were eight hundred acres of heath and common out of 1,467 acres in the parish as a whole. The squire owned the entire parish, except one small farm, which he proceeded to buy on liberal terms from the yeoman who owned it. Having obtained this, he set to work to enclose the parish and to re-arrange its landscape. The least fertile part of the heath was left as a common for the poor to collect firing from. The remainder, together with the open arable field, he divided into small squarish fields of eight to twelve acres each (sometimes more or less according to the convenience of the farmers) and parcelled out as farms among his tenants. He then laid out public roads for the convenience of the parish, and private roads and driftways for the individual occupiers, and so completed the transformation of the entire parish except his own park. Marshall, who gives these facts in his *Rural Economy of Norfolk*, supposes that three hundred acres of heathland were divided into thirty fields of ten acres each. Each field, he reckons, would require about seven hundred yards of quickset hedges, so giving a total of some twelve miles of hedgerow even on this comparatively small area of land. This was the visual transformation that enclosure brought about. In place of a sandy, open heath, supporting a rough pasture, there would be a dozen miles of flowering hawthorn in time, enclosing small fields that were being assiduously marled to produce corn crops.

The greatest transformation of heathland into corn fields was to be found on the estates of the famous Coke of Holkham, in the north of Norfolk. In the course of a long lifetime (1752-1842) he changed the entire face of this part of the country, through his own efforts and those of his imitators. When he began farming on his own account in 1778 he found an open and almost barren country, much of it worth only five shillings an acre. Chiefly by digging the underlying marl and spreading it over the sandy top-soil he converted it into rich cornlands and raised the value of his Holkham estate from £5,000 to £20,000 a year within fifteen years.[1] "Half a century ago," wrote Arthur Young in 1804, "Norfolk might be termed a rabbit and rye country. In its northern part wheat was almost

---

[1] Kent, *General View of the Agriculture of Norfolk*, 1794, says that the Holkham rental was "upwards of £20,000 a year . . . and is still increasing like a snowball."

unknown, in the whole tract lying between Holkham and Lynn not an ear was to be seen, and it was scarcely believed that an ear could be made to grow. Now the most abundant crops of wheat and barley cover the entire district." But even at the end of the eighteenth century there were still in Norfolk about 80,000 acres of unimproved common, and some 60,000 acres of warrens and sheep walks, most of which had been enclosed and converted to arable fields or woodlands by the middle of the nineteenth.

Hardly a county in England did not possess extensive heathlands. Much of them are unreclaimed to this day, as in Dorset, Hampshire, and Surrey. But more than two million acres of "waste" were successfully enclosed, divided into fields,

PLATE 47

A Yorkshire farmstead near Haworth created by the enclosure of the moorland "waste" in the early nineteenth century.

and brought under cultivation by act of parliament, mostly during the course of the nineteenth century. All this is a matter of statistics and arid generalities: but what the transformation of these local heaths meant to those who had grown up near them and upon them, what the change meant in *detail*, is revealed to us in the poetry of John Clare, who was born in 1793 on the edge of the heath country of northern Northamptonshire.

Clare was set to watch sheep and geese on Helpston heath as a child of seven, and spent years of his childhood, and of his later life, wandering over the heath and through the patches of woodland that survived in the parish. It was a small world of heath and wood, a few hundred acres at the most, but it was a separate world as Clare describes it, for example, in *The Village Minstrel*:

Swamps of wild rush-beds and sloughs' squashy traces,
Grounds of rough fallows with thistle and weed,
Flats and low vallies of kingcups and daisies,
Sweetest of subjects are ye for my reed:
Ye commons left free in the rude rags of nature,
Ye brown heaths beclothed in furze as ye be,
My wild eye in rapture adores every feature,
Ye are dear as this heart in my bosom to me.

O native endearments! I would not forsake ye,
I would not forsake you for sweetest of scenes:
For sweetest of gardens that nature could make me
I would not forsake ye, dear valleys and greens:
Though Nature ne'er dropped ye a cloud-resting mountain,
Nor waterfalls tumble their music so free,
Had Nature denied ye a bush, tree, or fountain,
Ye still had been loved as an Eden by me.

In Clare's brief Journal, too, are entries that reveal the detail of the heath landscape. On Wednesday 29 September 1824 he "Took a walk in the fields saw an old wood stile taken away from a favourite spot which it had occupied all my life the posts were overgrown with Ivy & it seemd so akin to nature & the spot where it stood as tho it had taken it on lease for an undisturbed existence it hurt me to see it was gone for my affections claims a friendship with such things but nothing is lasting in this world last year Langley Bush was destroyd an old whitethorn that had stood for more than a century full of fame the gipsies shepherds & Herdmen all had their tales of its history & it will be long ere its memory is forgotten."

Crabbe, in *The Village*, describes the heath land also, in a few savage lines. Doubtless they describe the hard life of the villager and the poverty of his surroundings as Crabbe saw them: but he was not a peasant, as Clare was, and he saw them from the outside as harsh, ugly, and wretched. Clare's view of the heathland is the truer one, for it is the peasant's view from the inside, born in it and part of it. Though he never idealized it or pretended it was anything but "the rude rags of nature," he saw things in it to which Crabbe was completely blind or hostile, and he felt their loss when change and "improvement" came:

Ye injur'd fields, ye once were gay,
When Nature's hand displayed
Long waving rows of willows grey
And clumps of hawthorn shade;
But now, alas! your hawthorn bowers
All desolate we see!

The spoiler's axe their shade devours,
And cuts down every tree.
Not trees alone have owned their force,
Whole woods beneath them bowed,
They turned the winding rivulet's course,
And all thy pastures plough'd

Clare is the only poet to describe the ragged, solitary heaths of England, though there is also Hardy's famous prose description of Egdon heath in Dorset. But what is even more remarkable is the entire absence of any poetry associated with the open fields, any lament in literature for their passing. There is indeed plenty in print about them, but it is economic, argumentative stuff, mostly condemnatory and lacking in any understanding of what this old world meant to the peasant, and of what he lost by its passing. Perhaps it is not remarkable, after all, that no poet should have described this world to us before it expired, described it in language that would bring home to us what kind of world it actually was and how its inhabitants looked upon it, for it was above all a peasant world and the peasant was inarticulate. Clare was the great exception, an articulate peasant, and he might have described that world for us in all its natural beauty and its deep associations for the human race—twelve or thirteen centuries of unbroken continuity—but he came almost too late for this kind of England. By the time he began writing, about the time of Waterloo, the open fields had nearly disappeared. In his own parish the changes had been begun immediately after the passing of the act in 1809,[1] while Clare was still a mooning youth. It is true that there were still considerable patches of open field left in some parts of the country: at Castor, which adjoined Helpston on the south, the fields remained open until 1898: but the Helpston fields had all been enclosed by 1820. One must have been born and have worked all one's life in such a landscape to understand its secret life, to be able to feel its poetry, and to express it. The English peasantry threw up only one John Clare, and he was born too late to experience this ancient world to the full. He saw only its remnants in the unenclosed heaths. The result is that we know nothing about it except its external face, how its economy worked, and that has mostly been described by unsympathetic observers. Of what it felt like to live in such a world we are, and must for ever remain, entirely ignorant.

Hedgerows and Trees

The new fields were hedged around with quickset, whitethorn, or hawthorn, to give its alternative names, with a shallow ditch on one side or both sides of the fence. In the upland stone country, dry-walling took the place of hedges (Plate 48). At first the hedges were no more than double rows of seedlings pro-

[1] J. W. and Anne Tibble, *John Clare*, 63. *The Prose of John Clare* (1951), by the same authors, gives a sketch-map of this heath country between Stamford and Peterborough, as it was in 1779, before much of it was enclosed.

tected by a rail on one side or both, but after twenty years the thorns had grown high enough to be cut and laid, a practice which William Marshall describes as the latest improvement in his *Rural Economy of the Midland Counties* in 1796. Throughout the East Midlands ash trees were planted along the hedges, less often the elm, usually spaced out at wide intervals. Possibly this comparative scarcity of trees in the East Midland hedgerows—in Northamptonshire and Leicestershire especially—arises from consideration for fox-hunting. In Leicestershire organized fox-hunting developed during the 1770s, in time to enjoy the exhilaration of galloping over miles of unfenced country. Enclosure made things more difficult, or perhaps we should say necessitated new and exciting skills, but

PLATE 48

In Derbyshire limestone walls take the place of the hawthorn hedges of the Midlands, but the fields created by parliamentary enclosure are of the same type. It is a landscape of straight lines, relieved only by the curve of the solitary hill behind.

at least there were no close ranks of trees to make the fences impossible. Indeed, the first effect of enclosure was to reduce the number of trees in thinly-wooded country, for the new fences—hundreds of miles of them—required vast quantities of oak, elm, and ash saplings for posts and rails. Clare, once more, was in no doubt about the diminution of woodland after enclosure:

> Ye fields, ye scenes so dear to Lubin's eye,
> Ye meadow-blooms, ye pasture-flowers, farewell!
> Ye banish'd trees, ye make me deeply sigh—
> Inclosure came, and all your glories fell:

E'en the old oak that crown'd yon rifled dell,
Whose age had made it sacred to the view,
Not long was left his children's fate to tell;
Where ignorance and wealth their course pursue,
Each tree must tumble down—old "Lea-Close Oak," adieu!

Fox-hunting had another effect upon the Midland landscape, and that was the creation of artificial fox-covers. The enclosure of heaths and commons reduced the extent of natural gorse patches where a fox could hide. Good arable farmers grubbed them up. To get more foxes and to get them distributed more evenly over the country, gorse covers and spinneys were started by hunting landlords in well-chosen spots. These were not less than two acres in size, and rarely more than twenty acres. Some of these covers were actually odd pieces of common land, old cow-pastures that had been allowed to get out of hand, taken over by the fox-hunters for fencing and preservation, in return for a money payment to the holders of the common rights. Such were Ashby Pastures or Cossington Gorse in east Leicestershire, in the "Quorn country."[1] These "gorses" filled up the odd corners of parishes, and may be quickly spotted on the Ordnance map. Other covers were planted with trees, and fenced around by large fox-hunting landlords like Lord Aylesford or Sir Francis Burdett, the radical politician, who hunted in Leicestershire in the 1820s. Most of these covers were made in the late eighteenth century or the early nineteenth, and often give away their date in their names. The famous Botany Bay cover of east Leicestershire dates from the 1790s, when the convict settlement was in the news. The one-inch maps of the East Midland counties are splashed all over with these shreds of green, usually distinguishable from true, ancient woodland by their small size and their regular shape. In the landscape itself, they are a very noticeable feature for they are often the only clump of trees anywhere in sight over thousands of acres.

The fox-hunting country was perhaps a special case. Over most of enclosed England, the small fields were hedged around with hawthorn fences, more or less thickly interspersed with ash and elm—the great trees of the Midlands—which when they were full grown gave the appearance of an almost continuous wood, especially when seen from an eminence. This is perhaps the most characteristic feature of any large view in the Midland Plain. Ash and elm were planted in the hedgerows, and the flashing grey-green willow along the banks of the streams. These are the three trees that dominate any Midland view in the deep country.

The greater part of the hedges is, however, made of white hawthorn (Plate 49). Some of these hawthorns, with their gnarled, twisted, and burnished trunks, probably date from the first enclosure of the fields five or six generations ago. The hawthorn is the oldest of the hedgerow trees, for it gets its name from the Old English word *haga*, "a hedge" or "an enclosure," and it was used from Saxon

[1]Ellis, op. cit., 60 et seq.

times onwards to make impenetrable fences—the hedge-thorn. In the Midlands it is the tree one sees most often: and for a brief spell in early summer it is the most beautiful of all the Midland trees, with its continuous miles of white may-blossom glimmering as far as the eye can see. W. H. Hudson says somewhere that May the eighteenth is the crown of the English summer: in the Midland fields on that day these miles of snowy hedges reach perfection, so dense and far-reaching that the entire atmosphere is saturated with the bitter-sweet smell whichever way the summer wind is blowing. From the hedgerow trees near and far come the calls of countless cuckoos, and the lesser sounds of an infinite number of small birds.

The thousands of miles of new hedgerows in the Midland countryside, when they came to full growth after a generation, added enormously to the bird population, especially with the extermination of the larger hawks and kites as pests, a process that is abundantly recorded in the churchwardens' accounts or the field-reeves' books of Midland villages. Millions of small birds now sing in the hedges and spinneys. But it was not all gain. The heathland birds have disappeared over large areas, and become rarer altogether. The whole balance of the bird-population altered where these changes were going on in the landscape. There were more hedges but fewer heaths; in some parts less arable than ever before, in other parts more than ever before; and the coming of the canals about the same time also introduced new varieties of birds to districts where they had previously never been known.

There is only one other thing to be said about the hedgerows of parliamentary enclosure, and that is when precisely they were made. Most enclosure awards, if not all, expressly stipulated that those who received allotments of land under the award were to fence these allotments within twelve months. This gives us, if we know the date of the award (which is easy enough to discover), the exact date of all the external fences or hedges, but it does not tell us the date of the internal fences on the bigger allotments. Where a biggish landowner received an allotment of two, three, or four hundred acres, he would put a ring-fence around the whole within the specified twelve months, but he might not divide up his allotment into smaller fields until some years later. It is a small point, perhaps, but not without some historical interest in the evolution of the English landscape. Henry Alken's hunting print *The Death*, dated 1824, appears to show such a landscape around Ab Kettleby, in the "wold" country to the north-west of Melton Mowbray. The parish had been enclosed as far back as 1761—two generations earlier—but Alken's view still gives a general impression of wide spaces and open views. There are indeed several hedges to be seen, but the hedged areas are mostly still very large and the landscape as a whole not unlike that of the Cotswolds in its feeling of great space and skies. But where a parish was mostly in the hands of a small peasantry, and this was true of a great many parishes in Midland and Eastern England, the effect would have been entirely different.

In such parishes as these the present field and hedge pattern was laid down in the year following the enclosure award, for the allotments would have been many and small. Not all parishes enclosed by parliamentary act immediately sprang fully-hedged into view. Indeed, the immediate effect of enclosure in most places must have been a feeling of nakedness and rawness in the landscape, until the hedgerow trees were well-grown:

> O samely naked leas, so bleak, so strange! . . .
> The storm beats chilly on its naked breast,
> No shelter grows to shield, no home invites to rest,

says Clare about his native Helpston in the years after its enclosure, and that must have been true of most parishes that underwent the great transformation.

Roads

A great number of new by-roads came into existence as a result of the enclosure movement. They are immediately recognizable on the one-inch map by the manner in which they run from village to village practically straight across country, with perhaps an occasional sudden right-angled bend and then on again. More significantly still, these straight roads sometimes do not run to the nearest village but continue for some miles through open country, reaching the villages by means of side-roads. There is none of that apparently aimless wandering in short stretches, punctuated by frequent bends, going halfway round the compass to reach the next hamlet or village, which characterizes the by-roads in country that has never been in open field or left it several centuries ago. On the six-inch and the twenty-five-inch maps, too, the parliamentary enclosure roads stand out conspicuously with their wide grass verges. The road runs like a grey ribbon between verges full of tall grasses, cow-parsley, and dog-roses, as may be seen above all in the Lincolnshire Wolds. But they are to be found in any of the "enclosure counties" and may be identified immediately as the work of the enclosure commissioners (Plate 49).

In the parish of Norton-by-Twycross, on the borders of Warwickshire and Leicestershire, the award of 1748 specifies that the road to London, which is here the main road between Burton-on-Trent and Atherstone, should be not less than thirty-three yards wide. The lesser main road from Twycross to the local market-town of Ashby de la Zouch was to have a minimum width of twenty-two yards; and the other roads of the parish were to be "of a proper width." The immense width of the two main roads, one with a minimum width of practically a hundred feet and the other of sixty-six feet, reflects the state of even the main roads before the days of the turnpikes and above all of the scientific roadmaking initiated by Metcalf and McAdam in the late eighteenth century. Roads that carried any considerable amount of through-traffic had to be wide enough, and could be wide enough in unenclosed country, to allow of detours around the impassable stretches that developed in unsurfaced roads by mid-winter. The main London to Exeter "road" was said to have been a quarter of a mile wide by the end of the winter where it crossed—or rather plunged through—the sticky morass of the chalk on Salisbury Plain. It seems to have been a fairly general rule in the later enclosure awards that the minimum width for inter-village roads should be forty feet between the ditches, though local roads carrying more than

PLATE 49

The landscape of parliamentary enclosure in Rutland, on the road from Empingham to Exton. Here oolitic limestone walls take the place of quickset, but hawthorn trees are planted at intervals and are at their best in late May. The photograph also shows the grass verge that is characteristic of by-roads laid out by the enclosure commissioners.

the average traffic for the district were often laid down forty-five or fifty feet wide. In Somerset, public roads were usually forty feet wide, of which—in 1795—twelve feet were stoned to a depth of a foot in the middle and nine inches at the sides.[1] This would leave verges of fourteen feet width on each side, if the paved road were dead in the middle. Often it was not, and the grass verge was very much wider on one side than the other. On most local roads today this width has hardly varied. All over the Midlands and Lincolnshire one finds roads with an overall

[1]Billingsley, *Agricultural Survey of Somersetshire*, 91.

width of forty feet, having a surface about fourteen or fifteen feet wide and grass verges of twelve or thirteen feet on each side.

It seems likely that a forty-foot width was regarded as the minimum for an unsurfaced road, allowing for detours as the winter went on, but when scientific roadmaking began these great widths were no longer necessary. Only a relatively narrow width was surfaced with stone, and the remainder was left under grass as we see it today. It is kept within bounds by county councils, but on the less frequented roads the cow-parsley, the dog-rose, and the blackberry bramble flourish by the wayside. Some of these by-roads have developed a heavier traffic since they were first laid out, and in these instances it has been an easy matter to take in more of the verges and to widen the road surface.

The established main roads that had been used for traffic between the medieval towns, and had made their own width with the usage of centuries, were generally left untouched by any parish awards. So the Fosse Way, which at one time had been the main road from medieval Coventry to Leicester, was ordered in the Sharnford award of 1765 to be "of the same width as it hath heretofore usually been." Even so, quickset hedges were planted on either side of these roads to fence them in, where formerly they had wandered at large.

It is sometimes said that the public roads laid out by the enclosure commissioners followed the lines of the medieval footpaths and bridle paths between the villages, paths that had been trodden out first in Anglo-Saxon times. But this is by no means always true. The strip-map of Barsby and South Croxton, already referred to, shows the public roads of these two parishes to be laid out on almost entirely new lines. Here and there they pick up and make use of the old common balks in the former open fields, which must have been the usual way of proceeding from one village to another in open-field country, but for the most part they are drawn straight across the old furlongs and strips regardless of all considerations but that of directness. Since the furlongs, strips, and balks were all to be swept away in the ensuing award and a new field-system devised, it was only natural that the commissioners should do this. The Stathern map of 1792 shows the same planning of new roads in more or less straight lines and judging by what the Ordnance map shows in other parts of the Midlands and eastern England the same thing happened fairly generally.

Often, however, it is clear that the commissioners took over an existing track between two villages and straightened it a little, without going to the extreme length of drawing entirely new roads. Where a road which bears all the marks of having been laid out by the enclosure commissioners makes, at longish intervals, a sudden right-angled bend, sometimes two bends in quick succession, one can be pretty certain that though it was planned by the commissioners it follows an even older line from one village to the next, a line which had deviated in the same way around the heads of medieval furlongs. There right-angled bends in the road, whatever the date of the enclosure award may be, reflect some stage in the medieval colonization of the parish when a new furlong, brought in from the waste perhaps in the twelfth or the thirteenth century, cut across the direct path to the next village and forced it to make a sudden turn for a few yards before resuming its onward course. Even a Roman road might be interfered with in this way and diverted from its ancient line; and in the course of time its exact line became lost and the subject of an archæological problem today. One sees all these little points of landscape in walking round the parish of Helpston, but they can be found in many parishes in these parts of England.

Farmhouses

With the enclosure of the open fields and the redistribution of the land mostly in compact blocks[1] instead of strips scattered all over the parish, one would have expected the old open-field village to disintegrate as the village farmers built new farmsteads on their allotments. Often, it is true, the commissioners drew the new boundaries so as to come to a point in the village where the ancient homestead lay, so that the farmer need not be disturbed from his old home. They did this, for example, at Middle Barton in North Oxfordshire. But it was not always possible to do this: the mere facts of topography were against it: and a great number of farms had to be created well away from the village. In such cases it was to the obvious advantage of the farmer to build himself a new farmstead in the middle of his lands.

This, indeed, is what happened in due course, but the old village was far from disintegrated by such new building unless it was already very small and decaying. Often many years elapsed before the village farmers built their new houses, however inconvenient it may have been to live in the centre of the parish and to farm on the boundaries. Enclosure had been an exceedingly expensive business, not only the heavy legal costs which worked out on an average at about £1 an acre (but were sometimes much heavier), but also the costs of making hundreds of yards of fences, which were heavier still. Many of the smaller farmers continued to live therefore in the ancestral homestead on the village street, but carried out no repairs to it and gradually allowed it to decay. When the old house was practically uninhabitable, they or their sons built a new farmstead in the midst of their own fields and migrated from the village. That is why one sees so many Victorian farmhouses in red brick in the midst of the fields in these parts of England.

On the other hand, the larger graziers, for the most part prosperous men, built themselves new farmsteads almost at once. In the adjoining parishes of Sileby and Seagrave, in mid-Leicestershire, one finds on the map such farm-names as Quebec, Belle Isle, Hanover, and Bunkers Hill, and New York not so

[1]The new allotments were not invariably made in one block, as is usually said. In some parishes the lands of the new farms were still scattered about, though to a much smaller extent than hitherto.

FIG. 15. THE PATTERN OF PARLIAMENTARY ENCLOSURE IN NORTH HERTFORDSHIRE AND SOUTH CAMBRIDGESHIRE

This "open" pattern of compact villages and few roads and lanes should be compared with Fig. 8, which shows the "close" pattern of early medieval colonization on the heavy London Clays of south-east Hertfordshire. Here, in north Hertfordshire and south Cambridgeshire, we are on the chalk land, cleared of its woodland cover in pre-Saxon times. It was settled by the Old English in compact villages such as Ashwell and Litlington, which were surrounded by large open fields. Many of these open fields survived into the nineteenth century, those of Bygrave and Ashwell into the twentieth century. Farmsteads are still rare ouside the villages: the few that exist were mostly built after the parliamentary enclosure of the parishes. The landscape of straight roads, often unfenced, and of small geometrical plantations, is characteristic of this late period.

Reproduced by permission from the 1-inch map of the Ordnance Survey.

far away, pleasant Georgian red-brick houses with white doorways gleaming across the home meadow. It is easy enough to guess when these parishes were enclosed. At Wiseton, in the Nottinghamshire plain between the Idle and the Trent, one landlord—Jonathan Ackham—built seven new homesteads on central sites on his estate after enclosure.

Yet the total number of farmsteads built out in the fields between the villages is very small. One would guess not more than half a dozen in the average parish, often fewer than that. There was rarely any sign of the village breaking up physically as a result of enclosure, whatever happened to it spiritually and culturally.

There were good reasons why the nucleated village should survive more or less intact. In the first place, the ownership of land and the occupation of farms was concentrated into far fewer hands in the eighteenth century than they had been in the medieval village. There is no need to labour this point, for every parish in England shows evidence of this tendency to concentrate ownership and occupation in the course of several centuries. Rider Haggard, in *Rural England*, gives a striking example of this: when the manor of Feckenham, in east Worcestershire, was surveyed in 1591, sixty-three different owners held some 2,900 acres. By 1900 there were only six owners, who held all this and another 3,000 acres besides.[1] Whatever the actual figures in any particular parish, the number of Georgian farmers was generally only a fraction of the number there had been in the medieval or Tudor village. In other words, there remained at the time of the parliamentary enclosure only half a dozen farmers who wished to build in the new fields.

Then again, the population of the country as a whole was rising fairly quickly at the time of the enclosure movement, especially in the industrial villages of the Midlands, and there was a demand for houses. Old and roomy yeoman farmhouses, those that had not been suffered to decay too far, were cut up into two or three cottages for a new class of "industrial poor." So far from disintegrating, the openfield village often grew larger after enclosure: larger, but often more squalid, for there was generally more poverty than there had been before.

Nevertheless, a new element had been introduced into the landscape in this part of England—the isolated farmstead. Nearly all the farm-houses we see between the compact villages of the country between the Yorkshire and the Dorset coasts date from the century 1750-1850. The few that are older may be either the result of Tudor or Stuart enclosure, or examples of monastic granges which have already been discussed. But probably four out of five of these farmsteads in the fields are the consequence of parliamentary enclosure.

On the vast tracts of Lincoln Heath, stretching north and south of the city for some seventy miles, Arthur Young found "a large range which formerly was covered with heath, gorse, etc., yielding in fact little or no produce, converted by

---

[1]Rider Haggard, *Rural England*, i, 405-6.

enclosure to profitable arable farms . . . and a very extensive country all studded with new farmhouses, offices, and every appearance of thriving industry . . ." On the map this Heath presents an absolutely typical picture of a planned landscape: dead-straight by-roads, almost empty spaces between the villages, solitary farmsteads sparingly dotted about and reached by occupation roads running off the public roads, a vast landscape utterly bare of woodland except for neat little fox covers, square or rectangular patches of green for the most part.

There is, too, another marked feature of this piece of country which is characteristic of all country enclosed from open fields or common of any kind. It is the complete absence of any *lanes*. It is this, more than anything else, which makes the map of this sort of country look so empty when compared with the map of anciently enclosed country in say mid-Sussex, Essex, or Devon. Lanes—true lanes that is, deep and winding—are characteristic of country fabricated piecemeal with small medieval implements. In recently enclosed country we have instead an open regular mesh of by-roads, and a few field-paths and bridle-roads to fill in the larger spaces between the villages. In Leicestershire, the man who wishes to forget income-tax, hydrogen bombs, and the relentless onward march of science, walks the field-paths, to which special maps and guides are provided; in Devon he takes to the deep lanes between the farms. It is a fundamental difference in landscape-history.

Such was the landscape created by the enclosure commissioners. But we must never forget that every few miles, even in the middle of this orderly landscape, an older scene may make its appearance. In passing from one parish to another, in simply crossing a nameless brook or a road, we may step back into fields that were created, not by the commissioners of Georgian times but by the Tudor squire or perhaps even by his monastic predecessors in the fifteenth century.

Thus if we are walking in the pastoral, remote country on the borders of Leicestershire and Rutland, following the Eye brook as it makes its way south through undulating fields to the Welland, we pass in a walk of nine or ten miles through a landscape modelled in five different centuries, and this in a part of England that is generally accounted somewhat dull, the monotonous product of parliamentary enclosure. We leave the main Uppingham to Leicester road at Allexton, a parish which is recorded as fully enclosed by 1555. Two miles or so to the south lies the village of Stockerston, now shrunk almost to a hamlet, with its attractive Perpendicular church standing alone on the hillside—a sure sign of some interesting change in village history. Here we know that the enclosure of the open fields began in the 1570s, and had been completed by some date in the seventeenth century. The field-pattern we see is three to four hundred years old. Another half hour's walk brings us to the site of a village which has disappeared altogether—the deserted village of Holyoak, now remembered by the solitary farmstead of Holyoaks Lodge. Here, in the winter of 1496, Sir Robert Brudenell evicted thirty people from their small, open-field arable farms to make way for his cattle-pastures. The record tells us that "they have departed thence, and are either idle or have perished." Holyoak was only a hamlet. Only five or six farms were involved in this tragedy; but for a few minutes at least we traverse fields brought into being by the high-handed action of a fifteenth-century squire, and pass by the mounds where the hamlet of Holyoak once stood. Up in the hills to our right lies Nevill Holt, now only a church, a park, and a great house. Here, too, the village has gone—probably deserted by Elizabethan times. Certainly all the fields were enclosed by the year 1572.

Then we emerge from these gentle hills into the broad levels of the Welland valley, and here, in the parishes of Great Easton and Bringhurst, we enter a landscape produced entirely (as far as we know) by the parliamentary enclosure of 1804-6. Another couple of miles up the valley and we are at Medbourne, the last bastion of the open fields in Leicestershire, enclosed in the year 1842. From Allexton to Medbourne is only five miles straight across the hills, yet we have passed through a period of some 350 years in the history of the landscape. Perhaps even longer: for Thomas Palmer had a grant of free warren at Holt as far back as 1448 and this may be the beginning of the park of Nevill Holt. If so, this piece of Leicestershire landscape is the product of various forces over a space of four hundred years. So, behind every generalization, there lies the infinite variety and beauty of the detail; and it is the detail that matters, that gives pleasure to the eye and to the mind, as we traverse, on foot and unhurried, the landscape of any part of England.

SELECT BIBLIOGRAPHY

CLARE, JOHN, various poems.
CURTLER, W. H. R., *The Enclosure and Redistribution of our Land* (1920).
ELLIS, C. D. B., *Leicestershire and the Quorn Hunt* (1951).
GONNER, E. C. K., *Common Land and Inclosure* (1912).
MARSHALL, WILLIAM, *Rural Economy of Norfolk* (1787).
MARSHALL, WILLIAM, *Rural Economy of Yorkshire* (1788).
MARSHALL, WILLIAM, *Rural Economy of Gloucestershire* (1789).
MARSHALL, WILLIAM, *Rural Economy of the Midland Counties* (1790).
    W. E. Tate's valuable Hand-lists to the enclosure acts and awards in most of the counties affected by the parliamentary enclosure movement have been published (usually) in the Transactions or Proceedings of the appropriate local historical or antiquarian society, and should be consulted for the detail about each county.

VII

The Industrial Revolution and the Landscape

The Early Industrial Landscape

ENGLAND was still a peaceful agricultural country at the beginning of the seventeenth century. Though she was passing through what has been called her first Industrial Revolution, there was as yet little to show for it in the landscape. Quarries and coal-pits were numerous in certain localities, salt-works and glass-works were flourishing, the cloth industry was growing; but so far as the visible signs upon the face of the country were concerned it was all a mere scratching on the surface. Neither Leland nor Camden has much to say about industry in England; and there was nothing that could be specifically called an industrial landscape. Perhaps the multitude of coal-pits near the Tyne were beginning to wear that look, and Camden observed in the 1580s that Sussex "is full of iron mines, all over it; for the casting of which there are furnaces up and down the country, and abundance of wood is yearly spent; many streams are drawn into one channel, and a great deal of meadow ground is turned into ponds and pools for the driving of mills by the flashes, which, beating with hammers upon the iron, fill the neighbourhood round about it, night and day with continual noise." The iron industry, centred in the Wealden woods, was steadily changing the face of the landscape in this region from the middle of the sixteenth century onwards, and a good deal remains to be seen by the historically-minded traveller.

By the end of the seventeenth century the industrial landscape was much more evident. Yarranton in 1677 thought there were more people within a radius of ten miles of Dudley, and "more money returned in a year," than in the whole of four Midland farming counties. This was pretty certainly an exaggeration, but it shows unmistakably that the Black Country (though this name had yet to be invented) was in process of creation.

The early industrial landscapes differed essentially from those that developed with steam-power. They showed a thick scattering of settlement, of cottages and small farmhouses dotted about all over the place, and a corresponding splitting-up of fields into small crofts and paddocks. It was a "busy" landscape, full of detail and movement, like one of Breughel's paintings, not a massive conglomeration of factories and slums. The Black Country in its early days was still country, "a countryside in course of becoming industrialized; more and more a strung-out web of iron-working villages, market-towns next door to collieries, heaths and wastes gradually and very slowly being covered by the cottages of nailers and other persons carrying on industrial occupations in rural surroundings."[1] The

[1]Court, *The Rise of the Midland Industries*, 22.

typical figure was that of the craftsman-farmer, combining, say, a smithy with a small-holding, living in his own small balanced economy: hence the minuteness of the detail in the picture. One still finds traces of this kind of landscape on the fringes of the Black Country, as for example in the hamlet of Lower Gornal, in the hills to the north-west of Dudley.

Defoe gives us a splendid picture of an industrial landscape in the time of Queen Anne or shortly after. It is the landscape of the cloth industry in the neighbourhood of Halifax before the revolutionary changes brought about by the invention of power-driven machinery:

> The nearer we came to Hallifax, we found the houses thicker, and the villages greater in every bottom; and not only so, but the sides of the hills, which were very steep every way, were spread with houses, and that very thick; for the land being divided into small enclosures, that is to say, from two acres to six or seven acres each, seldom more; every three or four pieces of land had a house belonging to it.
>
> . . . This division of the land into small pieces, and the scattering of the dwellings, was occasioned by, and done for the convenience of the business which the people were generally employ'd in . . .

This particular landscape had its origin in two sources—the outcropping of coal, and the presence of running water everywhere, even on the tops of the hills. Wherever Defoe passed a house he found a little rill of running water. "If the house was above the road, it came from it, and cross'd the way to run to another; if the house was below us, it cross'd us from some other distant house above it, and at every considerable house was a manufactory or work-house, and as they could not do their business without water, the little streams were so parted and guided by gutters and pipes, and by turning and dividing the streams, that none of those houses were without a river, if I may call it so, running into and through their work-houses."

The coal-pits near the tops of the hills were worked in preference to those lower down, for various reasons. The coal was easier to come at, water presented less of a drainage problem, and the pack-horses could go up light and come down laden. Every clothier kept a horse or two, to carry his coal from the pit, to fetch home his wool and his provisions from the market, to take his yarn to the weavers, his cloth to the fulling-mill and finally to the cloth market to be sold. He also kept two or three cows for the sustenance of the family, and so required two, three, or four pieces of enclosed land around his house.

> Having thus fire and water at every dwelling, there is no need to enquire why they dwell thus dispers'd upon the highest hills. . . . Among the manufacturers houses are likewise scattered an infinite number of cottages or small dwellings, in which dwell the workmen which are employed, the women and

children of whom are always busy carding, spinning, &c. so that no hands being unemploy'd, all can gain their bread, even from the youngest to the antient; hardly any thing above four years old, but its hands are sufficient to it self. . . . After we had mounted the third hill, we found the country one continued village, tho' mountainous every way, as before; hardly a house standing out of a speaking distance from another, and . . . we could see that almost at every house there was a tenter, and almost on every tenter a piece of cloth, or

PLATE 50

A late eighteenth-century weaver's cottage at Lumb, Yorkshire: a relic of the Domestic
System of industry when spinning and weaving were done at home. The long window
of the upper storey was designed to throw the maximum light on the loom at work.

kersie, or shalloon, for they are three articles of that country's labour; from which the sun glancing, and, as I may say, shining (the white reflecting its rays) to us, I thought it was the most agreeable sight that I ever saw, for the hills, as I say, rising and falling so thick, and the valleys opening sometimes one way, sometimes another, so that sometimes we could see two or three miles this way, sometimes as far another; sometimes like the streets near St. Giles's, called the Seven Dials; we could see through the glades almost every way round us, yet look which way we would, high to the tops, and low to the bottoms, it was all the same; innumerable houses and tenters, and a white piece upon every tenter.

The steep-sided valley of Stroud-Water in Gloucestershire must have presented much the same kind of picture, but Defoe does not attempt any description of it beyond saying that "the clothiers lye all along the banks of this river for near 20 miles"; and Celia Fiennes passed along the high road over the uplands from Gloucester to Bath and failed to notice it at all.

Water-Power and the Early Mills

Early inventions in most industries—except in those requiring large amounts of fixed capital, like the iron industry—benefited the small man, or at least kept him in business. Kay's flying shuttle (1733) and Hargreaves's spinning jenny (1767) multiplied the output of domestic workers in the textile industry without compelling them to enter mills or factories. Not until the application of water-power to machinery, and a consequent great increase in the size of machines, do we begin to see the large factory as an element in the landscape. Before that time the largest unit of production was what Defoe calls in Yorkshire the "work-house." But the great revolution was on its way.

The first true factory built in England was the silk mill built for John and Thomas Lombe at Derby in 1718-22. It was five or six storeys high, employed three hundred men, and was driven by the water-power of the river Derwent. It was, as Mantoux says, in every respect a modern factory, with automatic tools, continuous and unlimited production, and specialized functions for the operatives. Within fifty years there were several silk factories employing four hundred to eight hundred persons, but the silk industry was of secondary importance and did not initiate the Factory System. It was when Power reached the cotton, woollen, and iron industries that the face of the country really began to change on a large scale, and that was not until the 1770s.

Matthew Boulton opened his great Soho factory, in the still unravished country outside Birmingham, in 1765, and shortly afterwards began the manufacture of steam engines. Wedgwood's new large factory at Etruria in the Potteries was opened in 1769. Richard Arkwright, the greatest of the new industrial capitalists, erected his first spinning mill, worked by horses, at Nottingham in 1768, but his second factory, built on a much larger scale at Cromford on the Derwent in 1771, was driven by water power. In the 1760s, too, the Darbys enlarged their ironworks at Coalbrookdale in Shropshire to the largest works of any kind in the kingdom. With these four large-scale factories, the creation of the modern industrial landscape may be said to have begun.

The new mills, factories, and works tended to be in more or less remote places, partly because of the necessity for being near a falling stream for the supply of power, and later to escape too close an inspection and regulation of their un-inhibited activities. One finds these early mills therefore, often windowless and deserted today, in the upper reaches of the moorland valleys on either side of the Pennines. Coalbrookdale, then a romantically beautiful valley, was chosen by the Darbys for their ironworks because here a rapid stream entered the broad, navigable waterway of the Severn. Water was needed in the iron industry both for power and for the transport of heavy materials. It was not long before the ravish-ing of this scene attracted the lament of the poets. Anna Seward, "The Swan of Lichfield," mourned over "Coalbrook Dale" in a poem written about 1785:

> Scene of superfluous grace, and wasted bloom,
> O, violated Colebrook! in an hour,
> To beauty unpropitious and to song,
> The Genius of thy shades, by Plutus brib'd,
> Amid thy grassy lanes, thy wildwood glens,
> Thy knolls and bubbling wells, thy rocks, and streams,
> Slumbers!—while tribes fuliginous invade
> The soft, romantic, consecrated scenes . . .

Some ten years earlier, Arthur Young had already noted the discord between the natural beauty of the landscape and what man had done to it, but he saw, too—and painters also were on the verge of seeing it—that an unrestrained industrial landscape has a considerable element of sublimity about it. "That variety of horrors art has spread at the bottom [of Coalbrookdale]; the noise of the forges, mills, etc., with all their vast machinery, the flames bursting from the furnaces with the burning of the coal and the smoak of the lime kilns, are altogether sublime."

The scale of the new industries brought about a number of visual changes, some of them unexpected. The large sums of fixed capital sunk in the factory buildings and the machinery, and the fact that water-power, unlike human labour, needed no rest, demanded that the new buildings be used by night as well as by day. Shifts of labour were therefore organized, and these tall fortress-like structures were lit from top to bottom at night, and presented something new and dramatic to those who had the leisure to stay outside and contemplate it with detachment. So we get Joseph Wright of Derby as early as 1789 painting Arkwright's cotton mill by night—tiers of tiny yellow lights in the immemorial country darkness of the Derwent valley, the isolated forerunner of those tremendous galaxies of light that one now sees from the Pennine Moors after sundown.[1]

In the eighth book of *The Excursion*, Wordsworth sees the other side of this romantic scene:

[1]It was in 1792 that William Murdoch demonstrated the possibility of using coal gas for lighting, and night-work spread rapidly from the early years of the new century. But Wright's painting, done in 1789, definitely shows the Cromford mill illuminated at night.

When soothing darkness spreads
O'er hill and vale, and the punctual stars,
While all things else are gathering to their homes,
Advance, and in the firmament of heaven
Glitter—but undisturbing, undisturbed;
As if their silent company were charged
With peaceful admonitions for the heart
Of all-beholding Man, earth's thoughtful lord;
Then, in full many a region, once like this
The assured domain of calm simplicity
And pensive quiet, an unnatural light
Prepared for never-resting labour's eyes
Breaks from a many-windowed fabric huge;
And at the appointed hour a bell is heard,
Of harsher import than the curfew-knoll
That spake the Norman Conqueror's stern behest—
A local summons to unceasing toil!
Disgorged are now the Ministers of day;
And, as they issue from the illumined pile,
A fresh band meets them, at the crowded door—
And in the courts—and where the rumbling stream,
That turns the multitude of dizzy wheels,
Glares, like a troubled spirit, in its bed,
Among the rock below. Men, maidens, youths,
Mother and little children, boys and girls,
Enter, and each the wonted task resumes
Within his temple, where is offered up
To Gain, the master idol of the realm,
Perpetual sacrifice.

Arkwright's son built "a very elegant seat," after his father's death in 1792, commanding a view of his works, precisely as Josiah Wedgwood had built Etruria Hall within two hundred yards of his new pottery near Burslem (Plate 51). The early industrialists were proud of their achievements and liked to have them in full view. (Now they take good care to live well out of sight of them.) Matthew Boulton lived close to his works at Soho; but his son bought the estate and country house of Great Tew in Oxfordshire and went to and fro by the coach which is still preserved in the stables there. It was not long before the new factories generated their full powers of ugliness, dirt, and blight, and employers moved away. Etruria Hall still stands, in a landscape of demonic ugliness, backed not by tiers of green woods but by colliery tips higher than itself, and in front, not an ornamental sheet of water but a filthy "flash," dark with coal-dust, arising from subsidence due to coal-mining below.

In the textile districts the new industrial landscape lay in the valley bottoms, which had been comparatively ignored in Defoe's day, when the thickest settlement was on the hillsides. Now, down in the bottoms, arose the new many-storeyed mills, some of them handsome buildings not too unlike the plain country houses of the time. Around them grew up short streets of cottages for the workpeople, run up so quickly that they look as though they were planted flat on the surface, without any foundations; but still there was no congestion. The water-power age produced hamlets, at the most small villages, gathered around a new mill.

PLATE 51

Etruria Hall near Burslem: built by Josiah Wedgwood to face his new pottery (1769) then in open country. Now it has been engulfed in the squalor of coal-mining and is occupied by the Coal Board.

Around Ashton-under-Lyne, for example, where it was reckoned there were nearly a hundred cotton mills within a ten-mile radius—all on the river Tame or its tributaries—we find hamlets in the 1790s with the significant names of Boston, Charlestown, and Botany Bay.

Milford, in the Derwent valley just south of Belper, is a complete and almost untouched late eighteenth-century industrial village. Before 1781 it had consisted of only eight houses, but in that year the Strutts—who had gone into partnership for a time with the then-needy Arkwright—built the large cotton mill that still stands there. They built a great number of cottages for their work-people; a

Unitarian chapel for their spiritual welfare, a school for their children, and a mansion for themselves. It was what the Americans would call a "company town," and is worth seeing as an example of what enlightened employers were doing at the time.

A mile or so north of Milford is the little town of Belper. Until 1777 this was a poor place inhabited chiefly by nailers. Then came Mr. Jedidiah Strutt, who built

PLATE 52

Jedidiah Strutt's cotton mill at Belper (1776), driven by water-power. The round structure embodied some revolutionary ideas. It was an attempt to make a fire-proof building, the internal compartments being designed to localize any outbreak wherever it occurred. Further, the foreman sat at the hub of the wheel so to speak and could thence supervise the workers in each compartment.

a cotton mill on the Derwent and shortly afterwards three more. Here, too, the Strutts provided a chapel, and day-schools and Sunday-schools, and another mansion. At the north end of the town stands one of their great eighteenth-century mills, now under the name of the English Sewing Cotton Company, which incorporated several new and striking features (Plate 52). By 1811 Belper was the second largest town in Derbyshire.

The Derwent valley, which exemplifies along its bottom so much industrial history of the water-power age, attracted large mills from the beginning by reason of its fast-flowing river; but not everyone admired the result as Wright of Derby did. Uvedale Price in his *Essays on the Picturesque* (1810) observed: "When I consider the striking natural beauties of such a river as that at Matlock, and the effect of the seven-storey buildings that have been raised there, and on other beautiful streams, for cotton manufactories, I am inclined to think that nothing can equal them for the purpose of disbeautifying an enchanting piece of scenery; and that economy had produced, what the greatest ingenuity, if a prize were given for ugliness, could not surpass."

Mills arose in the remote valleys below the moors, and hamlets and villages quickly clustered around them. But established towns too were advancing over the surrounding fields. Trees and hedges were torn up, red-brick or gritstone streets, short and straight, multiplied every year, even before the Age of Steam: Sheffield, Birmingham, Liverpool, Manchester, all were on the move. According to Langford, "The traveller who visits [Birmingham] once in six months supposes himself well acquainted with her, but he may chance to find a street of houses in the autumn, where he saw his horse at grass in the spring." The population of the town doubled in the last forty years of the eighteenth century (35,000 people in 1760; 73,000 in 1801), but it was as yet far from being the dark and horrible landscape that it eventually became. Even in the early years of the nineteenth century the middle-class streets had "prospects" of the country and the older working-class houses at least still had gardens. The dirt and overcrowding came with the Steam Age in the nineteenth century.

Sheffield, on the other hand, was "very populous and large" in Queen Anne's time when Defoe traversed it, and its houses were already "dark and black" from the smoke of the forges. Two generations later the population had trebled and the pall of industrial smoke had become permanent. As Anna Seward saw it:

> Grim Wolverhampton lights her smouldering fires,
> And Sheffield, smoke-involv'd; dim where she stands
> Circled by lofty mountains, which condense
> Her dark and spiral wreaths to drizzling rains
> Frequent and sullied. . . .

In Lancashire and the Potteries the worst had still to come. Chorley was, when Aikin wrote (1795), "a small, neat market town" with its river flowing through a pleasant valley, turning "several mills, engines, and machines." It possessed the first water-driven factory to be erected in Lancashire (1777). Preston was "a handsome well-built town, with broad regular streets, and many good houses. The earl of Derby has a large modern mansion in it. The place is rendered gay by assemblies and other places of amusement, suited to the genteel style of the inhabitants." Aikin notes that the cotton industry had just come to the town. In the south of the county what was to be the most appalling town of all—St. Helens—was just beginning to defile its surroundings. The British Plate Glass Manufactory had been erected at Ravenhead, near the village, in 1773, and other glassworks followed. And about the year 1780 "a most extensive copper-work" was erected to smelt and refine the ore from Paris mountain in Anglesey. The atmosphere was being poisoned, every green thing blighted, and every stream fouled

PLATE 53

St. Helens, Lancashire. The chemical and glass industries produce more unusable waste than any other: hence this tormented landscape.

with chemical fumes and waste (Plate 53). Here, and in the Potteries and the Black Country especially, the landscape of Hell was foreshadowed.

Steam-Power and Slums

Water power in itself created no smoke or dirt. Only where industries used coal directly, like the forges of Sheffield, were towns yet blackened and the air poisoned; and only where they produced "waste" in great quantities, such as in coal-mining, glassworks, and chemicals, was the landscape beginning to acquire that sterile covering of "tips," that were destined to go on piling up until they produced a mountain landscape in miniature; until the vast range of coal-tips around the old town of Wigan, for example, could be sardonically nicknamed the Wigan Alps and be illustrated in later years under that name on picture postcards. But until steam-power became generally used, these landscapes did not achieve their final horrific form.

Although Newcomen had produced the first practical steam-engine in the early years of the eighteenth century, it was capable only of a simple back-and-forth or up-and-down motion and therefore disappeared underground to be used for pumping water out of mines. Nor, when Boulton and Watt began producing steam-engines, from 1775 onwards, was there much perceptible change in industry for many years. Between 1775 and 1800, when their patent expired, 321 steam-engines were built. Of these, nearly one-third went into cotton mills, and the remainder were distributed between ironworks, collieries, copper-mines, canals (for pumping), and breweries. Even with all the Newcomen engines that still continued to be made, and the piracies of Watt's engine, the use of steam power was neither general nor extensive in 1800. The Steam Age, with its dramatic impact upon the landscape, begins effectively in the early nineteenth century.

We are not concerned here with the general effects upon industry and the English economy of the use of steam-power, but with its visible effects upon the landscape, and these are now obvious enough. Steam-power meant a new and intense concentration of large-scale industry and of the labour-force to man it. It meant that manufacturers no longer needed to seek their power where there was fast-running water, especially in the higher reaches of lonely dales, but found it near the canals, which brought coal to them cheaply, or directly upon the coal-fields themselves. So emerged what Wordsworth called "social Industry." No longer need they go out into the wilderness and create a village or a hamlet to house their labour. Manufacturers ran up their mills, factories, and works on the edge of existing towns, and their workers were housed in streets of terrace-houses built rapidly on the vacant ground all around the factory.

Industry spread over the lower-lying parts of the towns, leaving the hills for the residences of the well-to-do, but this was not a conscious piece of "zoning." Large-scale industries in pre-railway days needed canal-side sites both for bringing in their coal and other raw materials and for taking away their heavy products. Thus they chose the flatter and lower ground where the canals lay. Moreover, it was the low-lying areas that were vacant when the industrialists appeared on the scene, for earlier generations had wisely avoided building on them wherever they could. The sites were there waiting. And again, it was easier and cheaper to build on a flat site than on a hillside. As a consequence most of the new streets of working-class houses were also built on land that presented difficult drainage problems (not that anyone except the victims gave much thought to this), and the sanitary conditions soon became appalling. The slums were born. The word *slum*, first used in the 1820s, has its origin in the old provincial word *slump*, meaning "wet mire." The word *slam* in Low German, Danish and Swedish, means "mire": and that roughly described the dreadful state of the streets and courtyards on these undrained sites. It need hardly be said that the industrialist of the Steam Age did not build his own house near the works, as the country factory owners had done. He went to dwell on the "residential heights" and walked down to the mill each day.

But there is more meaning in the word *slum* than simply a foul street or yard: it denotes also a certain quality of housing. In the early nineteenth century the quality of working-class houses, as structures, deteriorated rapidly. The industrialists of the water-power age, out in the open country, had put up houses for their work-people—as at Cromford, Mellor and Styal, where many of them may still be seen—which were, in Professor Ashton's words, "not wanting in amenity and comfort" and even possessed a certain quality of design and proportion.[1] These decent working-class houses were put up in the 1770s and 1780s, where land was cheap and when building materials were plentiful, wages in the building trades relatively low, and money relatively cheap.

With the outbreak of twenty years' war in 1793, the price of materials and wages in the building trades both began to rise steadily. Interest rates, too, increased and remained high for a generation. Since at least two-thirds of the rent of a house consists of interest charges, the rise in interest rates alone was sufficient to bring about a drastic reduction in the size and quality of working-class houses in order to preserve an "economic rent." Further, land inside the older towns was acquiring a scarcity value, above all in the towns that were surrounded by open fields, so that they could not grow outwards (see chapter IX), and a steady rise in the price of land for building was added to the rise in the price of borrowed money. Possibly, too, the building trade was invaded by a new class of speculator who made conditions even worse than they need have been by extracting high profits out of the unprecedented demand for cheap houses. No one has studied this particular class of parasite, how he worked, or what fortunes he made. One often wonders in what opulence his descendants live today forgetful, or perhaps ignorant, of the origin of their wealth. Their forebears would make a fruitful study.

Bad materials and fewer of them, and bad workmanship, reduced the costs of building. Houses run up in the courts of Birmingham in the 1820s and 1830s cost £60 each to build. Birmingham specialized in close, dark, and filthy courtyards: there were over two thousand of these in the town in the 1830s, and many of their houses were built back to back in order to get the maximum number on to each expensive acre. The local medical men did not object, but rather commended them for their cheapness. At first some of them had a deceptive brightness, but their abominable quality soon revealed itself and decay rapidly set in. Decent people moved out if they could, and the born-squalid moved in: the swamp of the slums spread a few years behind the speculative builder everywhere.

[1] Ashton, *The Industrial Revolution*, 160.

Open spaces inside the older towns vanished rapidly. The last remnant of Birmingham Heath was enclosed in 1799, and was built over forthwith with eight new streets. Precisely the same thing was happening around the Lancashire towns

PLATE 54

The Potteries landscape at Burslem, Staffordshire. This sad picture of an industrial landscape should be examined under a powerful reading-glass. There is the church, rebuilt in 1717, when the pottery manufacture was flourishing with 43 small manufactories, carried on by families until they were superseded in the Industrial Revolution. Next to the church-yard, children play around the Board School. All around, their homes lie intermingled with the filthy potbanks with their characteristic bottle shapes rising above the roof-tops. A blackened Anglican church, to cater for the enlarged Victorian population, stands in the middle of the view. Derelict ground occupies much of the scene. It is a formless landscape, usually thickly blanketed with smoke. The photograph was taken on a favourable day or it could not have been taken at all. Imagine being born amid this ugliness: or worse still, buried among it.

also, where the ancient commons were enclosed and grabbed by the private speculator for building, as at Oldham. Only Preston managed to save its commons from the vultures, and to transform some of them eventually into public parks. Not only the commons but the large gardens of the eighteenth-century bourgeoisie disappeared under bricks and mortar. The house of Baskerville, the eminent Birmingham printer, was sold in 1788 and the seven acres of land that surrounded it were advertised as "a very desirable spot to build upon." In these older towns, too, the large houses of the middle class were divided into tenements

PLATE 55

Cotton mills and Victorian housing for the working-class at Preston, Lancashire. Preston in the eighteenth century was "a rendezvous of fashion and society." Aikin in 1795 said that it was "a handsome, well-built town . . . rendered gay by assemblies and other places of amusement, suited to the genteel style of the inhabitants." The Earl of Derby had a town house here. When cotton spinning was introduced in 1777, there were six thousand inhabitants. A hundred years later there were ninety thousand, and the town had a bad reputation for strikes. The housing surely explains a great deal: neither good enough to promote happiness nor bad enough to produce hopelessness.

to house the swarming population, and factories and warehouses went up on their gardens and orchards. Slowly the other features of the industrial towns were added: Anglican churches, Nonconformist chapels, schools, and public houses. Public parks came in the 1840s, and public libraries a few years later; later still

perhaps the grandiose Town Hall, by no means always to be despised as architecture.

Entirely new towns grew out of hamlets in the industrial north and Midlands.
The germ of Middlesbrough was a single farmhouse near the banks of the un-
sullied Tees in 1830: by 1880 it was a town of more than fifty thousand people.
Barrow-in-Furness, too, sprang from a single house, grew into a fishing village of
about three hundred people by the 1840s, and by 1878 was a town of forty
thousand. South Shields, St. Helens, and Birkenhead all shot up quickly during
the first half of the nineteenth century. "Meanwhile," said Wordsworth in *The
Excursion* (1814):

> Meanwhile, at social Industry's command,
> How quick, how vast an increase! From the germ
> Of some poor hamlet, rapidly produced
> Here a huge town, continuous and compact,
> Hiding the face of earth for leagues—and there,
> Where not a habitation stood before,
> Abodes of men irregularly massed
> Like trees in forests,—spread through spacious tracts,
> O'er which the smoke of unremitting fires
> Hangs permanent, and plentiful as wreaths
> Of vapour glittering in the morning sun.
> And, wheresoe'er the traveller turns his steps,
> He sees the barren wilderness erased,
> Or disappearing . . .

Nor was the industrial landscape represented solely in the great towns, for
between them stretched miles of torn and poisoned countryside—the mountains
of waste from mining and other industries; the sheets of sullen water, known as
"flashes," which had their origin in subsidence of the surface as a result of mining
below; the disused pit-shafts; the derelict and stagnant canals. The train-journey
between Leeds and Sheffield shows one this nineteenth-century landscape to
perfection. In the Lancashire township of Ince there are today twenty-three pit-
shafts covering 199 acres, one large industrial slag-heap covering six acres, nearly
250 acres of land under water or marsh due to mining subsidence, another 150
acres liable to flooding, and thirty-six disused pit-shafts. This is the landscape of
coal-mining. As for the Black Country, one can hardly begin to describe it.
Dickens has an horrific description of it in *The Old Curiosity Shop* (1841), when it
had reached the rock bottom of filth and ugliness, and of human degradation.
The early industrialists were not "insensitive to the appeal of the country: the
beauty of Cromford and Millers Dale suffered little by the enterprise of Arkwright, and stretches of the Goyt and the Bollin owe something to Oldknow and

the Gregs."[1] But the later industrialists, the heirs of the Steam Age, were completely and grotesquely insensitive. No scruples weakened their lust for money they made their money and left behind their muck.

The industrial landscape is not confined to the north of England and the West Midlands. In Cornwall for instance one finds two distinct landscapes of industry, one dead, the other still active. Over central Cornwall, particularly to

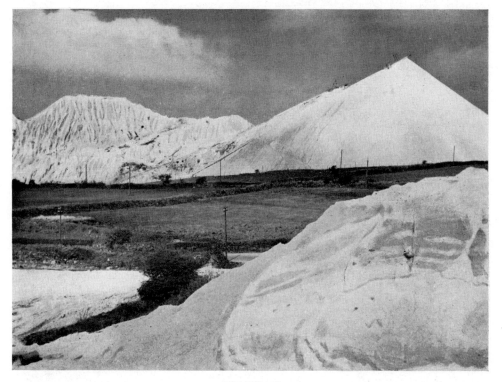

PLATE 56

The china-clay landscape near St. Austell: the industry produces vast quantities of sterile
waste on which nothing will grow, but it has the advantage of being white and of
sparkling in the sun. At a distance it is an almost lunar landscape.

the north-west of St. Austell, are the spoil-heaps of the china-clay industry, an almost lunar landscape that one sees gleaming on the horizon from almost any hill-top in the county (Plate 56). And there is the equally striking landscape of the vanished tin-mining industry: the windowless engine-houses, the monolithic chimney stacks against the skyline, the ruined cottages of an old mining hamlet, and the stony spoil-heaps—a purely nineteenth-century landscape, and perhaps

[1]Ashton, op. cit., 157.

because of its setting, the most appealing of all the industrial landscapes of England, in no way ugly but indeed possessing a profound melancholy beauty (Plate 57). Just across the Devonshire border is the old mining landscape of Blanchdown, west of Tavistock, where, in the middle decades of the nineteenth century, the Devon Great Consols was the richest copper mine in the world: now its miles of

PLATE 57

The derelict landscape of abandoned tin-mines, near St. Cleer, Cornwall: a complete settlement has disappeared here during the nineteenth century. Only roofless and windowless
ruins remain. Such a landscape is best seen towards sunset, when it becomes vastly melancholy and mysterious.

spoil-heaps have created a silent and desolate beauty of their own, and foxes and snakes haunt the broken buildings and the glades between.

There is a point, as Arthur Young saw, when industrial ugliness becomes sublime. And indeed the new landscape produced some fine dramatic compositions such as the railway viaduct over the smoking town of Stockport (Plate 58); or the sight of Bradford at night from the moorland hills to the north; or of the smoky silhouette of Nottingham on a winter evening as seen from the south-bound train on the Eastern Region line; or the city of Sheffield in full blast on a murky morning;

even (one thinks sometimes) the sight of long gas-lit streets of red brick working-class houses in a Victorian town with not a tree or a bush in sight: only the lamps shining on pavements blanched by the autumn evening wind.

PLATE 58

Stockport in 1848: industry and the railway together create fine new dramatic compositions in the town landscapes.

SELECT BIBLIOGRAPHY

AIKIN, J., *A Description of the Country round Manchester* (1795).
ASHTON, T. S., *The Industrial Revolution* (1948).
AUBIN, R. A., *Topographical Poetry in Eighteenth-Century England* (1936).
COURT, W. H. B., *The Rise of the Midland Industries, 1600-1838* (1938).
DEFOE, DANIEL, *A Tour through England and Wales* (Everyman ed., n.d.).
GILL, C., and BRIGGS, A., *History of Birmingham* (1952).
KLINGENDER, F., *Art and the Industrial Revolution* (1947).
MANTOUX, P. J., *The Industrial Revolution in the Eighteenth Century* (1928).

VIII

Roads, Canals, and Railways

Roads

THE roads of England have attracted a considerable literature, and it might seem difficult to say anything very new. It would be attempting the impossible to write about all the varieties of roads there are in England in the space of a few pages: such a wide-ranging discussion would be full of familiar generalizations and would make very dull reading. Let us take instead one comparatively small piece of country, which contains every variety of road from the prehistoric trackway to the modern by-pass, so that the detailed differences are brought out: for the interest of an enquiry such as this, and one cannot say it too often, lies in the detail of the subject. For this purpose I choose the country depicted on Sheet 145 of the Ordnance Survey (6th edition), which runs from the edge of Oxford northwards to a few miles beyond Banbury, and from Chipping Norton on the west to beyond Brackley in Northamptonshire on the east. One could find as much to write about on almost any other sheet of the Ordnance Survey; and one could indeed write a whole chapter about a single sheet of the $2\frac{1}{2}$-inch map, covering only some six miles each way.

A merely casual inspection of sheet 145 reveals a number of named roads suggestive of several different ages and uses. There are the Welsh Road, the Salt Way, the Port Way, Akeman Street, Traitor's Ford Lane, and Banbury Lane; and besides these named roads a considerable number of roads, lanes, and paths that excite our curiosity by their directness for miles across almost uninhabited country, or by their association with parish boundaries or ancient earthworks (like Aves Ditch), or some other suspicious circumstance.

Banbury Lane, now in part a main motor-road, is the oldest of the roads on the map, though there is little about it today to indicate its great antiquity. It is a part of the so-called Jurassic Way which runs along the junction of the upper Lias and the lower Oolite like a corridor, eventually linking the Bristol Avon with the Humber.[1] The course of this important trackway across sheet 145 is perfectly clear. It makes its appearance on the bold ridge by the Rollright Stones, where it forms the boundary between Warwickshire and Oxfordshire for part of its course. Keeping along the watershed between the Warwickshire Avon and the Cherwell, it runs past Oatley Hill Farm to Wigginton Heath. Thence it drops down to cross the Cherwell at Banbury. East of Banbury, where it has attracted the name of Banbury Lane for some twenty miles, it follows a winding course along the

---

[1]See the essay by W. F. Grimes in *Aspects of Archæology*, 144-71, and some pages in O. G. S. Crawford, *Archæology in the Field*, 81-5.

watershed between the Cherwell and the Great Ouse. For a considerable distance it is now followed by a main road (A.422 and B.4525), but near Culworth it becomes a narrow lane, running through almost deserted country, past Adstone Lodge and Foxley to Cold Higham. Here we are in the uttermost depths of the Midlands. After Cold Higham it crosses Watling Street, runs past the important Iron Age hill-fort of Hunsbury, and reaches the crossing of the Nene at North-ampton. There is no need to trace it farther. Mr. O. G. S. Crawford believes the

PLATE 59

The Ridgeway along the chalk downs of Berkshire, at Hackpen Hill. In this open country these ancient trackways retain something of their original character.

Jurassic Way to be of Iron Age date in view of its strong associations with hill-forts and finds of this period, though he does not dismiss the possibility of its being older. Whether it goes back to the Iron Age or the Bronze Age, however, it has lost its original character as a wide trackway across open country. To see what it was once like we have to turn to the chalk downlands, notably the ridgeway that follows the crest of the Berkshire Downs (Plate 59) or the Icknield Way near Royston in Hertfordshire.

In its present form the Banbury Lane represents a great narrowing-down of what was originally not a single track (so that one cannot be too precise about its prehistoric course) but a more or less open corridor, bounded on either side by dense forest, in places several miles wide. The narrowing-down of this primitive trade-route took place, perhaps in stages, in Saxon and early medieval times as more and more land was taken in for arable cultivation. On the chalk downlands, which have been under sheep pasture ever since the Iron Age, something like the original appearance of a similar trackway has been preserved, but in the arable Midlands it must have disappeared fairly early. We know that in the eleventh century the Jurassic Way in Oxfordshire was the main road to Northampton, probably joining it with the important town of Gloucester, and throughout the Middle Ages it was a market-road, linking one market-town with the next in a long series. Its present course can almost certainly be dated from late Saxon times. Northampton began life as a fortified position in the early tenth century—it is first recorded as a name in the year 917—and soon became the shire town. From this time we can probably date the development of Banbury Lane as a road rather than a wide corridor.

Deviations from ancient routes appeared at an early date. It is clear from the map (and other evidence) that the original trackway near Great Rollright ran due north, across the Stour and straight up Traitor's Ford Lane (this must be a medieval name), along the broken lip of the escarpment to Edge Hill. Thence it described a great arc through Fenny Compton and Byfield to rejoin the other road at Cold Higham (Crawford). Crawford considers that the Saxon road to Northampton was a later shortening of this ancient trackway; even so, parts of the Banbury "cut-off" are themselves prehistoric in date.

The other deviation, that from near Culworth to Watling Street, is of recent date. The old lane was in use down to comparatively recent times as a through-road from Northampton to Banbury. On the first edition of the one-inch map (1834) it is shown as boldly as the lanes linking the villages of Canons Ashby and Moreton Pinkney, and similarly on the map of 1887. The Lane must have fallen out of use in this stretch almost within living memory.

There is at least one other prehistoric ridgeway on sheet 145. This has continued in use to the present day and carries a vast traffic between Oxford and Coventry and Birmingham. It is now A.423, which began as a prehistoric ridge-way along the watershed between the Cherwell and the Evenlode. It ran from a crossing of the Thames at or near Oxford (perhaps ultimately from the Berkshire Ridgeway) northwards to join the Jurassic Way near Banbury. There are remains of long barrows and of megalithic tombs at various points along its course. Later it was taken over and paved by the Romans from a point north of Oxford to Sturdy's Castle, where it met the east-west road of Akeman Street. Medieval charters along its course refer to it as "the ridgeway." It apparently remained in continuous use throughout medieval times; it figures as the main road from Oxford to Banbury in Ogilby's road-book (1675); it was turnpiked in the eighteenth century, and it still follows its original course after some three thousand years. Because it has remained in use all this time, and has been continually adapted to heavier traffic, it has lost its original character except in two respects. It still commands extensive and airy views over the valleys to the east and west, and in places its broad grass verges betray something of its original width before the road was metalled.

Of the Roman roads of the district, one need say little. Akeman Street will serve as an example. A good deal of it to the east of the Cherwell remains in use as a main road (A.41 and A.4095), the only important break in the line being caused by the growth of the Saxon town of Bicester, a mile to the north, in place of the now-vanished Romano-British town of Alchester. Just short of the Cherwell, however, the line of the road disappears from the one-inch map, and to the west of the river for many miles it can be followed only as a continuous hedge-line, a field-path, and a bit of lane here and there. Its entire course can, however, be traced without much hesitation.

Among other features of the road it is interesting to see how it still forms the northern boundary of Kirtlington Park, to the east of the Cherwell, and the southern boundary of Tackley Park, on the other side of the river. The immense continuity of English boundaries is fascinating. Akeman Street was the boundary between what is now Tackley Park and Whitehill Farm as early as the year 1004 when King Ethelred gave the small estate of Whitehill to St. Frideswide's monastery at Oxford, and it is still a boundary though the Roman road has vanished from sight. Not many miles away, two estates meet, between Wootton and Steeple Barton, precisely where they met in a charter dated 958, and possibly for some considerable time before that.

The colonization of new land, and its demarcation into private estates, created thousands of miles of *boundaries* for the first time. Often these new boundaries followed a stream or a trackway that already existed; but very often they created their own boundary lanes or *meres* (from the Old English word (ge)maere, "boundary"). This is the origin of a great number of "green lanes" on the map which run for a few miles, separating parishes on either side but eventually petering out. They are to be distinguished, therefore, from the green lanes that run for more considerable distances, which are portions of through-roads dating from prehistoric times. Sometimes these ancient estate-boundaries took the form of deep V-shaped ditches, much more impressive than the ordinary ditch for drainage, and therefore puzzling until one realizes their special origin.

These green lanes are sometimes ten to fifteen yards wide, still entirely grassed over, and used only by tractors and cattle. An example of this kind is Dornford Lane, which runs parallel with the Banbury to Oxford road for some miles to the north of Woodstock. The age and original purpose of this road, like that of many similar green lanes, are puzzling. At its northern end it has no obvious beginning, but it assumes a recognizable course at Barton Lodge in Steeple Barton parish. Thence it runs directly southwards for $4\frac{1}{2}$ miles to Woodstock. For centuries the lane served no doubt as a cattle-road, but why did it come into existence at all, and when? It runs so near the ancient Banbury-Oxford road (within a quarter of a mile in places) that it cannot have served as another through-road. One might suspect then that it originated as a boundary—a green *mere* between two ancient

PLATE 60

The Fosse Way near Northleach in Gloucestershire: now a modern motor road which passes through no village for many miles. This is a characteristic of Roman roads where they have remained in use, for the Anglo-Saxons almost invariably founded their villages off these roads as a measure of safety.

estates—but there is no sign of a boundary along it today. The parochial and manorial boundaries (both very ancient) follow either the Banbury-Oxford road or else take a winding course between the main road and the lane. At no point on its way to Woodstock is it followed by a boundary that is known to be ancient.

It was not a through-road for Saxon or medieval traffic; it did not come into existence as a boundary; it was not originally a drove-road, for cattle-drovers took over existing tracks and lanes and did not create their own except in special circumstances. We are left with one possibility—that it originated as a road from one of the royal demesne farms to the royal hunting lodge of Woodstock. The Anglo-Saxon kings are known to have used Woodstock (now Blenheim) Park as a hunting-ground. It is first heard of about the year 1000, and a charter of 1005 speaks of the *Haga* or enclosure which existed here. At the other end of the lane lay the manor of *Bertone*: no amount of ingenuity can carry the lane any farther north than this.

Barton means literally "barley farm" or "corn farm," but later came to have the special meaning of "demesne farm." Although by 1086 the Barton estate had been split up into a number of manors, of which only one was still in the hands of the king himself, there can be little doubt that before the Conquest the Anglo-Saxon kings had had here an estate of some seven thousand acres which they kept in hand for their own supplies. Nor can there be much doubt that when they were in residence at Woodstock these supplies were called upon, and were carried in carts along the wide green track now called Dornford Lane. The lane came into existence for this special purpose not later than the tenth century: in no other way can we explain its peculiar and limited course. The fact that the lane runs so wide and straight also tells us that when it came into existence the open arable fields of Barton and Wootton did not yet extend so far. It clearly ran through uncultivated land originally.

I have dwelt upon this small piece of local topography in order to show how here and there, and possibly oftener than we think, roads came into existence to serve a special and limited purpose. Most of these curious little by-roads and lanes developed in Saxon times. In the same piece of country, for example, we read of "the wood way" in Saxon charters: these are the lanes that grew up between certain villages and the distant woods in which they had rights or pickings. Many of these tiny lanes survive, some incorporated into motor-roads.

It is likely that a considerable number of Romano-British by-roads came into existence in the same way for limited purposes and yet remain to be discovered on the map or on the ground. Mr. Margary's book on *Roman Ways in the Weald* was a revelation of how much can be unearthed by a patient and detailed examination of one region. There can be no doubt that on Sheet 145 of the Ordnance Survey, with which we are immediately concerned, there are by-roads which will prove eventually to be Romano-British in origin. We have been bemused too long by the great military roads of the Romans and have not given enough thought and research to the local "economic" roads that developed during the two or three centuries that followed the conquest and the brief phase of military occupation.

In many parts of England, roads marked as "Salt Way" may be found. On Sheet 145 there is a short stretch of lane so described immediately south of Banbury. Salt was one of the very few necessaries of life that could not be produced anywhere and had to be transported from the centres of production on the sea-coasts, on tidal rivers, and from certain inland centres. At Ingoldmells, to the north of Skegness, heaps of debris have been found to be the result of salt-workings in the late Bronze Age. In 1086 there were 278 salt-pools in Lincolnshire, in Sussex 285, and many other coastal counties had a considerable salt industry at this period.

At an early date, the inland brine springs of Droitwich and Cheshire were discovered and used for the manufacture of salt. The earliest reference to Droitwich salt occurs in 716, when King Ethelbald granted a salt-pit there to Evesham Abbey. By 1086, Droitwich salt was being widely distributed over the Midlands; King William himself had eighty-five salt pans here. According to Domesday Book, no fewer than sixty-eight manors and estates had the right to receive salt from Droitwich, including Princes Risborough, some seventy miles away in Buckinghamshire.[1] Mr. F. T. S. Houghton has worked out many of the salt-ways of the West Midlands, and considers that the short stretch of Salt Way near Banbury was part of the route taken between Droitwich and Princes Risborough, by way of Stratford-upon-Avon and Aynho. It is therefore of Saxon date, and is an example of a track used for a special purpose. It is doubtful, however, how far the salt trade created its own lanes and tracks. For the most part it made use of trackways already established and ancient, though it is possible that new pieces of track were trampled out where the direct line required it. Certainly the crossing of the Avon at Stratford is extremely ancient.

Salt ways present no special features that distinguish them from other roads and lanes on the map or on the ground. Nor have the medieval market-roads that developed all over England, particularly in the twelfth and thirteenth centuries, any special characteristics. Most of these, too, developed along existing paths, the paths that ran from village to village in Saxon times, though here and there they may have called for a new piece to complete the chain of paths. Many medieval market-towns were originally villages of little note, and have sunk back again into obscurity, but their former importance is betrayed by the spider's net of roads that still converge upon them. Deddington, in north Oxfordshire, is an example of such a village, and there are several similar examples in every English county.

Few new roads were created between Saxon times and the turnpike and "enclosure" roads of the eighteenth century. Like the salt traffic, the cattle trade that developed so strongly from the sixteenth century onwards moved along existing green lanes and trackways. Since most of England south of the Trent was now in a state of cultivation, there was little opportunity for drovers to strike across country and create new lines of movement, though on the moorlands north of the Trent they may have done so. The drovers' roads of the Midlands were particularly important, for it was along these that the great traffic in cattle from

[1] F. T. S. Houghton, Salt Ways, *Birmingham Archæological Society Transactions and Proceedings,* vol. 54 (1932).

Wales to London and the Midland markets found its leisurely way. The Welsh Road, which occurs here and there on the map of the Midlands, refers to this cross-country traffic. This road can be picked up just outside Kenilworth, whence it runs in a south-easterly direction through Offchurch across country to Southam, and thence through an almost uninhabited landscape towards the Northampton-shire uplands. Near Marston Doles the route turned south, past Priors Hardwick, Upper and Lower Bodington, to Aston-le-Walls, near which it crosses the Banbury-Daventry road. It goes on to Culworth, where it meets Banbury Lane, and may have proceeded along this Lane to the great markets of Northampton, where cattle were sold in large numbers for fattening on the rich Midland pastures. In the other direction, one can trace the route vaguely from the Welsh border into the Midlands. The Anchor Inn, on the border of Wales and England, high up on the far western side of Clun Forest, was the great point of assembly for drovers coming out of Wales. Thence one recognized route led on to Ludlow, and so due east through Bewdley and Bromsgrove, through the country south of Birmingham, to the point near Kenilworth where we previously picked it up on the map.

The drove-roads of England have yet to be identified and pieced together. They have been written about in Scotland and Wales, and a fascinating piece of field-work and historical research awaits someone in this country who is not afraid to use his feet as well as his head. For many miles along the Leicestershire-Lincoln-shire border there runs a green lane known as Sewstern Lane or The Drift. This road has a continuous history from the Bronze Age onwards. After it had been superseded in the seventeenth century by the Great North Road, which runs to the east of it through more inhabited country, Sewstern Lane became a recognized route by which cattle from Scotland and the North of England reached the Midland pastures and London: hence its later name of The Drift (Plate 62). Parts of it have been taken over for a secondary motor-road, but much of it remains remote and quiet, rarely disturbed by a human voice.

The old drove-roads made their own contribution to the landscape in the way-side inns that grew up to cater specially for drovers in lonely stretches of country, and in the "stances" beside them where the cattle were shut up and rested for the night. After the middle of the nineteenth century, animals were moved by train (and now by lorry), and the drovers' lanes were deserted for good. Now they make some of the quietest walking in England away from the high moors. For they always avoided towns and traffic; they avoided also the larger roads which became turnpikes in the eighteenth century and were subject to tolls, and they were short-turfed for the cattle and sheep, grazing as they went.

The turnpikes, though important in the history of roads, contributed little to the landscape that did not exist before. For the most part they took over existing routes, though in the hillier parts of the country they were responsible for the making of entirely new stretches of road where the older roads tackled gradients suitable only for foot-passengers and pack-horses. These new roads may often be

PLATE 61

Packhorse track and bridge in Wasdale, Cumberland. Bridges of this primitive style and construction are undatable: they are an almost ageless type, like the clapper bridges on Dartmoor.

recognized by the fact that they run for miles without passing through a village, or indeed much habitation at all apart from their own toll-houses (their most notable addition to the scene) and an inn or two attracted to the roadside by the prospect of traffic. In the industrial counties such as Lancashire the new towns called for entirely new turnpike roads between them, and the old road pattern was more drastically altered.

Certain important roads, too, were altered out of all recognition. The Roman

PLATE 62

Sewstern Lane, otherwise called The Drift. The counties of Lincolnshire and Leicestershire meet along this ancient track for many miles. It began as a Bronze Age trackway linking the navigable Welland at Stamford with the Trent near Newark and was continuously used down to recent times. In the eighteenth century, the cattle-drovers used this track . (hence its alternative name of The Drift) in preference to the Great North Road on which they would have had to pay tolls.

Watling Street, which had become the London to Holyhead road, was vastly improved and largely remade by Telford between 1820 and 1828. Cuttings were made to ease the original gradients, causeways laid down in difficult places, and the roadway widened. Much of this engineering work was wasted at the time, for it was done on the eve of the Railway Age and never put to good use—not until the twentieth century. An incidental effect of the turnpike movement was the construction of fine bridges to carry heavy coach-traffic. There is a notable series over the Thames from Lechlade down to Staines, and there are innumerable others up and down the country. Near Exeter, the old Exeter to Crediton road had been doubled in width (from 9½ to 20 feet) and so made necessary a new bridge over the Creedy. This bridge (Cowley Bridge), built by James Green (the county surveyor) in 1813-14, is so fine in design that it has already been scheduled and protected as an ancient monument.

Milestones make their appearance along the roads during the reign of Charles II. They were known to the Romans, but no one afterwards used them until the Dover Road was given mile-marks in 1663. Stones were also set up along the Great North Road in 1708, but the first true milestone to be set up in Britain since Roman times was that at Trumpington, just outside Cambridge, in 1727, where it is still to be seen. The earliest milestones were the result of private enterprise. Official milestones were authorized on the London to Chester road in 1744, but they did not become compulsory until 1773. An act of that year ordered all turnpike trusts to provide guide-posts and milestones on their roads.

Guide-posts of a sort are much older than milestones. Rough granite crosses, for example, marked the track across Dartmoor in the thirteenth century; and a German traveller in 1598 found a pre-Reformation wayside cross acting as a guide-post in Kent. A few new guide-posts appeared here and there in the late seventeenth century, and an act of 1698 ordered justices to erect standing-posts at cross-roads; but the act seems to have been ineffective. Guide-posts did not become compulsory until the act of 1773. One of the earliest private guide-posts stands on Broadway Hill, in the Cotswolds, set up by Nathan Izod in 1669. A post dated 1705 stands at Hopton in Derbyshire; and at Bicton, in East Devon, is a fine brick pillar dated 1743, with directions and scriptural texts on its four sides. Yorkshire has many early guide-posts. The older guide-posts stood several feet high for the benefit of travellers in coaches and on horseback, but in recent years those on the main roads have been considerably reduced in height for the convenience of motorists.

In recent years, too, other changes have been made in English roads. Great by-pass roads, like the East Lancashire By-Pass, now plunge straight across the country, regardless of contours, using cuttings and embankments to keep as even a gradient as possible. They are entirely without beauty. Is there anything uglier in the whole landscape than an arterial by-pass road, except an airfield? Old roads have been straightened, and have lost all their character, historic and otherwise. Sheet 145 of the Ordnance Survey, with which we began, furnishes an excellent example to finish with. The main road from Oxford to Bicester (A.43) runs dead straight for several miles and might well be taken for a fine piece of Roman road. But the first edition of the one-inch map, dated 1833, shows a very different sort of road, a narrow Saxon road winding and zig-zagging every few yards. Only in recent years has it been straightened.

Canals

The canals of England are mainly the creation of the last forty years of the eighteenth century and the first quarter of the nineteenth, and they introduced a number of distinctive changes into the landscape. Not only did they bring stretches of water into country often lacking in them, as in many parts of the Midlands, with consequent changes in bird and plant life, but they also brought—mostly for the first time—aqueducts, cuttings and embankments, tunnels, locks, lifts and inclined planes, and many attractive bridges, and they greatly influenced the growth and appearance of many towns. One town, indeed, was entirely the creation of canals (Stourport in Worcestershire) and is worth seeing solely on that account (Plate 64).

It is true that the Romans had constructed two or three artificial waterways in this country large enough to be regarded as canals: the Car Dyke that winds from Peterborough up to Lincoln, the Foss Dyke joining the Witham and the Trent, and perhaps the Itchen Dyke from Winchester to the Itchen. But these were hardly distinguishable from drainage channels, having none of the features that we associate peculiarly with canals. The first true canal, with locks and a towpath, was that constructed by the municipal authorities of Exeter between 1564 and 1567 to allow barges to pass around the weirs on the river and to reach the city. On this canal pound-locks were used for the first time in England, *i.e.*, an upper and a lower gate fitted with sluices and enclosing a chamber into which boats passed to be raised or lowered to the next level. The Exeter canal had three locks of this type. It was a small undertaking, only sixteen feet wide, three feet deep, and about three miles long, but it was a remarkable work for its time, all the more so because it was a municipal enterprise. Since then it has been three times enlarged, in width, length, and depth. It became a favourite walk in the eighteenth century for the citizens of Exeter and remained so until recent years. Perhaps it still is, for it still winds peacefully between the elm-shaded meadows of the Exe valley past congenial inns.

The Exeter canal remained the only one of its kind for almost two hundred years, until James Brindley made his first canal for the Duke of Bridgewater in 1760-1. In the meantime more than a thousand miles of rivers had been made navigable, but these made no noticeable change in the landscape. But Brindley's canal from the coal-mines at Worsley to Manchester had several features hitherto unknown. His principle was to keep his canal as level as possible. To achieve this he carried it over roads and streams by means of aqueducts, of which the most notable was that at Barton (two hundred yards long and nearly forty feet above the Irwell), crossed valleys by embankments, cut through hills where they were unavoidable, and followed the contours where possible. At times the Worsley canal followed a most circuitous route in order to maintain a level course, and this excessive winding remained a feature of the early canals. On reaching Worsley the canal tunnelled into the sandstone cliff to reach the coal workings some three-quarters of a mile inside the hill, where it divided into channels that eventually reached a length of several miles. The village of Worsley was transformed by this undertaking, the first of many to be so affected by canals. When Josiah Wedgwood visited it in 1773 it had "the appearance of a considerable Seaport town. His Grace has built some hundreds of houses, and is every year adding considerably to their number."

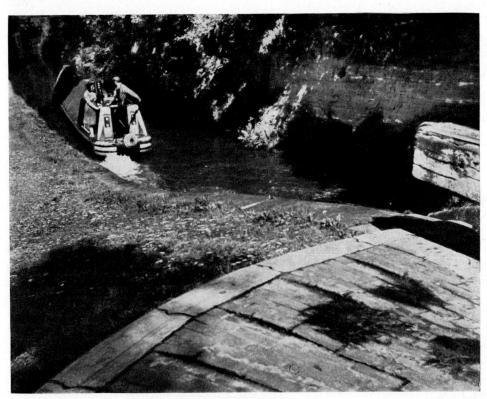

PLATE 63

A cutting near Market Drayton, Shropshire, on Telford's Birmingham and Liverpool Junction Canal, now called the Shropshire Union. "All the elements of canal scenery are here," says Eric de Maré, "lock platform and balance beam, painted Narrow Boat, towpath, tree overhang and dark tunnel entrance."

Later canals became more daring in their engineering as experience was gained. The Grand Trunk Canal (1766-77) not only made use of aqueducts, cuttings, and embankments, but was carried through the hill-country between the Mersey and Trent basins by means of five tunnels, of which the Harecastle Tunnel near Kidsgrove was 2,880 yards long and more than two hundred feet beneath the surface at its deepest point. One can still see this triumph of Brindley's engineering skill, though it is now disused, having been superseded by a second tunnel, parallel with the first, which was constructed by Telford in 1827. Altogether the Grand Trunk Canal had five tunnels and seventy-six locks on its ninety-three mile course from the Mersey to Shardlow, near which it entered the Trent. Shardlow was transformed from a quiet farming village into an inland port like Worsley, but with even wider connections. Wharves were constructed to handle the coal and timber traffic, and tall red-brick warehouses arose after 1777 for iron, for cheese, for corn and salt. By the early nineteenth century three "large carrying establishments" had made their headquarters here, of which Sutton & Co. carried on a great trade with Hull and Gainsborough, Liverpool and Manchester, the Cheshire salt works and the Potteries, and with Birmingham, Dudley and the Black Country. For many years Shardlow was "an improving place," but the Derbyshire directory for 1857 observes that business had declined greatly after the opening of the Midland and other railways. But one can still go to Shardlow, which has sunk back into obscurity, and see the tall warehouses, the wharves, and the late Georgian Shardlow Hall where the prosperous James Sutton lived, and all the other evidences of a place that was virtually created by the Canal Age.

More striking, however, than Shardlow is Stourport, at the confluence of the Stour with the Severn (Plate 64). Before 1772 only a little ale-house stood here, on a sandy waste. With the completion of the Staffordshire and Worcestershire Canal in that year, and the refusal of the town of Bewdley to have anything to do with it, a new town shot up at the point where the canal joined the Severn. Soon there were extensive wharves and basins, tall warehouses, boat-building yards, and "a considerable iron foundry belonging to Messrs. Baldwin." Just as Shardlow was a great inland distributing centre for the East Midlands, where mining, industry, and agriculture mingled their products, so Stourport became the emporium for the West Midlands, connected by river and canal with most parts of the kingdom.

Some notable canal engineering was carried out by men like Rennie and Telford. Rennie built the beautiful aqueduct carrying the Lancaster Canal over the Lune; but even more striking was the Pontcysyllte aqueduct, constructed by Telford between 1795 and 1805, carrying the Ellesmere Canal over the Dee. This, perhaps the greatest monument in stone of English canal engineering, is over a thousand feet long and 121 feet above the river. On the same canal may be seen the Chirk aqueduct and tunnel. Telford's canals took a much more direct course than Brindley's, and so involved much more dramatic engineering, of which a splendid example is the bridge over the deep cutting near Tyrley, on the Shropshire Union Canal (Plate 65).

Tunnels, too, became bolder in conception. The Sapperton tunnel (1789) at the summit of the Thames and Severn Canal bores through the Cotswolds for more than two miles. The Pennines presented the most formidable obstacles of all to the canals, but even they were successfully overcome. The Standedge tunnel, at the highest point (637 feet) of the Huddersfield Canal, was 5,415 yards long. On the little canal linking Tavistock with the navigable Tamar in Devon, the Morwell Down tunnel (1804-17) was a mile and a half long and emerged at its

PLATE 64

Street along the canal at Stourport, Worcestershire. Stourport is the only town in England to be created entirely by canals, and it still contains much purely canal architecture.

western end nearly 240 feet above the river meadows. This drop was overcome by means of an inclined plane, up and down which the loaded barges were carried on trolleys. For many years the quay at Morwellham was "a scene of busy industry,

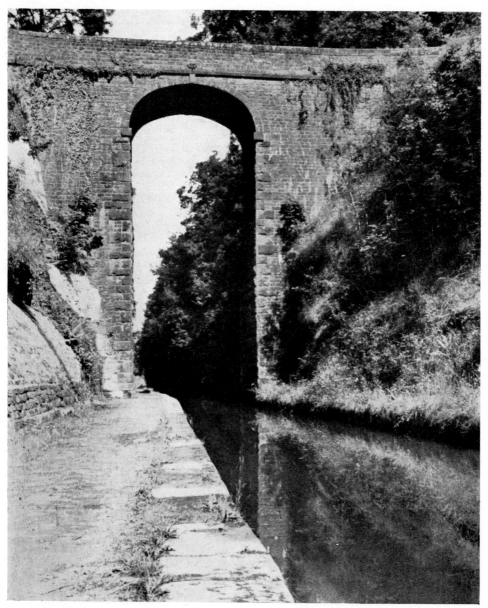

PLATE 65

A bridge across a deep cutting on Telford's canal (now called the Shropshire Union) near Tyrley in Staffordshire. Telford preferred as direct a course as possible in contrast to the indirect course favoured by Brindley, and such cuttings and dramatic bridges are characteristic of his work.

with its unloading barges, and shouting sailors, and hammering workmen, and train of waggons ascending or descending the inclined plane. A quantity of ore is here shipped off to distant smelting-houses. It is curious to enter the well-swept

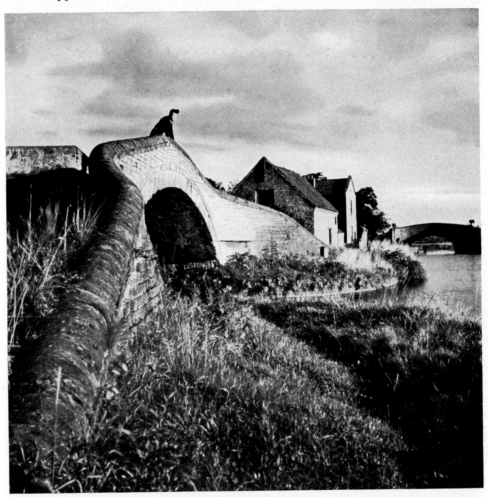

PLATE 66

The canal junction at Great Haywood, Staffordshire, where two of Brindley's canals meet —the Trent and Mersey and the Staffordshire and Worcestershire. Such a scene as this gives a truer and more evocative picture of canal landscape than any dramatic aqueducts or bridges.

yard, and observe the different wooden shafts down which distinct ores from various mines are poured. Then it is to be collected, and placed on board the vessels bound for distant quarters. These ships in return bring coals, and limestone, and many other commodities." By the end of the nineteenth century the quay was deserted; and now it is a grass-grown waste covered in part with the ruins of houses and other buildings. The canal was derelict for many years, but now flows again to produce electricity for the neighbourhood; and it still makes a pleasant summer evening walk from Tavistock to the tunnel mouth.

By the 1820s some three thousand miles of canals had been made, the industrial districts in particular being a network of grimy waterways. But all over the pastoral Midlands and the south of England too, the canals flowed clear and sparkling in the sunshine, something new in the landscape with their towpaths, lock-keepers' cottages, stables for canal horses, their *Navigation* or *Canal* Inns where they met a main road, and their long and narrow gaily-painted boats. The early canals were contour canals, winding about for miles in order to circumvent a hill; but the later ones were made as straight as possible by means of cuttings and embankments. Sometimes an older canal was straightened by later engineers. The Oxford Canal, for example, was shortened by $13\frac{1}{2}$ miles between 1829 and 1834. The old course and the new can be seen particularly between Hawkesbury Lock, where it joins the Coventry canal, and Hillmorton near Rugby. In 1868 the Fenny Compton tunnel, on the same canal, was removed and replaced by a cutting.

By vastly cheapening the carriage of heavy materials over long distances, the canals also brought about indirect changes in the landscape. Thomas Pennant observed in 1782 that the Grand Junction Canal, between Trent and Mersey, had brought in new building materials: "the cottage, instead of being half covered with miserable thatch, is now covered with a substantial covering of tiles or slates, brought from the distant hills of Wales or Cumberland. The fields, which before were barren, are now drained, and by the assistance of manure, conveyed on the canal toll-free, are clothed with a beautiful verdure." But it was left mainly to the railways to break down finally the various regional traditions of building in England, and to put an end to the use of age-old local building materials in favour of standardized brick and slate.

Railways

Two generations of canal-building brought about great alterations in the landscape of England, now matured by centuries of slow growth, but these changes were highly localized. They were confined for the most part to the close proximity of the waterways and some parts of the country hardly knew them at all. The railways made a more massive impact. Not only were they greater in mileage, penetrating to remote places unknown to the canals and sometimes even to the roads, but they began—from an engineering point of view—where the canals left off. Striking though the tunnels and cuttings and aqueducts of the canal engineers had been, they were soon surpassed in size and grandeur by those of the railways. The canals had indeed created two classes of people without whom the railways could not have been built—the civil engineers at one end of the scale, and the navvies (the "inland navigators" of the canal era) at the other. Almost from the start therefore the railways manipulated the landscape on a grand scale. Nothing like their earthworks had been seen since the earlier Iron Age of pre-Roman times. We take the railways so much for granted. Indeed, we see little of their grandeur from the line itself as we cross the Wharncliffe Viaduct on the Great Western

PLATE 67

The first impact of the railway on the landscape: horse-drawn coal wagons on a track made of wooden rails resting on logs for sleepers. Some other elements of railway scenery are already here—the shallow cutting in the background and the primitive timber viaduct. (The drawing is taken from the title-page of A. F. Tait's *Views on the London and North Western Railway (Northern Division)* published in 1848.)

Railway, or the beautiful bridge over the Thames at Maidenhead, and plunge into the Classical-Renaissance portal of the Box Tunnel (Plate 69); or as we traverse the great Tring cutting on the old London and North Western. We must walk to see all this, and it is more difficult to walk along the railways than along the canals with their sequestered towpaths. The early lithographs of J. C. Bourne and A. F. Tait and others show us best the magnitude of the physical changes that the railways brought about in both town and country.

In *Dombey and Son*, too, Dickens—an incomparable reporter of the contemporary scene—makes us feel what a convulsion the making of a railway was. Here is Camden Town in the year 1836 when the London and Birmingham Railway was under construction in a locality which Dickens calls Staggs's Garden:

> The first shock of a great earthquake had, just at that period, rent the whole neighbourhood to its centre. Traces of its course were visible on every side. Houses were knocked down; streets broken through and stopped; deep pits and

PLATE 68

The making of the Edge Hill tunnel on the Liverpool and Manchester Railway, about 1829, one of several notable engineering achievements on the line. The Olive Mount cutting which leads to this tunnel was "the first extensive stone cutting executed on any railway and to this day one of the most formidable." It is nearly two miles long, and in parts nearly eighty feet deep.

trenches dug in the ground; enormous heaps of earth and clay thrown up; buildings that were undermined and shaking, propped by great beams of wood. Here, a chaos of carts, overthrown and jumbled together, lay topsy-turvy at the bottom of a steep unnatural hill; there, confused treasures of iron soaked and rusted in something that had accidentally become a pond. Everywhere were bridges that led nowhere; thoroughfares that were wholly impassable; Babel towers of chimneys, wanting half their height; temporary wooden houses and enclosures, in the most unlikely situations; carcases of ragged tenements, and

fragments of unfinished walls and arches, and piles of scaffolding, and wilder-
nesses of bricks, and giant forms of cranes, and tripods straddling above nothing.
There were a hundred thousand shapes and substances of incompleteness,
wildly mingled out of their places, upside down, burrowing in the earth,
aspiring in the air, mouldering in the water, and unintelligible as any dream.
Hot springs and fiery eruptions, the usual attendants upon earthquakes, lent
their contributions of confusion to the scene. Boiling water hissed and heaved

PLATE 69

Box Tunnel on the Great Western Railway near Bath. Railway builders, says Mr. Christian
    Barman, gave a special dignity and significance to the treatment of tunnel entrances.
    This western portal to Box tunnel is nearly twice the height required for modern traffic.
    Even the short tunnels on this part of the line are treated on a grand scale.

within dilapidated walls; whence, also, the glare and roar of flames came
issuing forth; and mounds of ashes blocked up rights of way, and wholly changed
the law and custom of the neighbourhood.

In short, the yet unfinished and unopened Railroad was in progress; and,
from the very core of all this dire disorder, trailed smoothly away, upon its
mighty course of civilization and improvement.

But as yet, the neighbourhood was too shy to own the Railroad. One or two bold speculators had projected streets; and one had built a little, but had stopped among the mud and ashes to consider farther of it. A bran-new Tavern, re-dolent of fresh mortar and size, and fronting nothing at all, had taken for its sign The Railway Arms; but that might be rash enterprise—and then it hoped to sell drink to the workmen. So, the Excavators' House of Call had sprung up from a beer-shop; and the old-established Ham and Beef Shop had become the Railway Eating House, with a roast leg of pork daily, through interested motives of a similar immediate and popular description. Lodging-house keepers were favourable in like manner; and for the like reasons were not to be trusted. The general belief was very slow. There were frowzy fields, and cow-houses, and dunghills, and dustheaps, and ditches, and gardens, and summerhouses, and carpet-beating grounds, at the very door of the Railway. Little tumuli of oyster shells in the oyster season, and of lobster shells in the lobster season, and of broken crockery and faded cabbage leaves in all seasons, encroached upon its high places. Posts, and rails, and old cautions to trespassers, and backs of mean houses, and patches of wretched vegetation, stared it out of countenance. Nothing was the better for it, or thought of being so. If the miserable waste ground lying near it could have laughed, it would have laughed it to scorn, like many of the miserable neighbours.

Bourne's lithograph of the excavation at Park Village near Camden Town, showing the works in progress in September 1836, must be the identical scene described by Dickens (Plate 70).

The railway pushed on to Birmingham, the army of navvies departed, the convulsion subsided, and within a very few years

there was no such place as Stagg's Gardens. It had vanished from the earth. Where the old rotten summerhouses once had stood, palaces now reared their heads, and granite columns of gigantic girth opened a vista to the railway world beyond. The miserable waste ground, where the refuse-matter had been heaped of yore, was swallowed up and gone; and in its frowsy stead were tiers of warehouses, crammed with rich goods and costly merchandise. The old by-streets now swarmed with passengers and vehicles of every kind; the new streets that had stopped disheartened in the mud and waggon-ruts, formed towns within themselves, originating wholesome comforts and conveniences belonging to themselves, and never tried nor thought of until they sprung into existence. Bridges that had led to nothing, led to villas, gardens, churches, healthy public walks. The carcasses of houses, and beginnings of new through-fares, had started off upon the line at steam's own speed, and shot away into the country in a monster train.

As to the neighbourhood which had hesitated to acknowledge the railroad in its straggling days, that had grown wise and penitent, as any Christian might in such a case, and now boasted of its powerful and prosperous relation. There were railway patterns in its drapers' shops, and railway journals in the windows of its newsmen. There were railway hotels, office-houses, lodging-houses, boarding-houses; railway plans, maps, views, wrappers, bottles, sandwich-boxes, and time-tables; railway hackney-coach and cabstands; railway omnibuses, railway streets and buildings, railway hangers-on and parasites, and flatterers out of all calculation. There was even railway time observed in clocks, as if the sun itself had given in. Among the vanquished was the master chimney-sweeper, whilom incredulous at Staggs's Gardens, who now lived in a stuccoed

PLATE 70

Excavations for the cutting at Park Village, Camden Town, 1836: on the London and Birmingham Railway. This splendid lithograph by Bourne gives one a vivid idea of the impact of the railway on urban landscapes. It is the scene of the "earthquake" description in *Dombey and Son*.

house three stories high, and gave himself out, with golden flourishes upon a varnished board, as contractor for the cleansing of railway chimneys by machinery.

To and from the heart of this great change, all day and night, throbbing currents rushed and returned incessantly like its life's blood. Crowds of people and mountains of goods, departing and arriving scores upon scores of times in every four-and-twenty hours, produced a fermentation in the place that was always in action. The very houses seemed disposed to pack up and take trips.

Wonderful Members of Parliament, who, little more than twenty years before, had made themselves merry with the wild railroad theories of engineers, and given them the liveliest rubs in cross-examination, went down into the north with their watches in their hands, and sent on messages before by the electric telegraph, to say that they were coming. Night and day the conquering engines rumbled at their distant work, or advancing smoothly to their journey's end, and gliding like tame dragons into the allotted corners grooved out to the inch for their reception, stood bubbling and trembling there, making the walls quake, as if they were dilating with the secret knowledge of great powers yet unsuspected in them, and strong purposes not yet achieved.

But Staggs's Gardens had been cut up root and branch.

Dr. Johnson had deplored the effect that canals would have upon the privacy of the landed class. The railways aroused an even greater opposition for this as well as for numerous other reasons, and not only among those who quietly enjoyed the amenities of a large estate. At Helpston in Northamptonshire, Clare recorded in his diary for 4 June 1825:

> Saw three fellows at the end of Royce Wood, who I found were laying out the plan for an iron railway from Manchester to London. It is to cross over Round Oak spring by Royce Wood corner for Woodcroft Castle. I little thought that fresh intrusions would interrupt and spoil my solitudes. After the enclosure they will despoil a boggy place that is famous for orchises at Royce Wood end.

Nothing came of this particular project, not at least for many years, and Clare continued to enjoy the orchises of Royce Wood undisturbed. But the battle to preserve beloved solitudes flared up repeatedly in patches all over the country, precisely as it does today with the threat of new airfields and military training areas. The price of solitude in the modern world is eternal vigilance. In 1844 Wordsworth was aroused by the proposal to construct a railway from Kendal to the shores of Lake Windermere

> Is then no nook of English ground secure
> From rash assault?

His two long letters to the *Morning Post* marshal every conservative argument against the proposal, and conclude

> We have too much hurrying about in these islands; much for idle pleasure, and more from over activity in the pursuit of wealth, without regard to the good or happiness of others.

> Proud were ye, Mountains, when, in times of old,
> Your patriot sons, to stem invasive war,
> Intrenched your brows; ye gloried in each scar:

Now, for your shame, a Power, the Thirst of Gold,
That rules o'er Britain like a baneful star,
Wills that your peace, your beauty, shall be sold,
And clear way made for her triumphal car
Through the beloved retreats your arms enfold!

Heard YE that Whistle? As her long-linked Train
Swept onwards, did the vision cross your view?
Yes, ye were startled;—and, in balance true,
Weighing the mischief with the promised gain,
Mountains, and Vales, and Floods, I call on you
To share the passion of a just disdain.

PLATE 71

The Wolverton embankment under construction in 1837. Here the London and Birmingham
Railway is crossing the meadows of the Great Ouse valley. No wonder Ruskin spoke of
"your railroad mounds, vaster than the walls of Babylon." To discover earthworks of
comparable magnitude in England we have to go back to the Early Iron Age, to the
builders of hill-forts like Maiden Castle in Dorset.

But the conservatives, however right they were—and we have lost nearly all our
privacy and silence since they wrote—lost all along the line. The new railways
"slashed like a knife through the delicate tissues of a settled rural civilization. They
left their scars on park and copse; they raised high walls of earth across the
meadows—'your railroad mounds, vaster than the walls of Babylon,' Ruskin
called them; they brutally amputated every hill on their way."[1]

The magnitude of the early railway works was enhanced by the severe limitation
the engineers placed upon themselves as regards gradients. Brunel would have
nothing steeper than 1 in 660 for the first eighty-five miles out of Paddington;
Robert Stephenson planned the London and Birmingham Railway with no

[1]Barman, *Early British Railways*, 25.

gradient steeper than 1 in 330 (except the first rise from Euston to Camden); and Locke nothing steeper than 1 in 250 on the difficult London and Southampton line. So we get on the London and Birmingham route the vast cuttings at Tring ($2\frac{1}{2}$ miles long and at times nearly sixty feet deep) and Roade ($1\frac{1}{2}$ miles long and nearly seventy feet deep), and the embankments at Boxmoor and Wolverton (Plate 71). On the London and Southampton line sixteen million cubic feet of earth were moved in making the cuttings and embankments, mostly between

PLATE 72

Brunel's railway viaduct at Chippenham on the Great Western Railway. The whole line from Paddington to Bristol is marked by splendid engineering and architecture, so well done that most of it survives and cannot be improved upon. Much of it is invisible from the line itself.

Basingstoke and Winchester: some of the most extensive cuttings in the world are on this stretch of line. On the Great Western route we have such major engineering achievements as the Wharncliffe Viaduct over the Brent valley at Hanwell, the Sonning cutting, the embankment west of Chippenham (and the fine viaduct over the town itself) (Plate 72), the Box tunnel, and the series of tunnels, cuttings, and embankments between Bath and Bristol.

At times the railway altered almost the whole aspect of a town, or at least of distant views of it. The Great Western Railway's embankments and viaducts changed the prospect of Bath (Plate 73); the viaduct over the Mersey at Stockport brought a fine geometrical composition into the urban landscape (Plate 58). Indeed the railways created as much beauty as they inadvertently destroyed, but of a totally different kind. The great gashes they inflicted on the landscape in their cuttings and embankments healed over, and wild flowers grew abundantly once more. Going down to the south-west in spring, the cuttings through Somerset and Devon sparkle with primroses. Even in Clare's own country, the railway has been absorbed into the landscape, and one can enjoy the consequent pleasure of trundling through Rutland in a stopping-train on a fine summer morning: the barley fields shaking in the wind, the slow sedgy streams with their willows shading

PLATE 73

The Great Western Railway approaching Bath by means of great embankments and viaducts. As at Chippenham (Plate 72) and Stockport (Plate 58) the urban prospect was transformed, in part at least, by the architecture and earthworks of the new railways.

meditative cattle, the elegant limestone spires across the meadows, the early Victorian stations built of the sheep-grey Ketton stone and still unaltered, the warm brown roofs of the villages half buried in the trees, and the summer light flashing everywhere. True that the railway did not invent much of this beauty, but it gave us new vistas of it.

Or there is the grander scenery, and the more spectacular engineering, of the railway from Settle up to Carlisle, some of the finest railway landscape in Britain; and the route over Shap with its visions of the Lakeland Mountains; and there are the superb night scenes from the railway viaducts that span the industrial towns of Lancashire and Yorkshire. There are the elaborate tunnel entrances like Box and Bramhope and others, the great viaducts like Monsal Dale and Dutton, the bridges like Saltash and Severn; and the charming survivors among early railway stations that one comes across unexpectedly almost anywhere in England. All the convulsions and brutal gashings of the rural landscape by the railway engineers have long been smoothed over and forgotten; and we take the railway earthworks and monuments as much for granted as we do the hedges and fields of the enclosure commissioners or the churches of our medieval forefathers.

The railways not only made a direct physical impact on the landscape: their

PLATE 74

Crewe station in 1848. The early railway stations were often a pleasure to contemplate—imposing sometimes, and sometimes faintly romantic, like the first Crewe station. Few stations of the first generation survived the vast increase of railway traffic, but some did and they are well worth seeing. Railways added a vast amount of detail to the English landscape, besides manipulating it at times on a large scale.

indirect effects were equally powerful and far-reaching. The diary of a Middlesex parson (the Rev. B. J. Armstrong) shows us what a devastating effect they were having as early as the 1830s.[1] His father had decided in the year 1830 to move out of London and to take a small house in the country.

It was thought advisable to take some small place in the country for the benefit of our health . . . He took a very pretty and rather commodious cottage-

[1]Michael Robbins, "A Middlesex Diary," *Trans. London and Middlesex Archæological Society*, XI, Part II.

residence at Southall Green, Middlesex, about a mile out of the high road to Uxbridge, and exactly 10 miles from Tyburn Gate. Our intention was to reside half the year at Southall, and the remainder in London, and I remember we moved there on the 26th June, 1830 . . . My delight at everything I saw was beyond bounds—gardens were allotted my sister and self—there was the canal to fish in—a pony to ride—besides animals of different kinds. . . . Having been long pent up in town, Annie and myself viewed Southall as a second Paradise, and I remember I nearly hung myself on my pin-before the very first morning after our arrival, in attempting to scale the yard gates to see the country beyond them.

Eight years later the main line from Paddington to the West was opened through Middlesex. West Drayton (for Uxbridge) was the first station; and in the following year stations were built at Ealing, Hanwell, and Southall. The effect on Southall is duly recorded in Armstrong's diary:

A remarkable change for the worse took place about this time in the hitherto retired neighbourhood of Southall Green. The railway spread dissatisfaction and immorality among the poor, the place being inundated with worthless and overpaid navigators [*i.e.,* "navvies"]; the very appearance of the country was altered, some families left, and the rusticity of the village gave place to a London-out-of-town character. Moss-grown cottages retired before new ones with bright red tiles, picturesque hedgerows were succeeded by prim iron railings, and the village inn, once a pretty cottage with a swinging sign, is transmogrified to the "Railway Tavern" with an intimation gaudily set forth that "London porter" and other luxuries hitherto unknown to the aborigines were to be procured within.

These immediate effects were observable only near the stations, but as the railways extended rapidly to all parts of the country their effects on local building and building materials grew correspondingly wide. In Middlesex the impact came soonest, and was most violent. The older houses had been built of a homely and native brown stock brick, and the farm-buildings largely of wood. Between 1800 and 1850, however, a hard soapy-looking yellow brick was pouring up the Thames from Suffolk, and most of the new Middlesex churches were built of it. "From 1850 onwards"—with the triumph of the railways—"every kind of material was poured on to the unprotesting soil: harsh red bricks, sometimes glazed; in the north, yellow-green brick from Three Counties, near Hitchin; slates, pantiles, green tiles; stucco, artificial stone, and concrete."[1] What happened in Middlesex eventually happened all over England, and as Midland bricks and Welsh slates— and later more unspeakable materials like asbestos and corrugated iron—flooded into every corner of provincial England, the ancient local materials that fitted

[1]Robbins, *Middlesex*, 165.

their own regions so well, for they came out of their very soil, disappeared one by one. In Oxfordshire the Stonesfield slate-pits and mines shut down one by one during the second half of the nineteenth century;[1] in Leicestershire the Swithland slate-quarries, which had been worked since Henry III's time, shut down altogether in 1887; and so it was in nearly every county in England. All regional styles and all local materials were exterminated except where the well-to-do could afford to build deliberately in the old manner, with the aid of an architect. What had been the living style of a whole region, modified to suit all classes of people, became a piece of pleasant antiquarianism for a rich man.

[1] The Duke of Marlborough managed to keep a pit open until 1909. Arkell, *Oxford Stone*, 140.

SELECT BIBLIOGRAPHY

Architectural Review, Special Canals Number, July 1949.
BARMAN, CHRISTIAN, *Early British Railways* (1950).
BOURNE, J. C., *History and Description of the Great Western Railway* (1846).
BRITTON, JOHN, *Drawings of the London and Birmingham Railway* (1839).
BUTTERWORTH, EDWIN, *Views on the Manchester and Leeds Railway* (1845).
CRAWFORD, O. G. S., *Archæology in the Field* (1953).
HADFIELD, CHARLES, *British Canals* (1950).
HOUGHTON, F. T. S., "Salt Ways," *Birmingham Archæological Society Transactions*, vol. 54, 1932.
JACKMAN, W. T., *The Development of Transportation in Modern England* (1916).
MARGARY, I. D., *Roman Ways in the Weald* (1948).
NOCK, O. S., *The Railways of Britain* (1948).
PRATT, E. A., *History of Inland Transportation and Communications in England* (1909).
TAIT, A. F., *Views on the London and North-Western Railway* (1848).
WILLIAMS, F., *Our Iron Roads* (1875).

IX

The Landscape of Towns

THERE are many different ways of looking at a town for the first time. One of them—a little old-fashioned perhaps, for I do not see many people doing it nowadays—is to walk around it guide-book in hand, best of all with one of those old Murray's *Handbooks for Travellers*, the most catholic, the most informative, the most solid guide-books ever written in this country: still well worth buying though the last one came out nearly fifty years ago and one must hunt for them with increasing difficulty in the second-hand bookshops.

We may study with our guide-books all the historic, individual features of a town and get to know them. But then—if we are taking our time and stay to look at the town as a whole, walk around it in the cool and quiet of the evening when the shops are shut, and the traffic has gone home, and we can really see its contours and its bone-structure—other questions begin to arise in the mind, which even the best of guide-books does not answer. Why is the town just like this, this shape, this plan, this size? Why do its streets run in this particular way and not in some other way that seems more logical to us? Why are there sometimes two market places, why are the ancient churches just where they are?—and so on. In short, what gives the town this particular landscape?

Here even the best of guide-books fails us. Indeed, there are no books at all to answer our question. The historians also fail us—in this country, at least—for they have not studied the topography of towns as they have in Germany and France. We have nothing like Louis Halphen's great topographical study of the growth of Paris; or the work of Keussen and Koebner on the physical development of Cologne, or of Des Marez on the city of Ghent. This lack is astonishing when one thinks of the innumerable ancient towns of England that richly deserve such a study. There are, of course, many scholarly books on boroughs in their institutional aspects, their political history, and their administration. But one looks in vain for any discussion of their physical growth, where their original core lay, of the directions in which they grew, and when and why, and of what accounts for their street plan and their shape today. The nearest we have to this in England is one chapter by the American scholar Carl Stephenson in his book *Borough and Town*. Written twenty years ago, it is admittedly a tentative sketch put out in the hope that some English historians and archæologists would set to work in a more expert way and on a bigger scale. But still very little has been done: only medieval Lincoln and modern Brighton have had some attention recently.

What is the point of studying towns in this way? For me, at least—and I think for most people who travel around this country for pleasure, that is, to see things—

it is simply that one gets a greater depth of pleasure out of knowing the anatomy of a town and why it takes that particular form, and not just its superficial features, however attractive they may be individually. It may well be that when the archæologists and historians have studied a sufficient number of towns intensively in this country, as they have done abroad, we shall add something appreciable to our knowledge of English history, knowledge which we could get in no other way. But this is looking a long way ahead. In the meantime one studies them as landscapes, so to speak, simply to heighten one's pleasure in sight-seeing, to get behind the superficial appearances, to uncover the layers of the palimpsest and to see, for example, a piece of the tenth century in the way a street makes an abrupt turn or does something else unexpected.

The Planned Town

Street-plans raise a multitude of questions. Why are certain English towns, for example, laid out on a gridiron pattern with straight streets crossing each other at right angles, sometimes at fixed distances apart, like a mid-western American city? Towns, moreover, so utterly dissimilar in other ways—Salisbury and Middlesbrough, Barrow-in-Furness and Winchelsea? From a topographical point of view, these planned towns are the simplest towns to understand: but even here we are confronted with a number of questions at the outset. Why are there so few planned towns in this country? Why were most English towns left to grow up in more or less haphazard fashion? What determined that a particular town should be planned with this regular layout of streets and building-plots? Why, again, are the planned towns scattered about the country in so haphazard a way, and so different in age and social type—Salisbury's plan belongs to the thirteenth century (Fig. 10), Middlesbrough's to the nineteenth. And why are certain parts of a great city like Birmingham planned on the gridiron pattern, and the rest of it just a jumbled, inchoate mess?

We look into the records and another question emerges. While some, indeed most, planned towns established themselves successfully, others proved completely abortive, never came to life at all despite all the activity of the planners, including the king himself. For the viability of towns depends in the last resort on a solid economic foundation, and planned towns especially were deliberate attempts to exploit the economic possibilities of a site: and like any other investment could go wrong. On the southern shore of Poole Bay in Dorset, directly opposite the ancient port of Poole, is the site of a completely still-born royal town—Nova Villa. King Edward I, that great town-planner, gave it a charter in 1286, conferring upon it all the liberties and privileges of the City of London. A site was chosen, two town-planners appointed (one of them a parson), the town marked out on the ground: but all in vain. Nothing happened. In Elizabethan days, three hundred years later, the solitary farm of Newton, standing upon the heath that petered out in the muddy flats of the bay, alone marked the site of Edward I's "New Town."

Leaving aside the Romans, whose tradition of town-planning had been completely forgotten after their departure, the earliest piece of town-planning that we know of in England is that carried out by Abbot Baldwin at Bury St. Edmunds, between 1066 and 1086. This plan is still very easily picked out today as one walks about the streets of Bury. The little border town of Ludlow may well be a twelfth-century example of planning on a smaller and more rudimentary scale, but the most notable examples come from the thirteenth century—Salisbury, New Winchelsea, the five bastide towns laid out by Edward I in North Wales, and part of Kingston-upon-Hull, laid out by Edward from 1293 onwards. Hull was already an important seaport in the twelfth century. Edward did not create it from nothing, but he founded a new town—King's Town—on the old site, which he manipulated especially on the western side. At Stratford-upon-Avon, the Bishop of Worcester (who owned the entire manor) obtained the grant of a market in 1196 and proceeded to lay out a new town forthwith. He set aside an area of one hundred and nine acres to the east of the original Saxon village (called Old Town to this day) and on it laid out a regular plan of streets—three running parallel with the river and three others crossing them at right-angles. This elementary plan survives unchanged as the core of the modern town.

The impulse to produce planned towns, such as it was, had died out by 1300. Then we get no more until the planned development of more or less large estates in the late eighteenth-century towns—notably, of course, the spas, but also in such unlikely places as Birmingham and (early in the nineteenth century) Ashton-under-Lyne. Finally, in the middle decades of the nineteenth century, we get once again whole new towns created on the gridiron pattern, of which the outstanding examples are the iron and steel towns of Middlesbrough and Barrow-in-Furness. It is curious, by the way, that the gridiron plan should have gone on so long. It is the simplest and most obvious layout, but there are, of course, other patterns—such as the radial pattern of so many modern housing estates—and it is odd that these others should not have been tried out until within our own time.

When we study the planned towns of England, we arrive at the first, and obvious, conclusion that to make a planned town required the absolute ownership of the site by one man or corporation. This immediately limited the number of towns that could be planned, for most English towns have developed from villages, and their sites had been partly built on for centuries before they developed into towns. More important than that (for medieval village buildings could have been swept away as easily as the Romans had swept away the native British buildings for their planned towns)—a variety of ownerships and rights had grown up that precluded a unified plan even as early as the twelfth or thirteenth century. True, these property rights could have been dealt with by a determined planner, but the fact remains that they were not. At Bury, for instance, the abbey owned the whole site and could lay it out as it pleased. At Salisbury, in the 1220s, the bishop of Sarum was able to plan a complete new city on his own meadows by the Avon (Fig. 16). At New Winchelsea and in North Wales, the king was dealing with his own land, as he was also on the abortive site of New Town beside Poole Bay. In Birmingham the planned area—all that part to the west of Snow Hill station today—was formerly the New Hall estate of the Colmore family. Their park was given over as

PLATE 75

Middlesbrough: a nineteenth-century planned town, begun in 1830, on a site of 600 acres to the north of the railway station (bottom right). The photograph does not show the earliest growth, which is a fascinating piece of early Victorian social history: broad streets running at right angles to each other and to a large square at the centre. Above we have the mid-Victorian expansion to the south of the railway station, but the grid-iron plan is still adhered to until one gets well out.

a whole for building development, and laid out on the gridiron pattern in the middle decades of the eighteenth century. At Barrow-in-Furness the site of the new town was owned by the Dukes of Devonshire, one of whom was responsible for its planning in the middle decades of the nineteenth century. At Middlesbrough in 1829 a syndicate of six Quakers bought a site of five hundred acres beside the Tees, and created their planned town upon the empty farmland, drawing their straight lines and making their rectangles without hindrance from any legal or physical obstacle (Plate 75).

But to say that the planned town required a single ownership of the site does not go to the root of the matter. Most English towns have grown from Anglo-Saxon villages, but, particularly in the twelfth and thirteenth centuries, land-owners were founding new towns all over England—and indeed all over Europe. In the one county of Devon, for example, sixty or so boroughs were created by optimistic landowners, of which one half failed to come to anything. Population was increasing, trade and industry growing; it was an expanding economy with wonderful new opportunities for making money if one could only strike the right spot.

So landowners, from the king down to relatively small provincial lords, founded boroughs right and left, especially where they saw merchants and traders already congregating at some convenient spot—near the protection of a castle or an abbey, which were considerable markets also, at some important river-crossing, and so on. Why, then, were only half-a-dozen of these new towns properly laid out on a predetermined plan, and the vast majority left to grow haphazard with narrow, irregular, winding streets, odd little lanes everywhere, and all the other attributes of the picturesque today? There were two principal reasons for this: one was that medieval men had no *a priori* love of symmetry. The planned town is an aberration, not the norm. Secondly, the planning of a new town—laying out the lines of streets, lanes, markets, churches, and house-plots over a considerable area re-quired, after all, the investment of a large amount of capital, and a greater degree of economic optimism than most landowners could contemplate. The planned town is the product of the big capitalists—kings, bishops, abbots, in medieval times; town corporations, dukes and Quaker syndicates in modern times. And today, only the State can afford to lay out a complete new town.

Most landlords, even bishops and abbots, made no attempt to lay out their new towns. They gave them charters, sometimes supplied building materials, offered low rents and other inducements, but they were content to let the town grow—if it was to grow—as it liked within the prescribed area. And when that area was satisfactorily filled, they were prepared to extend the boundaries of the borough by granting more land for building, as happened at Scarborough in 1256 (Plate 76) or at Newcastle-on-Tyne in 1298. To plan a whole town at once was a highly risky investment. We know, for example, that at Kingston-upon-Hull fewer than half the building plots in the royal town had been taken up by 1320, a generation after the original planning. At New Winchelsea many of the thirty-nine squares or chequers into which the town-site had been divided in the 1280s were never built upon, but remained under grass and can be seen to this day.

These were all royal foundations. Few other landowners could afford to wait a generation for the return of their money, if it was to come back at all. It was far safer to start a town off with a charter, a market, and a fair, and a few other practical inducements to settlers, and then to sit back and hope for the best. Let it grow automatically as new groups of traders and merchants directed their steps there and decided eventually to settle and build there. No landowner—not even

PLATE 76

Scarborough: the first settlement can be precisely dated. It was in 966 or 967 that the Norseman Thorgils *Skarthi* (hare-lip) founded it below the great fortified headland that was thereafter called "Skarthi's *burh* or stronghold." The earliest village probably lay along the water-front of the inner harbour (called Old Harbour). With the building of the castle on the headland in Stephen's reign (1135-54) a town grew up to the west, across the neck of the peninsula. By 1155 this was sufficiently viable to get a charter from Henry II. Within a hundred years the town had grown westwards almost to the limit of this view, and in 1256 Henry III granted land outside the walls for an extension of the borough. This extension is today marked by the street called Newborough.

the king—could create a new town if people did not want it. It remained empty or half-empty despite all the inducements.

We do not know why New Town, on Poole Bay, failed so completely to come off. It is one of those nice little problems of local history. In a general way, I suppose it was still-born because the town of Poole lay only four miles across the bay, founded about forty years before by William Longsword, Earl of Salisbury, and the new town of Edward's, for all its royal backing and privileges of the City of London, could not compete with it. The earl had got in first on this wonderful anchorage, and the advantage remained with his town.

Down in Cornwall, the chief problem was to attract the natives into the new towns at all. Like all Celtic people they preferred to live in the country. So, though medieval landowners founded nearly forty boroughs in the county, few of them ever got going as towns. Most were futile experiments. In fact, they became the rotten boroughs of later centuries. Even those that succeeded in coming alive were populated in their early days mostly by foreigners, that is, by non-Cornish-men, or they too would have failed.

There were in fact great risks in starting a new town, or at least in investing money in it. One needed considerable capital and a long-term view to risk a completely planned town, and preferably also the certainty that the demand was there and could not fail—as in New Sarum in the thirteenth century or Middlesbrough and Barrow in the nineteenth. And so, for these and other reasons, the planned town has always been the exception in England, and derives most of its special interest from that fact.

The Open-Field Town

The planned towns are the easiest kind of urban landscape to understand, and perhaps for that reason the least interesting to the curious traveller—however attractive they may be to look at. They satisfy our curiosity too soon. Now let us explore what lies behind the contemporary appearance of quite another group of towns: towns which reveal nothing at first sight of their secret, physical history, and which indeed seem to have little or nothing in common as one looks at them and around their streets. As we explore the ramifications of their anatomy we shall encounter a good deal of the stupidity, the greed, and self-interest, the plain conservatism—just human resistance to change of any kind—as well as the pure evil of human nature, working itself out in bricks and stone and mortar.

Let us look at those towns that grew up in the midst of their own open fields, that entered the nineteenth century with their population rising at a phenomenal rate, but were wholly unable to expand their building area to meet this rise in numbers. They were still held within the vice of their own fields, with all the complicated property rights which made it impossible to secure land for building development. Most effective of all in stopping any new building were the Lammas pasture rights—that is, the right of burgesses, or some of them, to graze their cattle and sheep over the open fields after the harvest had been taken in. The town fields might well be private property and held by only half-a-dozen farmers. The burgess might have no land at all in the fields; but he had this right to graze his cattle after Lammas over any man's lands, freely and wherever he liked. It sounds a trivial thing—this common pasture right for six months of the year—but it had the most devastating effect on town development, in the Midlands above all. The consequences are almost unbelievable until one follows out their sequence.

There are, in the east Midlands, three towns lying fairly close together that illustrate well the physical consequences of this situation—Nottingham, Leicester, and Stamford. Until about 200 years ago, they had developed along pretty much

PLATE 77

Stamford from the meadows of the Welland. Founded in the fifth century on the rising of a hill above the meadows, Stamford almost became a university town in the thirteenth and fourteenth centuries. It is still rich in medieval architecture, and in domestic building of the sixteenth to nineteenth centuries. It is a museum-piece from a pre-industrial England.

the same lines. They differ very markedly from each other today. For in each instance the problem of expansion was solved or evaded in a different way, and produced as a result towns with very different characteristics. Nottingham failed to solve the problem until too late and created as a consequence some of the worst slums in any town in England. Leicester solved it just in time and produced a town that spilled widely across the surrounding fields and gave its working class

bigger and better houses, and wider streets, than almost anywhere else in industrial England. Stamford failed entirely to solve the problem of its open fields;
but whereas Nottingham created its slums, Stamford fossilized into the beautiful
seventeenth- and eighteenth-century town we see today, a museum piece from a
pre-industrial England (Plate 77).

Some two to three hundred years ago, Nottingham was one of the most beautiful
towns in England. All travellers were agreed about this. Thomas Baskerville,
who saw it in the sixteen-eighties, called it "Paradise Restored, for here you find
large streets, fair built houses, fine women, and many coaches rattling about, and
their shops full of merchantable goods." For Celia Fiennes, a few years later, it was
a favourite town by which she judged all others—and generally found them wanting. It was, she said, the neatest town she had ever seen. And Dr. Charles Deering,
who settled there after a wandering career, said that "were a naturalist in Quest
of an exquisite Spot to build a Town or a City, could he meet with one that would
better answer his Wishes?"

Three generations later, Nottingham had become a squalid mess. "I believe,"
said the commissioner who reported on it to the Health of Towns Commission in
1845, "that nowhere else shall we find so large a mass of inhabitants crowded into
courts, alleys, and lanes as in Nottingham, and those, too, of the worst possible
construction. Here they are so clustered upon each other; court within court,
yard within yard, and lane within lane, in a manner to defy description. . . .
Some parts of Nottingham [are] so very bad as hardly to be surpassed in misery
by anything to be found within the entire range of our manufacturing cities." In
an England that contained the slums of Manchester and Liverpool, Leeds and
East London, this was strong language indeed.

What had happened to destroy so utterly the Paradise Restored of Thomas
Baskerville, the neat town of Celia Fiennes, the exquisite spot of Charles Deering,
to destroy it in the short space of three generations? To the north and south of
the town, gripping it along three-quarters of its circuit, lay nearly eleven hundred
acres of open fields, far more than enough land for housing the new industrial
population. But until these fields were enclosed, until their multitudinous strips
were reallotted in large compact blocks of land, and until the rights of common
pasture over them were extinguished, it was impossible to get a single acre for
building. The burgesses with pasture rights steadfastly refused to allow the
enclosure of the fields. Borough elections were fought on this issue. Candidates who
wanted enclosure were burned in effigy, their supporters wheeled about in muck-
carts in the robust eighteenth-century fashion. Even the freeholders in the fields—
who were willing to have enclosure so that they could farm more efficiently or sell
land for building—were helpless in the face of the burgesses who might have no
land but who hoped to get a piece in time, or who already held these rights to
graze their cattle and sheep.

This "Cowocracy," as they were called, were not entirely blind to the evils of

PLATE 78

A Nottingham court as it was in 1913. This view was taken on a sunny day or it would have
been incomparably grimmer. After a hundred years of wrestling with the problem, the
city of Nottingham has almost got rid of everything like this. Such slums (and many
worse than this) were largely the product of the land-shortage of the early 1800s when the
population rose rapidly but the town could not expand outwards.

slums and overcrowding. But they had a lively fear that enclosure might rob them of their valuable rights—rights which made a real difference to their

FIG. 16

Plan of a typical court in Nottingham (taken from the *Report of the Royal Commission on the State of the Large Towns, 1845*) showing the intense pressure on building land as a result of the failure to enclose the surrounding open fields. Notice the back-to-back houses, the tunnel entrances to the completely enclosed court, and the primitive sanitation.

standard and their mode of living—in the interests of the large freeholders and a corporation known to be corrupt. Then, too, there were those who opposed enclosure because there was no guarantee that any open spaces would be reserved for the public benefit; and, as things stood, the slum-dweller in Nottingham could at least walk in the adjacent fields and get some fresh air. Enclosure might result in every acre being grabbed by private owners, who would sell for speculative building.

Most of the opponents of enclosure at Nottingham were not, therefore, mere villains. They had some good reason on their side. But their refusal to enclose had the effect of creating another class of opponents of a blacker hue—the owners of slum property. The town could not grow outwards. So every garden, every orchard, every foot of open space within the old confines, was doled out piecemeal at exorbitant prices for building. Even streets were too extravagant of space: courts and alleys enabled more houses to be packed into a given area: and where, in Deering's day, the apple or the cherry orchard had blown in springtime, courts of back-to-back houses now faced each other across an open drain (Fig. 16). In some parts there were eight hundred persons living—if that is the word—on one acre of ground: one person to every six square yards.

Even the schools were built in the corners of crowded burial grounds, or over public sewers into which they slowly sank. Rents for these appalling houses— eight thousand back-to-backs, rising three storeys with single rooms piled one on top of the other—took a high proportion of a working-class income. Nottingham's own historian, Dr. Chambers, reckons that altogether the slum property of the town produced an annual return of forty thousand pounds, some of which went to building-clubs financed by small artisans. Not all the slum-owners were big men.

So an unholy alliance of cow-keepers and slum-owners repeatedly elected the kind of corporation that would fight to the death "the unsightly monster" of enclosure—as the mayor called it in 1825. When, at last, the reformed corporation carried through the enclosure in 1845, and the town could burst outwards, the damage had been done. Three times as many people had been packed into the old confines as could prudently be housed there, even by the low standards of a hundred years ago, and the slums of Nottingham have remained a byword down to our own day. Not until the nineteen-twenties and thirties could a real clearance be made of this formidable mess, and a newer Nottingham begin to appear out of it.

At Leicester, twenty miles away, with much the same kind of industrial and population history, things happened quite differently. Here the three open fields which practically surrounded the ancient town had all been enclosed before the need for more building land had become desperate. One great field, lying to the east and north-east of the town, had been enclosed in 1764—in good time for the population-increase—and the town proceeded to grow comfortably in that direction. There was almost unlimited space for Leicester to expand; and in 1845 the commissioners were able to report that the town "was spread over an unusual extent of ground in proportion to its population." Many large gardens were still

FIG. 17.—HOUSING DEVELOPMENT IN NOTTINGHAM AFTER THE ENCLOSURE OF THE
OPEN FIELDS IN 1845.

The map shows the development of part of Clay Field after the enclosure. The heavy black
lines represent the boundaries of the separate allotments made to private owners by the
Enclosure Commissioners. There were about four hundred of these allotments, most of
which were immediately "developed" by their owners without the slightest reference to
neighbouring allotments and owners. The pattern of the roads and streets was largely
determined by the medieval footpaths and furlongs of the open fields. Thus Victorian
Nottingham is largely built upon lines determined many centuries ago (see J. D.
Chambers, *A Century of Nottingham History, 1851–1951*).

The above map is reproduced by permission of Dr. J. D. Chambers and of the Ordnance Survey.

to be seen, even in the centre of the town. The newer streets were wider than the average of manufacturing towns. The wind could blow through them and the sun shine upon them, unlike the courts of Nottingham. The working-class homes seldom rose above two storeys. Moreover, these houses had four rooms, and each room was bigger than its Nottingham counterpart; and there was rarely more than one family per house. They generally had ample yards, often little gardens, and were better built than those of most industrial towns. Leicester was no Paradise Restored: its flat site led to difficult drainage problems and mortality was high even by the standards of the time, but there was nothing remotely resembling the horrors of Nottingham.

Stamford presented quite another case again. The open fields hemmed in the town along its entire northern side, while on the southern side Burghley Park and the farmlands of the Cecils offered not an acre for expansion. Here the open fields survived until 1872. Until that late date, the Cecils successfully opposed any move to enclose the fields, for reasons which were never fully disclosed at the time. But the main reason is clear enough. The borough of Stamford returned two members to Parliament, the franchise being restricted to householders. Since the end of the seventeenth century the Cecils, at Burghley House just outside the town, had controlled the election of both members by a combination of methods that seemed to leave no loophole for a mistake. There was, indeed, one possible loophole. Squatters on the waste of the manor, at the fringe of the open fields, erected hovels and tried to stake a claim. But the Marquess of Exeter (as the Cecils had become in 1801) pulled down these hovels instantly, and prosecuted the squatters. Why? Because every house that went up and stayed up represented a certain vote against his political nominees. With all his elaborate political machinery—his control of all the tradesmen in the town and of all the town's six advowsons, his ownership of some two hundred houses each carrying a vote, his absolute control of the Mayor, the corporation, and all the corporation offices—the Marquess of Exeter could not be absolutely certain that the remaining voters would not one day oust his candidates. There were too many houses he did not own; and he could not afford to see any more built. In a town that chafed under this tyranny, every new house that went up was a vote against the Cecil interest.

For the same reason, therefore, he could not allow the open fields to be enclosed. That would have meant some twelve hundred acres freed for building, a catastrophic thought. True, he owned a good deal of this land and could stop any building on his own acres. But there was much he did not own. As lord of the manor, his consent was necessary to the procuring of any Act of Parliament for the enclosure of the town fields: and that consent was never forthcoming. If Stamford had been a vigorous industrial town like Nottingham or Leicester, the results of this feudal control would have been disastrous for the health and housing of the population. But Lord Exeter also saw to it that Stamford should never attract any industry. In 1846 there was a good chance that the new main line of railway from London to York would pass through Stamford instead of Peter-borough, then a place of no consequence. The people of Stamford were passion-ately anxious that the railway should come their way, for it was plain enough that the great coaching trade, by which they lived, was doomed. For reasons we need not go into, Lord Exeter successfully prevented the main line from entering the town: it was taken through Peterborough instead. Stamford was killed: in the eighteen-fifties, its population, which until then had been rising steadily, actually began to fall. There was no housing problem here. The open fields remained open for another generation—until the secret ballot came in 1872, but by then grass was growing in the streets of the town.

Other towns in the Midlands, towns such as Coventry for example, faced the same problem of how to get building land for their physical expansion. Some towns, like Leicester, solved the problem with no difficulty. Others, like Notting-ham and Stamford, failed—though the failure was due to entirely different political circumstances. At Nottingham it was the short-sighted conservatism of the towns-people themselves, fighting a minority who wanted change and improvement; at Stamford it was an aristocratic landlord fighting for his archaic political privileges against the townspeople. And there at Stamford, the beautiful town that Celia Fiennes and Defoe had admired so much remained almost exactly as they had seen it: but fossilized, moribund. Peterborough became the great railway and engineering centre that Stamford might well have become. But now that the human misery of the transition is over and forgotten, and now that we see modern Peterborough, we may perhaps be grateful to the Cecils for the feudal obstinacy which kept their town from growing, and preserved it for our pleasure today. There are too many Peterboroughs, and not enough Stamfords, in modern Eng-land.

The Market Town

The majority of old towns have grown up as market towns, and they all present their own special problems. This makes them more varied to look at, and in general perhaps more picturesque, but it is not easy to make them intel-ligible to someone who has not seen them. The market-place was the growing point of most towns, and they have taken their shape around it. Standing in the market-place, we are—not always but very often—at the origin of things. As we study its shape, its size, its lay-out in relation to the parish church, and the details of its topography, we are confronted by a whole series of questions. If we could answer these, I feel we should know a lot more than we do about the earliest history of the place and the way it has grown. What accounts for the differences from town to town, or the similarities between them?

In the Midlands, even in the large industrial towns, we find markets still being carried on with stalls pitched in a large open space, covering perhaps a couple of acres, exactly in the medieval fashion. The covered stalls with their piles of goods of every description, the traders shouting their wares from every stall under the open sky, all this is purely medieval; and around these open markets stand the lordly twentieth-century shops, the nearest to the London shops that the town can show. It is a curious survival: the Middle Ages incapsulated in the twentieth-century industrial town. Such great open-air markets can be seen at Northampton, Newark, and Leicester, for example, and most notable of all was that at Nottingham,

PLATE 79

Marlborough, Wiltshire. The great size of this street, which was also a market-place from time immemorial, is perhaps due to the fact that Marlborough lay in the heart of the Wiltshire downlands, which provided extensive sheep-pastures from Saxon times onwards. Space on this scale would be needed for a sheep market.

where the vast triangular market-place covers five-and-a-half acres and was once even larger. Only in recent years has it been taken over as the civic centre, and the Goose Fair relegated to the outer suburbs; but for something like a thousand years it was the market-place. At Leicester the market-place occupied the whole of the south-eastern quarter of the walled town. It has shrunk a little since it first started there, perhaps in the tenth century, but it is still one of the largest open-air markets in the country.

15

Yet at Stamford, thirty miles away, not an industrial town but indeed always
a market-town for a very rich countryside, the market-place has shrunk to a
fraction of its original size. Red Lion Square, covering about half an acre at the
most, and mostly taken up by the Great North Road, represents just the shrunken
remains of a market-place that once covered about five times that area.

Not all market-places were vast squares or rectangles or triangles, set aside for
the purpose. At Marlborough and Thame, both ancient Saxon towns, the present-
day main street—of immense width and length—once served as the open-air
market. Stalls were set up to a considerable depth on either side of the main road,
which swelled out like a sausage-shaped balloon for half a mile or so and then
closed in again. All this must have taken shape before there were any houses on
the scene. Not until much later were these immense spaces lined with buildings,
and even then the houses and shops were kept well back so as not to interfere with
the immemorial rights of the stall-holders. In such towns as Marlborough and
Thame—and many others—the market-places were never built upon, but remain
wide and open to this day (Plate 79). Probably they owe their exceptional size
to the fact that Marlborough was a great sheep-market from the earliest times,
and Thame possibly a great cattle-market. Both needed all the space they could
get. In scores of other towns, on the other hand, the market-places have been
partly built over, so that one gets a broad main street, a block of buildings down
one side and behind that again a narrow street running parallel to the main street.

There seem to be no discoverable rules about the shape of market-places, why
some take the form of a large open square—often set rather apart from the main
flow of traffic—and some a swelling, a sort of aneurism, in the main artery of
trade. The triangular shape is also common: starting with a broad base, narrowing
steadily as one goes away from it for a quarter to half a mile, until one reaches the
outlet in a main road of the normal width. St. Albans is a good example of this
type, if we think away the large block of building that lies between the present
market-place and the street called Chequer Street that lies behind. One would like
to know what these various shapes mean. Perhaps they reflect nothing at all except
the accidents of conception: but I suspect that there is often, in fact, a buried clue
here, and that if we could unearth it we should know something about the early
growth of many market-towns that no documents will ever tell us.

Very occasionally indeed, there is a document that gives us a clue. Thus the
chronicler of St. Albans monastery tells us that about the year 950 Abbot Wulsin
laid out the rudimentary town outside the north gate of the abbey. It took the form
of an open space tapering from a broad base outside the abbey walls, northwards
to a point at which he built St. Peter's Church. Facing this triangular space,
created for the benefit of traders, the abbot divided up the land on either side into
a series of narrow plots on which traders and others were encouraged to settle
permanently, building their houses with timber and other materials provided by
him. The triangular plan of the market-place, which determined the shape of the

town here, is now seen to be a perfectly rational shape for its purpose. Traders would naturally regard stall-sites close to the abbey wall as the best for business. As many as possible would cluster at that end, and the stalls would thin out quickly as one went northwards away from the abbey towards the open country, with all its dangers for the peaceful trader. The triangular shape gave the maximum protection for the greatest number of traders; but whether it represents a fairly general type of early plan—say pre-Conquest—I do not know.

Such a market-place was covered with booths and stalls for different types of traders. The next stage developed when the stalls were covered over and became permanent. The last stage was reached when the permanent stalls became houses or shops. At this point it might well happen that a block of shops and houses would be built down one side of the market-place, taking the place of a number of stalls, and so creating a plan which is frequently seen today—that is, where the original open space is reduced to a broad main street, with a detached block of buildings down one side, behind which is a narrow back street as at St. Albans, or Kimbolton in Huntingdonshire, to speak of only two examples. This happened at Stamford, also, though the buildings put up in the market-place there formed irregular blocks. And the records at St. Albans and Stamford show that these permanent buildings had made their appearance by the early fourteenth century. We should be safe in saying that this building-over of ancient market-places was the result of the great expansion of trade and population in the boom of the thirteenth century. But why did they choose to build on their own valuable market-places instead of expanding outwards into suburbs? After all, suburbs have a very respectable antiquity. They were well developed outside the walls of many English towns by the thirteenth century, even a little earlier in some places.

The relationship of market-place and church raises yet other questions. That the two are almost invariably found together is a commonplace; but why, at Market Harborough, does the church of St. Dionysius spring grandly up from the market-place without any green space around it, without a vestige of a church-yard? The answer to this question takes us back to the very origins of the town in the middle years of the twelfth century. Before that it was simply a part of the open fields of Great Bowden, a village a mile or two away. With the expansion of trade and industry in the twelfth century—perhaps the most prolific of all centuries for new towns until we come to the nineteenth—a few traders assembled periodically near a crossing place over the river Welland. An informal and unofficial market began to develop. In such a casual way many an English town was conceived. This is no guesswork; we know from the records that it often happened like this.

By the year 1203 the casual assembly at Harborough was sufficiently well established and viable to attract the notice of the Crown—ever on the lookout for revenue—and the infant township was called upon to pay three marks into the Exchequer for the right to hold a regular weekly market. Some forty years later, the town had grown big enough to call for a church of its own, instead of attending the mother church of Great Bowden. But the new town church, large and imposing though it was, was allowed only to be a dependent chapel of the mother church, without the right of burial of the dead. This right, which was a source of income to the medieval rectors, was carefully reserved to the mother church. When the men of Market Harborough died they were carried back to Great Bowden for burial, back to the country village on whose fields their town had

PLATE 80

Boston, Lincolnshire: the market-place and the parish church of St. Botolph which gives the town its name ("Botolph's *tun*"). Boston was founded by a Breton overlord soon after the Norman Conquest and grew rapidly to become one of the leading towns in medieval England.

sprung up. Their own church of St. Dionysius was allowed no churchyard. Wherever we see an ancient town church without a churchyard, we may well suspect that the town is the daughter of some mother village near by—now completely overshadowed by its offspring—and that it came into existence at a comparatively late date, since the Norman Conquest anyway, and most probably in the twelfth or thirteenth century.

At King's Lynn one's curiosity is immediately aroused by two great market-places with a splendid church beside each: the Saturday market shadowed by St. Margaret's church, the Tuesday market by St. Nicholas. Here again, we are taken back to the very beginning of the town, to the years just after the Norman Conquest—for King's Lynn is not really old by English standards. It was a town created on the marshland by the first Bishop of Norwich (Herbert Losinga, 1091-1119), to whom the site belonged and who saw its wonderful possibilities. It was he who created the Saturday market and built the church of St. Margaret beside it, just before the end of the eleventh century. And it was his successor,

PLATE 81

The main street of a dockyard town about 1830: Devonport (now part of Plymouth). The naval dockyard here was founded in the 1690s. Each of the successive wars down to 1815 enlarged both the dockyard and the town. Here is a street and a town of tremendous character and dignity.

William de Turbe (1146-74) who, two generations later, had to extend the limits of the successful town over the marshland to the north, where he established another market-place and built the church of St. Nicholas beside it. Hence the two: the Saturday market in the original town, the Tuesday market in its twelfth-century extension. Each symbolizes a distinct phase in the physical history of Lynn.

This is much too bald an account of what lies behind the landscape of this fascinating town: and across the grey waters of the Wash lies another town of the same type and date and manner of origin—Boston (Plate 80). Lynn was the creation of a Norman bishop, Boston of a great Breton lord almost simultaneously.

But they did not get in each other's way: more than twenty miles of water lay between them and they drew their vigour and their sustenance from different parts of England.

What I have tried to do in this chapter is to suggest a way of looking at towns as though they were a special kind of landscape—as indeed they are—to get behind the guide-books and the individual buildings to the secret history of these places: to draw attention to what I think are some of the significant bits of urban landscape that point the way into this secret history. But there is—for all our reflection—so much we do not know about even the simplest town scene.

There are so many towns to be seen, and each must be—or ought to be— approached for the first time on foot: certainly all the smaller towns. For only on foot does one detect the subtle rise and fall of ground to which the earliest settlers were so sensitive, or alignments in the town scene that may throw light on some fundamental change of plan: or the names of streets and lanes that set the mind working at once. No one could see Old Town Street, at Plymouth, without beginning at once to speculate about the significance of a name like this: and in fact the name takes us back to the very beginnings, to the poverty-stricken little Saxon village of farmers and fishermen, well down behind the Hoe, out of which this great naval city has grown. And then there are all the seaside towns and the dockyard towns, about which I have said nothing. The Landscape of Towns, indeed, requires a whole book to itself.

One needs the published histories of the towns and behind them the town records themselves. And slowly one pieces together from the records, from the archæological finds in the local museum, and from the evidence of one's own eyes, what has happened. It would be an interminable occupation were it not for the fact that what one learns about the landscape of one town often throws a flash of light upon a topographical puzzle in another. A pattern begins to form. It is still too early to generalize much about this subject—if indeed one will ever be able to. But in the meantime how pleasant it is to find oneself arriving in the evening for the first time in some lively little English market-town, where one can forget for a while the noisy onward march of science, and settle down to meditate upon the civilized past.

SELECT BIBLIOGRAPHY

BALLARD, A., *British Borough Charters*, 1042-1216 (1913).
BALLARD, A., and TAIT, J., *British Borough Charters*, 1216-1307 (1923).
BELOE, E. M., "Freebridge Marshland Hundred and the Making of Lynn," *Norfolk Archæology*,
CHAMBERS, J. D., *Modern Nottingham in the Making* (1945).   [xii, (1895).
BRIGGS, A., and GILL, C., *History of Birmingham* (1952).
FOX, LEVI, *Stratford-upon-Avon* (1953).
GILBERT, E. W., *Brighton* (1954).
HILL, J. W. F., *Medieval Lincoln* (1948).
HYDE, F. E., and MARKHAM, F. S., *A History of Stony Stratford* (1948).
LITTLE, B., *The City and County of Bristol* (1954).
SAVAGE, SIR WILLIAM, *The Making of our Towns* (1952).
STEPHENSON, CARL, *Borough and Town* (1933), esp. Chapter VII.

X

The Landscape Today

THE industrial revolution and the creation of parks around the country houses have taken us down to the later years of the nineteenth century. Since that time, and especially since the year 1914, every single change in the English landscape has either uglified it or destroyed its meaning, or both. Of all the changes in the last two generations, only the great reservoirs of water for the industrial cities of the North and Midlands have added anything to the scene that one can contemplate without pain. It is a distasteful subject, but it must be faced for a few moments.

The country houses decay and fall: hardly a week passes when one does not see the auctioneer's notice of the impending sale and dissolution of some big estate. The house is seized by the demolition contractors, its park invaded and churned up by the tractors and trailers of the timber merchant. Down comes the house; down come the tall trees, naked and gashed lies the once-beautiful park. Or if it stands near a town, the political planners swarm into the house, turn it into a rabbit-warren of black-hatted officers of This and That, and the park becomes a site for some "overspill"—a word as beastly as the thing it describes. We may indeed find the great house still standing tidily in a timbered park: but it is occupied by what the villagers describe detachedly as "the atom men," something remote from the rest of us, though not remote in the sense they themselves like to think. And if the planners are really fortunate, they fill the house with their paper and their black hats, and their open-cast mining of coal or iron ore simultaneously finishes off the park. They can sit at their big desks and contemplate with an exquisite joy how everything is now being put to a good use. Demos and Science are the joint Emperors.

Beyond the park, in some parts of England such as East Anglia, the bull-dozer rams at the old hedges, blots them out to make fields big and vacant enough for the machines of the new ranch-farming and the business-men farmers of five to ten thousand acres. Fortunately, the tractor and the bull-dozer cannot easily destroy the great hedgebanks and stone walls of the anciently-enclosed parts of England; nor is it worth doing, for the good farmer knows the value of these banks and walls as shelter, and of the hedges for timber. Much of the old field pattern therefore remains, with its tangle of deep lanes and thick hedges.

What else has happened in the immemorial landscape of the English country-side? Airfields have flayed it bare wherever there are level, well-drained stretches of land, above all in eastern England. Poor devastated Lincolnshire and Suffolk! And those long gentle lines of the dip-slope of the Cotswolds, those misty uplands

of the sheep-grey oolite, how they have lent themselves to the villainous requirements of the new age! Over them drones, day after day, the obscene shape of the
atom-bomber, laying a trail like a filthy slug upon Constable's and Gainsborough's
sky. England of the Nissen hut, the "pre-fab," and the electric fence, of the high
barbed wire around some unmentionable devilment; England of the arterial
by-pass, treeless and stinking of diesel oil, murderous with lorries; England of

PLATE 82

The completed English landscape: near Wantage in Berkshire. A fertile strip of the Upper
Greensand runs along the foot of the chalk downlands. A string of villages were founded
in Saxon times on this narrow belt of water-bearing sands between the porous chalk of
the hills and the impervious Gault clay of the Vale.

the bombing-range wherever there was once silence, as on Otmoor or the marshlands of Lincolnshire; England of battle-training areas on the Breckland heaths,
and tanks crashing through empty ruined Wiltshire villages; England of high
explosive falling upon the prehistoric monuments of Dartmoor. Barbaric England
of the scientists, the military men, and the politicians: let us turn away and
contemplate the past before all is lost to the vandals.

The view from this room where I write these last pages is small, but it will serve as an epitome of the gentle unravished English landscape. Circumscribed as it is, with tall trees closing it in barely half a mile away, it contains in its detail something of every age from the Saxon to the nineteenth century. A house has stood on this site since the year 1216, when the bishop of Lincoln ordained a vicarage here, but it has been rebuilt over and over again, and last of all in 1856. Down the garden, sloping to the river, the aged and useless apple trees are the successors of those that grew here in the time of Charles I, when the glebe terrier of 1634 speaks of "one orchard, one backside, and two little gardens." Beyond the apple trees and within a few feet of the river is a large raised platform, visible in winter before its annual submergence in weeds, part of a vanished building, and there are clear lines of stone walls adjoining it. Almost certainly this is the site of one of the three water-mills recorded on the estate in Domesday Book. Below it flows the Dorn, known to the Saxons as the Milk, from the cloudiness of its water after rain: and one still sees it as the Saxons saw it a thousand years ago, as I saw it a few minutes ago in the thin rain drifting down from the Cotswolds.

Across the stream, tumbling fast on its way to Glyme and Evenlode, one sees a wide sedgy hollow planted with willow saplings, from which flocks of goldfinches rise with a flash of wings on sunny mornings. This hollow, enclosed by a massive earthen bank, was the fishpond begun by the lord of the manor before his death in 1175, and completed by his son:

Odo de Berton grants to Roger de St. John the land between the garden of Roger and the road to the bridge, together with the moor where Thomas de St. John began to make his fishpond, rendering yearly a pair of spurs or twopence.

This was about the year 1200 (the charter is undated), but there is the fishpond today. And there is the lane dropping down to the stone bridge that was rebuilt in 1948, but unquestionably on the site of the stone bridge which is mentioned as a landmark in an even earlier charter. And "the moor" is the description of the scene before it had been claimed for cultivation. We catch a sight of an earlier world in the bare words of this charter.

Beyond the fishpond, the ground rises to form the other side of the valley, fields with their broken hedges of twisted hawthorns. What age are these hedges? They were not here in 1685, when another glebe terrier shows that the parish still had its open fields. But they were probably made before 1750, by which date the enclosure had apparently been accomplished. One or two hedgebanks are, however, medieval in origin, for the St. Johns had a separate enclosed pasture called Grascroft from the early 1200s onwards, and this ancient field comes into the view also.

A little to the right, on the other side of the lane, the eye dwells upon a small park, with a boating-lake catching the light, and some modest landscaping; and through the bare winter trees one sees the chimneys of a seemly Victorian "big house." The house and park were made as late as the 1870s. It must be one of the last parks to be made in England, for landowners began to feel the pinch of falling rents soon after that. The house, in fact, is older, for the work of the 1870s, though apparently a complete rebuilding, is merely a stone casing around a house originally built by a successful merchant of the Staple, whose inscription is still over the door: "*Thinke and Thanke Anno 1570.*" Three hundred years later his house was remodelled by another successful bourgeois—this time a wealthy Oxford brewer.

But this was an old, long-cultivated estate when John Dormer the merchant stapler acquired it, with a history stretching back to pre-Conquest days, when it was one of the demesne-farms of the Anglo-Saxon kings. When they hunted in Woodstock Park, five miles away, in the tenth and eleventh centuries, they called upon the produce of this large estate (about seven thousand acres then) to feed their household; and one can walk, after a morning's writing, along the broad green lane that was first made to connect the estate with the hunting-park. It was a royal estate in Saxon times, but how far back into that age? What was it when the Saxons captured Eynsham, not many miles away, in the year 571? We do not yet know, but here in this room one is reaching back, in a view embracing a few hundred acres at the most, through ten centuries of English life, and discerning shadowy depths beyond that again.

By opening the window and leaning out, the parish church comes into view across the lane, a lonely building now, empty and cold and bare except for one hour each week. It was rebuilt about the year 1300, when the village was large and flourishing: this was the High Farming period of the Middle Ages. But the font is of the twelfth century, so there was a church here then; and deep in the churchyard to the east of the chancel is a buried wall which is perhaps the east wall of a Saxon church. For though it stands so isolated today from human kind, St. Mary's church was a mother-church for a wide area round about, as befitted the spiritual centre of a royal estate; and we do not know how far back a building stood on this site. A Roman coin came from under the tower at the restoration of 1855, but one cannot make too much of that.

And then, finally, out of sight but only fifty or sixty yards from this room, in the field next the garden, there lies buried the main street of the old village that was wiped out by the Black Death. One walks between the banks that show where the houses stood, marking how blocks of squared masonry thrust in one place out of the turf (a more important building than most of them), and how the tree-roots twist among the rubble footings of the peasant dwellings; and one picks up pieces of twelfth- and thirteenth-century pottery—mere sherds, bits of rim, of sides, of bases, but all dateable: nothing later than the Black Death, when the Great Silence descended.

Not every small view in England is so full of detail as this, upon the oolite of north Oxfordshire, for this was a rich and favoured countryside that was beloved of owners of Roman villas, even in places of Bronze Age men. The cultural humus of sixty generations or more lies upon it. But most of England is a thousand years old, and in a walk of a few miles one would touch nearly every century in that long stretch of time.

Know most of the rooms of thy native country before thou goest over the threshold thereof. Especially seeing England presents thee with so many observables.

Index

Abbotsham, 28
Abingdon bridge, 106
Ab Kettleby, 153
airfields, 231
Akeman Street, 180, 182, 183
Allexton, 160, 161
Althorp, 116, 131
Alton Priors, Wilts., 57
Ambion, Leics., 93
Andred, forest of (Andredes Weald), 62
Anglo-Saxons, 45
　cemetery at Wigston, 59
　estate boundaries, 55-8
　　boundary banks, 55
　paths, 156
　villages, 19
Apethorpe park, Northants., 131
aqueducts, 191
Arden, Forest of, 109
Arkwright, Ric., 165, 168, 176
Arncliffe, 62
Asgardike, 78
Ash trees, 37, 69, 122, 152
　planted in hedges, 151
Ashby-de-la-Zouch, 107, 154
Ashmore, N. Dorset, 43, 44, 45
Ashridge park, 75, 130
Ashton-under-Lyne, 212
Ashwell, 67, 158
"assarts," 70, 74
Asterleigh, Oxon., 93
Asthall, iron-working settlement, 32
Audley End, Essex, 129
Aunby, Lincs., 92, 93, 95
Avon, the Bristol, 180
　the Wilts., 89, 213
Axholme, Isle of, 39, 42, 138
Aylesbury, Vale of, 117

Babeny, 22-5, 81
Bagshot Heath, Surrey, 110
Bakewell, Robt., 81, 145
Baldock, Herts., 54
balks, 41, 42
Banbury, 180, 182, 183
　Lane, 180-2, 187
Barnet, Herts., 48
Barrow-in-Furness, growth of, 176, 211, 212, 213, 216
Barsby, Leics., 144, 156
Barton Abbey, Oxon., 132
Bath, 34, 165, 200, 205, 206
Beech forest, 37, 69
Belgae, the, 29, 34, 35, 37
Belper, 168, 169
Berkshire, 62, 73, 110, 141, 181
Bewdley, 187, 193
Bexhill, 63
Bicester, Saxon town, 183
Bicker Haven, 76, 77
Biddisham (Tarnuc), Axbridge, 45
Bideford, 90, 105-6
Birkenhead, growth of, 176
Birmingham, 109, 170, 182, 187, 193, 201, 211, 212, 213
　courts, 173
　heath, 174
Bishops Cleeve, 70
Black Country, the, 162, 163, 171, 176, 193
Black Death, the, 13, 69, 84, 93, 234
Bladon, Oxon., 88
Blanchdown, Devon, 178
Blanchland, Northumb., 49
Blandford, 134

Blenheim Palace, 129, 130, 136
　Park, 130, 132, 135, 136, 185
Bodmin, 106
　Moor, 20, 81
Bolton abbey, 83
　Castle, 106
Bosigran farm, Zennor, 24, 25
Boston, Lincs., 34, 69, 76, 77, 228, 229
Bottoms, Almondbury, Yorks., 164
Boulton, Matt., 165, 167, 172
Bourne, 33
Bourne, J. C., 198, 201, 202
Box Tunnel, 198, 200, 205, 206
Boxmoor embankment, 205
Brackley, Northants., 180
Bradgate Park, Leics., 75
Bradley, Devon, 104
Bradworthy, W. Devon, 53
Braunton, N. Devon, 42, 138
Breckland, 61, 92, 95, 232
Brentwood, Essex, 48
bricks, 107
bridges in medieval England, 90-1, 100
bridle paths, 30
Brighton, 22, 210
Brindley, Jas., 191, 192, 193, 195, 196
Bringhurst, 161
Bristol, 29, 114, 205
Brixworth, Northants., 65
Broadway Hill, 190
Bromsgrove, 187
Bronze Age, 22, 30, 181, 186, 187
Brown, Lancelot (Capability), 128, 135, 136
Brudenell, Sir Robt., 160
　family, 131
Buckinghamshire, 97, 141, 145
Burghley House, Northants., 128, 135, 223
　Park, 128, 130, 131, 223
　lake in, 128, 135, 137
Burslem, 167, 168, 174
Burton Agnes, Yorks., 29
Burton Constable, Yorks., 133
Burton-upon-Trent, 69, 91, 154
Bury St. Edmunds, 212
Buttermere, Wilts., 45
Bygrave, Herts., 158

Calceby, Lincs., 95
Calleva (Silchester), 34
Callington, E. Cornwall, 46
Cambridge, 33, 34, 190
Cambridgeshire, South, 158
Camden Town, 199, 201, 202, 204
Camel Estuary, the, 105, 106
canals, 153, 172, 191-7
Canons Ashby, 182
Canterbury Cathedral Priory, 80
Car Dyke, the, 33, 191
Careby, 95
Carew, Ric., 105
Cary, Geo., 98
Castallack farm, 24, 26
Castle Drogo, Devon, 129
Castle Hill, Devon, 137
Castle Howard, 129
castles, 91, 100, 126
Castor, 150
Catfoss, 63
cattle-field, early Celtic, 24
Celliwic, 46
Celtic estates, 14, 26, 28
　farms, 22, 28
　farmsteads, 23, 24
　fields, 22, 23, 24, 28, 33
　hamlets, 27, 42

Celtic hedges, 28, 49
　landowners, 26, 28
　monastic communities, 47
　names, 46
　place-names, 26, 45
　saints, 46
Chalk downlands, 22, 23, 141
　sites on, 31, 158
Challacombe, 81
chapels, medieval (see oratories)
Chedworth, Roman villa at, 80
Cheltenham, 70, 80
Cherwell, the, 180, 181, 182, 183
Cheshire, iv, 141
　salt works, 193
Chiltern Hills, 71, 75, 141
Chippenham, 205, 206
Chirk aqueduct and tunnel, 193
Cholwich Town, 81, 84
church, the country, appearance of, 65
　spires, first appearance of, 85
　towers and spires, 66, 101
churches in S.W. England rebuilt, 101
　two or more in one village, 60
Chysauster, 21, 22, 24, 25, 31
Cistercian monasteries, 80-1
　granges, 93, 114
clapper bridges on Dartmoor, 188
Clare, John, 109, 148, 150, 206
　quoted, 138, 149, 151-2, 154, 203
clearance of woodlands, 48, 62, 69-76
Clovelly, Devon, 98, 99
coal gas for lighting, 166n.
　mining, 171
　pits, 163
Coalbrookdale, Salop, 165, 166
Coalville, 61
Colchester (Camulodunum), 34
Colkirk, Norf., 95
Colly Weston, Northants., 121
　slates, 123, 125
Combe, Oxon., 93
common pasture, 138
　rights, 111
commons enclosed for building, 174
Compton Superior, 126
　Wynyates, 126
coppice fences, 113
Cornwall, 23, 38, 42, 45, 46, 47, 65, 90, 105, 111, 122, 141, 216
　church towers, 101
　industrial landscapes, 177
　moorlands, 81
　rotten boroughs, 216
Cotswolds, the, 35, 45, 70, 80, 153, 190, 193, 231, 233
Country Houses and Parks, 126-37
country house building, 119
　origin of the, 126
Courteenhall House and Park, 130
Coventry, 114, 156, 182
　expansion of, 224
　Canal, 197
Cowley Bridge, Devon, 190
Crabbe, Geo., quoted, 149-50
Granborne Chase, 33, 42, 44
Crawford, O. G. S., 43, 45, 76, 181, 182
Crewe Rly. Station, 207
Crimscote, Warws., 43
Cromford, 173, 176
　Arkwright's spinning mill at, 165, 166n.
Crowndale farm, Tavistock, 93
Culworth, 181, 182, 187
Cumberland, Norwegian place-names in, 59

Danish conquest, 92
  partitioning of land, 60
  soldier settlers, 59, 77
Darby, Abr., ironworks, 165, 166
Dartmoor, 26, 63, 75, 81, 82, 190
  central waste of, 18, 62
  clapper bridges on, 188
  hut circles on, 20
  prehistoric monuments, 232
Dean, Forest of, 109
Defoe, D., 109, 117, 165, 168, 170
demolition of country houses, 231
Derby (formerly Northworthy), 59, 165
Derbyshire, 109, 129, 151, 169
Derwent, the, 63, 165, 168, 169, 170
deserted villages, 93-7
Devon, 38, 42, 46, 61, 63, 65, 66, 67, 70,
  74, 75, 90, 105, 111, 114, 121, 123,
  141, 142, 178, 206, 214
  castles, 91
  church towers, 101
  early enclosure, 139
  Great Consols copper mine, 178
  lanes, 160
  medieval field pattern, 82
  new towns in 12th and 13th cen-
    turies, 214
  wastes, 110
Devonport, main street, 229
disafforestation, medieval, 75
Dishley, 81
ditches, Fenland, 34, 36
Ditchley, Oxon., 31, 45, 132
Domesday Book, 46, 47, 49, 52, 60, 61, 62,
  63, 64, 65, 66, 69, 77, 80, 82, 92,
  186, 233
  boroughs, 67
Dorset, 34, 42, 121, 123, 138, 141, 148, 159
double ditch, 28, 56
drainage of marsh and fenland, 59
Drift, The (Sewstern Lane), 187, 189
drove-roads, 52, 184, 186, 187
Droitwich brine springs, 186
Dudley, 162, 193
Dutton viaduct, 206

Eagles and ravens, 62
Earls Barton, Northants., 65
Easington, Gloucs., 134
East Anglia, 142
  population, 61, 92
  Roman roads in, 29
East Barsham, Norf., 126
Edge Hill, Warws., 124, 182
  tunnel, Liverpool, 199
Ellesmere Canal, 193
elm tree, the, 69, 122, 152
  planted in hedges, 151
Ely, monks of, 75
Empingham, Rutland, 155
enclosure, 111-13
  by agreement, 118, 139
  expense of, 157
  fields, size of, 145
  of the Midland fields, 114-19
  parishes affected, 139
  parliamentary, extent of, 138-42
  roads, 154-7, 186
English boundaries, continuity of, 183
Epping Forest, 109
Epworth, Isle of Axholme, 138
Essex, 38, 50, 61, 62, 70, 73, 88, 142
  early enclosure, 111, 139
  lanes, 160
  woodlands, 111
Etruria, Burslem, 165
  Hall, 167, 168
Evelyn, John, his *Sylva*, 135
Evenlode, the, 32, 182, 233
Evesham, Worcs., 33, 186
evictions by landlords, 96-7
Exe, the, 42, 55, 191
Exeter (Isca Dumnoniorum), 34, 35, 69,
  72, 104, 114, 155, 190, 191

Exeter (*contd.*)
  abbey of St. Mary and St. Peter, 55,
    56, 57, 58
  bp. of, 103
  bridge, 91
  canal, 191
Exmoor, 63, 75
Exton, 130, 155
Eynsham, Oxon., 45, 90, 234

factory working introduced, 165
farmhouses, building of, 13
  enclosure, 157-61
farmsteads, granite, of Cornwall, 13
  Lincolnshire, 54
  Norwegian, 59
  of Saxon origin, 46
Felbrigg, Norfolk, 147
Fens, the, 54, 61, 62, 78
  and marshes, 46
Fenland, the, 33, 36, 63
  landscape, 76-7
  parishes, 85
Fenny Compton, 182, 197
field-patterns, 22
    created by enclosure, 144, 146
Fiennes, Celia, 165, 218
Finchingfield, Essex, 49, 50
Fingest, Bucks., Norman church at, 71
fishing villages, 97
"flashes," 167
Fleet, 78
  Haven, 76
Flitteris Park, 130
forest laws, Norman, 73
  clearings, Roman villas in, 31
Forest of Dean, 109
forests, 30
formal gardens, 135
Fosham, 63
Foss Dyke, Roman canal, 34, 191
Fosse Way, the, 156
Fotheringhay church, Northants., 100, 101
Fountains abbey, 83
fox-hunting in Leics., 151, 152
  coverts, 152
fragmented villages, 49, 53-4
Fullbrook castle, 126
fulling mill, the, 65
fulling establishment, Roman, 80
Fyfield Down, Wilts., 22, 23

General Enclosure Act, 1845, 143
geology, books on, 13
Georgian farmhouses, 159
  hedges, 119
  mansions, 129, 130
glass-works, 162
Glastonbury, 45, 79
  abbey, 83, 80
glazing becomes general, 123
Gloucester, 165, 182
Gloucestershire, 90, 141
  abbeys, 85
Godney (Goda's island), 79
Gothic Revival, 129
Grand Junction Canal, 197
  Trunk Canal, tunnels on, 192, 193
granite boulder walls, 24, 25, 26
  crosses as guide-posts, 190
  dry-walling, 21
  surface (moorstone), 27
grass verges, 154, 155, 156
gravel, sites on, 31
graziers, prosperous, 124, 157
grazing rights in open fields, 111, 216, 218
Great Bowden, Leics., 227, 228
  Haywood, Staffs., 196
  North Road, 187, 189, 190, 226
  Tew, Oxon., 167
"green lanes," 183
green-village, the, 49, 50, 53, 54
Greenstead, Essex, 66
Greyston bridge, Devon, 105

Grimsby, 60, 79
guide-books, 210
guide-posts, 190

Hackpen Hill, Berks., 181
haga (hedge, enclosure), 152, 185
Halifax, 110, 163
  parish, 88, 104
hamlets, 31, 66
  Anglo-Saxon, 46-8
  Norwegian, 59
Hampshire, 61, 73, 141
Hampstead Marshall Park, Newbury, 76
Hanwell, 205
Harecastle Tunnel, 192
Hassock Dike, 78
Hatfield Park, Herts., 75, 130
Hatton, Sir Chris., 128, 129
Hawkesbury lock, Oxford Canal, 197
Haxey, Isle of Axholme, 39, 42, 138
heathen cemeteries, 49, 77
heath-lands of W. Norfolk and Lincs., 147
heathland birds, disappearance of, 153
hedgerows, planting of, 150
Helpston, 150, 154, 157, 203
  heath, 148
Helston, W. Cornwall, 46
Hengrave Hall, Suff., 126, 127
Henley-in-Arden, Warws., 49, 124
Hertfordshire, 75, 97, 158
Heythrop Park, 132
Hindhead, 110
Hitchin, 45
Holdenby, 128
Holderness, 80
  place-names in, 63
Holkham, Norf., 147, 148
"hollow way," 28
Holt (Nevill Holt), 161
Holyoak, deserted village of, 160
Holywell, Lincs., 92, 95
homesteads, isolated, Danish, 60
Honeychurch, Devon, 85, 101
Huddersfield Canal, 194
Hull, 69, 193, 212: *and see* Kingston-upon-
  Hull
Humber, the, 37, 59, 180
Hunsbury, Iron Age hill-fort, 181
Huntingdon bridge, 104
Hurstmonceaux Castle, Sussex, 107

Icknield Way, 54, 181
Ince, Lancs., coal-mining landscape, 176
industrial landscape, early, 162-5
  19th century, 176-9
  Revolution, 85, 231
    villages, 66
  "sublime ugliness," 178
  towns, amenities added, 175-6
  villages, 18th century, 159, 168-9
Ingoldmells salt workings, 186
Iron Age, 181, 182
  earthworks, 198, 204
  field boundary, 26
  houses, 24
  village sites, 22
  villages of W. Cornwall, 19, 24
iron-mining in the Weald, 30, 162
ironstone, 123, 124, 125
Izod, Nathan, 190

Jacob of Mountsorrel, 74-75
Jurassic Way, the, 180, 181, 182

Kelham bridge, 91
Kendal, 203
Kenilworth, 187
Kensington Gardens, 135, 137
Kent, Wm., landscape gardener, 135, 137
Kent, 38, 61, 62, 114, 122, 142, 190
  abbeys, 85
  castles, 91
  early enclosure in, 67, 111, 139
  marshes, 80, 97

Kent, Roman roads in, 29
    square plots in, 67
    windmills, 88
Kettering, 61
Ketton, Rutland, 87
    stone, 206
Kew Gardens, 135
Kilkhampton, N. Cornwall, 46
Kimbolton, Hunts., 227
King, Gregory, 108, 109, 138
Kings Lynn, 69, 148, 229
Kingston-upon-Hull, 212, 214
Kirby Hall, 129
    Muxloe castle, 107
Kirkby Lonsdale, 105
Knaptoft, Leics., 117–18
Knole, Kent, 129
Knowsley Park, 75, 130, 131

Lake District, 124, 206
Lammas pasture rights, 216
Lancashire, 38, 121, 170, 189, 206
    enclosure, 111
    moorland, 88
    towns, 174
Lancaster Canal, 193
Langley Bush, 149
Lapford, Devon, 104
large parishes, 88
Launceston, 103
    castle and town, 68, 91
    church, 103
Lavenham, Suff., church tower, 101
Lawling, Essex, 70, 71
Laxton, Notts., 41, 42, 138
Leeds, 176
    slums, 218
Leicester, 156, 160, 217, 221-23, 224, 225
Leicestershire, 42, 61, 75, 117, 119, 122,
    130, 145, 147, 151, 160, 187, 189,
    209
    deserted villages, 93, 94
    field paths, 160
Leighfield, forest of, 130
Leland, John, 105, 106, 110, 111, 162
lime trees, 69
limestone belt of Northants., 66
    boundary walls, 83
    walls, 151, 155
Lincoln, 33, 34, 67, 85, 143, 191
    medieval, 210
    bp. of, 233
Lincolnshire, 42, 54, 61, 62, 65, 92, 186,
    187, 189, 231
    deserted villages, 93
    heath country of, enclosed, 143, 159-
    60
    marshland, 60, 64
    monasteries, 85
    Wolds, 93, 95, 154
Litlington, Ashwell, 45, 158
Little Wenham Hall, Suff., 107
Liverpool, 69, 88, 170, 193
    slums, 210
    and Manchester Rly., 199
Lombe, John and Thos., silk mill, 165
London, 33, 67, 114, 155, 187, 189, 190,
    208
    East, slums, 218
    Elizabethan, 125
    as a food market, 122
    natural landscape of, 20
    Roman, 34
long barrows, 182
Long Melford, Suff., "street-village," 49
Longleat, 128
Looe bridge, 106
Losinga, Herbt., bp. of Norwich, 229
lost villages in Lincs., 13
    identification of, 95-6
Low Church vandals, 101
Lower Gornal, 163
Ludlow, 90, 91, 187, 212
Lydford, Devon, 67

lynchets, 22
Lyveden, 129

Maiden Castle, Dorset, 204
Maidenhead Rly. bridge, 198
Maidenwell, Lincs., 93
Manchester, 170, 191, 193
    slums, 218
maple, the, 69, 121
market-place, position of, 224
    relation to church, 227
market-roads, 182, 186
market towns, 90, 186, 224-30
Market Harborough, 69, 125, 227, 228
Marlborough, Wilts., 22, 23, 226
    market-place, 225
Marsh, Fen, and Moor, 76-83
marshland, 63, 79
    Lincs. and Norf., 76
    parishes, 85
    villages, 78
Marsh Chapel hamlet, 79
Marshall, Wm., Rural Economy of Norfolk,
    113, 142, 145, 147, 151
medieval hedges, 119
    housing, 120
    peasants, 36
megalithic tombs, 182
meres, 183, 184
Mersey, the, 192, 193, 197, 206
Mevagissy, Cornwall, 97
Michaelstow church, Cornwall, 102
Middle Barton, Oxon., "fragmented-
    village," 49, 52, 157
Middle Carlton, Lincs., 93
Middlesbrough, growth of, 176, 211, 212,
    213, 216
milestones, 190
Milford, Belper, 168, 169
mills, 65, 88, 165
Milton Abbas, Benedictine monastery,
    Dorset, 133-4
    "planned-village," 49, 134
Minchinhampton Common, 80
monasteries, 85
Monkton royal estate, Devon, 55-8
Monsal Dale viaduct, 206
Montacute, 128
moorstone (surface granite), 27
Morwellham, 194
mother churches, 104
Moulton Seas End, 76
Mountsorrel, Leics., 74
Mow Cop, iv
Muchelney abbey, Somerset, 63, 80

Navigation or Canal Inns, 197
navvies ("inland navigators"), 198, 201,
    208
Nevill Holt, 161
New Bridge, Devon, 105
    Buckenham, Norf., 76
    Forest, 73, 93
    Hall Estate, Birmingham, 213
    Quay, Cornwall, 97
    Sarum (Salisbury), 89
Newark, 61, 91, 189, 225
Newbury, Berks., 69, 76
Newcastle-on-Tyne, 69, 91, 214
Newtown, Dorset: see Nova Villa.
Norfolk, 61, 65, 114, 141, 147
    Breckland, 61, 92, 142
    difference between E. and W., 142
    deserted villages, 93
    marshland, 61
    parishes, 60
Norman Forests, 74-5
Normanton Park, Rutland, 133
Northampton, 181, 182, 187
    market, 224
    Saxon road to, 182
Northamptonshire, 61, 115, 116, 117, 119,
    122, 141, 145, 147, 148, 151, 187
    deserted villages, 93

Northumberland enclosure, 111
Norton-by-Twycross, Leics., 154
Norwegian settlement in N.-E. England,
    59
Norwich, 61, 62, 67, 85, 109, 114
Nottingham, 91, 178, 217, 223, 224, 225
    Arkwright's spinning mill at, 165
    Clay Field after enclosure, 222
    opponents of enclosure, 219-21
    plan of a typical Court, 220
    slums, 218-21
Nottinghamshire, 61, 109, 131
Nova Villa ("Newtown"), Dorset, 211,
    212, 213, 215
nucleated village, 33, 38
    survival of the, 159

Oak forest, 37, 69
Offa's Dyke, 76
Old Podike, 79
    Sarum, 89
    Sea Bank, 77
    West Water, 33
Oldham, 174
Olive Mount cutting, 199
oolitic limestone ("Cotswold stone"), 31,
    32, 80, 85, 90, 120, 123, 234
open-cast mining, 231
open fields, 60, 66, 70, 71, 138, 158
    area at parliamentary enclosure,
    138
    enclosure of, 139
    in Midlands, 111
    Saxon, 38, 46
    system, 38, 39, 42
    2- and 3-field systems, 40
    villages, 54
    or commons, land without, 112
Open Field Town, The, 216-24
oratories, private, 100, 101
Otford, Kent, 31
Ouse, the, 33, 104
    the Sussex, 33
    the Great, 181
Overstone Park, Northants., 130
Oxford, 61, 180
    canal shortened, 197
    St. Frideswide's monastery, 183
Oxfordshire, 62, 66, 80, 123, 141, 180,
    182, 183, 209
    North, 35, 235
    distribution of parks in, 132

Packhorse track and bridge, 188
Paddington station, 204, 208
parish boundaries, 58, 180
park enlargements, 132-4
    medieval, tracing boundary of, 76
    "park," orig. enclosure, 75, 113, 129
Park Village, Camden Town, 201, 202
parks, expansion of, 131
    made in 19th century, 137, 231
    private, for hunting, 75
    round country houses, 129
parliamentary enclosure, 38, 138-61
    absence of lanes, 160
    date of, 142-3
    extent of, 138-42
    farmhouses, 157-61
    the fields, 145-50
    hedgerows and trees, 150-4
    the new landscape, 143-4
    roads, 154-7
pastures, large, 117
    disadvantages of, 118
peasant building, 122
Pennines, the, 193
    moorland valleys of the, 166
Penwith peninsula, 21, 25, 27
Pershore, 67
Peterborough, 33, 191, 224
Pevensey Levels, "inning" of, 63, 64
Pewsey, Vale of, Wilts., 58
Pickworth, 93

planned town, the, 211-16
    villages, 18th century, 49
plough, heavy wheeled, 29, 31
    types of, 67
ploughing, open-field, 42
Plymouth, 88, 229, 230
Plympton, priors of, 88
Polperro, Cornwall, 98
ponds, 43, 44
Pontcysyllte aqueduct, 193
Poole, Dorset, 211, 215
population, prehistoric, 29
    neolithic, 20
    at Roman conquest, 29
    at 1086, 61
    on eve of Black Death, 84
    in 1500, 108
Porthmeor, 21, 22, 24, 25
Portsmouth, 69, 88, 110
Port Way, the, 180
Potteries, the, 165, 170, 171, 174, 193
pound-locks on canals, 191
Powderham (polder-ham), 63
power-driven machinery, 163
Preston, Lancs., 170, 174
    mills and housing at, 175
Price, Uvedale, *Essays on the Picturesque*,
    quoted, 170
Priors Hardwick, 187

Quarries, 162
Queen Hoo Hall, Herts., 46
"Quorn country," 152

Raby castle, Durham, 107
Raddon Hills, Devon, 55
Radipole, Dorset, 143 *n.*
railways, 197-209
    impact on landscape, 197-8
Railway Age, the, 189
    earthworks, 198
    gradients, 204-5
    stations, early, 206, 207
reclamation of marshes from the sea, 77,
    79-80
    of fens, 78, 79-80
    of moorland, 81-3
Renaissance style building, 127
Rennie, John, 193
repair of dikes and ditches, 78
Repton, Humph., 135
reservoirs, construction of, 231
Revesby, Lincs., 59
ridge-and-furrow, 42, 43
Ridgeway, the, Berks., 181, 182
Rievaulx abbey, Yorks., 86
rivers made navigable, 191
Roade cutting, 205
roads, 180-90
Roman Britain, 29-37
"Roman Bank," 64, 76, 77, 78
    canals or dykes, 29, 191
    dykes, 33
    roads, 29, 31, 157, 183
    towns, 34, 35, 67
    villa-estates, 35
    villas, 30, 33, 45, 235
        decay of, 36
        in N. Oxon., 132
        sites of, 29
    walls, 69
Romano-British by-roads, 185
    ironworking at Asthall, 32
    villages, 30, 31, 33, 45
Romans, the, 63, 77, 182, 190, 212
Romney marsh, reclaiming of, 63
roodscreens, 101
Rousham, Oxon., 135
Roxford, Hertingfordbury, 46
royal demesne farm of Anglo-Saxon kings,
    185, 234
Royston, Herts., 181
Rutland, 19, 85, 130, 141, 155, 160, 206
Ryedale, 86

St. Albans (Verulamium), 34, 67, 226, 227
St. Austell, Cornwall, 177
St. Brioc, 47
St. Helens, 171
    growth of, 176
St. Ives, Cornwall, 24
    bridge, Hunts., 104
St. Neots, 81, 106
Salisbury (New Sarum), 69, 114, 212,
    213, 216
    the medieval plan of, 89, 90, 211
    Plain, 33, 155
Salt Way, the, 180, 185-6
Saltash bridge, 207
Sapperton tunnel, 193
Saturday Dike, 78
Saxon charters, 46, 80
    estate, 28
    hawthorn hedges, 152
    landmark at Alton Priors, 57
    town of Bicester, 183
Scandinavian names, 57, 92
    settlement, 42, 57-60
    settlers, 60, 64
Scarborough, 214, 215
"Scenery," taste for, 109
Schools in villages, 124-6
    science, onward march of, 232
sea-banks, 78
Sea Dike, the, Lincs., 64
Seagrave, Leics., farmhouse names, 157
Seebohm, F., *The English Village Com-
    munity*, 45
Severn, the, 141, 166, 193
Seward, Anna, "The Swan of Lichfield,"
    quoted, 166, 170
Sham ruins, iv, 137
Shardlow, 193
sheep in 1500, 108
    and cattle farming, 117, 118
    grazing, 63
    grazing in East Anglia, 92
    on reclaimed marshland, 80
    -walks, 36
Sheffield, 109, 170, 171, 176, 178
Sherwood Forest, 17, 109
Shropshire Union Canal, 192, 193, 195
Sileby, Leics., farmhouse names, 157
silt bank, Old English settlers on, 77
    ridge, villages on, 54
Silverton, E. Devon, 51, 56
Skegness, 186
Sleaford, 34, 143
slums, growth of, 172-3
Somercotes, 64
Somerset, 45, 58, 61, 63, 65, 85, 111, 141,
    155, 206
    Levels, 62, 79, 80
Somerton, 57
South Berks., forest, 31
    Croxton and Barsby, Leics., 144, 156
    Damerham, Wilts., 80
    Shields, growth of, 176
Southall Green, Middlesex, 208
Spencer, John, 115, 116, 117, 135
"Stagg's Gardens," 199
Staithes, Yorks., 97
Stallingborough, 60
Stamford, 74, 100, 189, 217, 223-4, 226
"stances," cattle, 187
Standedge tunnel, 193
Stathern, Leics., 144, 156
steam engines, 172
    -power and slums, 171-9
Steeple Barton, Oxon., 52, 93, 183, 184
    fishpond, 233
    main street, 234
    park and house, 234
    St. Mary's parish church, 234
Stephenson, Carl, *Borough and Town*, 210
Stockport railway viaduct, 178, 179, 206
Stonesfield slate-pits, 209
Stourport, Worcs., 191, 193, 194
Stowe Park, Bucks., 135

Stratford-upon-Avon, 69, 88, 90, 186
    Old Town, 88, 212
street-plans, 211
    -villages, 40, 49, 53
Stroud-Water valley, Glos., 165
Strutt, Jedidiah, 168, 169
Suffolk, 61, 65, 92, 142, 231
    church towers, 101
    enclosure, 111
    East, woodlands, 111
Surfleet Seas End, 76
Surrey, 141, 148
    enclosure, 111
Sussex, 61, 62, 142
    downs, 22, 33, 35, 36
    iron mines, 162
    lanes, 160
    marshes, 64
    Roman roads in, 29
    windmills, 88
Sweden, place-name, 48
Swithland, Leics., 48
    slate-quarries, 209
sycamore trees, 69, 121

Tackley Park, 183
Tait, A. F., *Views on L. and N.-W. Rly.*, 198
Tamar, the, 194
    bridges over the, 105
Tattershall Castle, Lincs., 107
Tavistock, 93, 178, 194, 197
    abbey estates, 113
Telford, Thos., 189, 193, 195
Terrington, 78
Tetney, 79
Thames, the, 74, 106, 182, 189
    and Severn Canal, 193
Thoresby, North, 64
    Park, 131, 133
Thornbury Castle, Glos., 126
Thorverton, E. Devon, 51, 53, 56
Thunderbarrow Hill, Shoreham, 31
thwaites, 59
Tilgarsley, Oxon., 93
timber, destruction of, in Midlands, 117
    famine, 135
    use of, 48
    value and use of, in 1500, 108
tin boom, *c.* 1200, 75
tinners of Widecombe, 101
toll-houses, 189
Torksey, Lincs., 34
town gardens built over, 175
towns in 1086, 67
    of medieval England, 88-90
    from Saxon villages, 212, 214, 230
trackways, prehistoric, 30
    pre-Roman, 30
    wide, 180, 181, 182
Treable farm, Cheriton Bishop, 26, 27, 28
Trecarrel, Robt., 103
    chapel, 103
tree-planting in 17th and 18th centuries,
    135
trees cut down for fencing enclosure, 151
Trent, the, 34, 35, 104, 111, 159, 186,
    189, 191, 193, 197
    bridges, 91
    Valley, 33, 192
    and Mersey Canal, 196
Tring cutting, 198, 205
Tudor enclosers, 117, 118
    enclosures, 38
    hedges, 119
tunnels, canal, 193-4
    railway, 198-200, 206
turnpike roads, 186, 187, 189
two-field system, 38, 114
Tyrley, Staffs., 193, 195

Ugborough, S. Devon, 53

Vanbrugh, Sir John, 135, 136
Venta Belgarum (Winchester), 30, 34

Verulamium (St. Albans), 34
Victorian farmhouses, 157
  hedges, 119
  "restorers," 101
village greens, 50
  rare in West, 50, 52
villages, Anglo-Saxon, 38, 42
  around a perimeter, 52-3
  Bronze Age, 20
  changes in plan of, 54
  continuously inhabited, 42-4
  Danish, 59
  in Domesday Book, 49
  and their fields, 38-46
  fragmented, 49, 53-4
  green-, 49, 50, 52, 53, 54
  Iron Age, of W. Cornwall, 19, 24
  Iron Age sites, 22
  native, 31
  new Norwegian, 59
  new Scandinavian, 58
  nucleated, Anglo-Saxon, 33, 38, 159
  Romano-British, 45
  settled, appearance of, 20
  shape of English, 48-54
  street-, 40, 49, 53
  united, 95

Wadebridge, Cornwall, 105, 106
Wainfleet, 76, 77
Walla Brook, the, 22-3, 25
Wansdyke, 76
Warmington, Warws., 123
Warwickshire, 115, 123, 141, 145, 154, 180
  deserted villages of, 93
Wasdale, Cumb., 84, 188
Wash, the, 64, 76, 77, 78, 229
  place-names, 76, 77
  rivers of, the, 37
"waste," industrial, 171
Water-mill, the, 65
Water power and early mills, 165-71

Watling Street (Holyhead Road), 29,
  181, 182
Weald, the, 30, 109
  Kentish, 63, 111
  Sussex, 97, 111
Wedgwood, Josiah, 165, 167, 168, 192
Welbeck Park, 131
Welland, the, 77, 160, 161, 189, 217, 227
Welsh border counties, 111, 141
  road, 180, 187
Westcott Barton, Devon, 47
western farmsteads and fields, 23-9
Westmorland, Norwegian place-names in,
  59
Westwood Common, Laxton, 41
Whalley parish, 88, 104
Wharncliffe viaduct, 198, 205
Whatborough, E. Leics., 117
Widecombe-in-the-Moor church tower,
  101
Widford, 73
width of enclosure roads, 154-6
Wigan, 172
willow-trees, 152
Wiltshire, 42, 45, 61, 62, 81, 141
  downs, 22, 36, 225
  N.-W., 119
  villages ruined, 232
Wimpole, Cambs., 133, 134
Winchelsea, 211
  New, 212, 213, 214
Winchester (Venta Belgarum), 30, 34, 67,
  191, 205
windmill, the, 65, 88
Windover Hill, 22
Wiseton, Notts., 159
Witham, the, 33, 34, 191
Woburn Park, Beds., 131
Wolverhampton, 170
Wolverton embankment, 204, 205
Woodchester, Glos., 45
Woodcott, 70
Wood Eaton, Romano-British temple at, 32

Woodhall, 70
woodland clearings, 46, 47, 48
woodlands, destruction of, 109, 135
  extent of, in 1500, 108
Woodmancote, 70
Woodstock, Oxon., 69, 88, 183, 184
  hunting park, 73, 130, 185, 234
Wordsworth, W., 69, 121, 172, 203
  Guide through the District of the Lakes, 17
  The Excursion, quoted, 166-7, 176
  letter to Morning Post, quoted, 203-4
Wormleighton, Warws., 115-16
Worsley, 191, 192, 193
Wrangle, 77
Wright, Jos., of Derby, 166, 170
Wulsin, abbot of St. Albans, 67, 226
Wychwood Forest, Oxon., 31, 93, 109, 130

Yardworthy, Devon, 81
Yelland, Yellaton, Yellowland, Yellow,
  mead, Devon farm names, 36
Yeoman, Elizabethan, rebuilding, 120-1,
  123
York, 34, 67, 114
  vale of, 81
Yorkshire, 61, 106, 109, 121, 123, 138,
  159, 190, 206
  church towers, 101
  Cistercian abbeys, 86
  dales, 81
  East Riding, 141
  East Riding deserted villages, 93
  monasteries, 85
  moors, 20, 63, 88
  North Riding enclosure, 111
  Scandinavian settlement of, 59
  Wolds, 33
Young, Arthur, quoted, 143, 147, 159-60,
  166, 178

Zennor parish, 24, 25